Organizational Theory and Aesthetic Philosophies

Diverse philosophies constitute the theoretical ground of the study of the aesthetic side of organization. In fact, there is not a single unique philosophy behind the organizational research of the aesthetic dimension of organizational life. *Organizational Theory and Aesthetic Philosophies* will illustrate and discuss this complex phenomenon, and it will be dedicated to highlighting the philosophical basis of the study of aesthetics, art and design in organization.

The book distinguishes three principal "philosophical sensibilities" amongst these philosophies: aesthetic, hermeneutic and performative philosophical sensibility. Each of them is described and critically assessed through the work of philosophers, art theorists, sociologists and social scientists who represent its main protagonists. In this way, the reader will be conducted through the variety of philosophies that constitute a reference for aesthetics and design in organization.

The architecture of the book is articulated in two parts in order to provide student and scholars in philosophical aesthetics, in art, in design and in organization studies with an informative and agile instrument for academic research and study.

Antonio Strati is a senior professor of sociology of innovation and organization at the University of Trento, Italy, and chercheur associé at i3-CRG, École polytechnique, France.

Routledge Studies in Management, Organizations and Society

This series presents innovative work grounded in new realities, addressing issues crucial to an understanding of the contemporary world. This is the world of organised societies, where boundaries between formal and informal, public and private, local and global organizations have been displaced or have vanished, along with other nineteenth century dichotomies and oppositions. Management, apart from becoming a specialized profession for a growing number of people, is an everyday activity for most members of modern societies.

Similarly, at the level of enquiry, culture and technology, and literature and economics, can no longer be conceived as isolated intellectual fields; conventional canons and established mainstreams are contested. **Management, Organizations and Society** addresses these contemporary dynamics of transformation in a manner that transcends disciplinary boundaries, with books that will appeal to researchers, students and practitioners alike.

Recent titles in this series include:

For a full list of titles in this series, please visit www.routledge.com

Organizational Theory and Aesthetic Philosophies

Antonio Strati

Routledge
Taylor & Francis Group

NEW YORK AND LONDON

First published 2019
by Routledge
605 Third Avenue, New York, NY 10017

and by Routledge
2 Park Square, Milton Park, Abingdon, Oxon, OX14 4RN

First issued in paperback 2020

Routledge is an imprint of the Taylor & Francis Group, an informa business

© 2019 Taylor & Francis

The right of Antonio Strati to be identified as author of this work
has been asserted by him in accordance with sections 77 and 78
of the Copyright, Designs and Patents Act 1988.

Library of Congress Cataloging-in-Publication Data
A catalog record for this book has been requested

ISBN 13: 978-0-367-73225-7 (pbk)
ISBN 13: 978-1-138-09826-8 (hbk)

Typeset in Sabon
by Apex CoVantage, LLC

Contents

Figures and Table

Figures

Table

Author Biography

Antonio Strati, senior professor of sociology of innovation and organization at the Department of Sociology and Social Research of the University of Trento, Italy, and chercheur associé at i3-CRG, École polytechnique, CNRS, Université Paris-Saclay, France, is both a sociologist and an art photographer.

He is a founder member of the Research Unit on Communication, Organizational Learning and Aesthetics (RUCOLA), University of Trento, and of the international network of academics and practitioners Standing Conference on Organizational Symbolism (SCOS).

His academic work focuses on organizational symbolism and the aesthetic approach to study organizational life, while his artistic research focuses on conceptual photography.

He is the author of *Organization and Aesthetics* (Sage, 1999)—which also appeared in French (PUL, 2004), Portuguese (FGV, 2007) and Italian (Mondadori, 2008)—and of *Theory and Method in Organization Studies* (Sage, 2000).

He is co-author (with Silvia Gherardi) of *Learning and Knowing in Practice-Based Studies* (Elgar, 2012).

His artistic research in conceptual photography, Photopoesia, has been published in books and photographic journals, and collected at museums and international collections.

Acknowledgments

I would like to thank, first of all, the artists, organizational scholars and practitioners who produced the rather vast literature and the vital debate regarding the aesthetic dimension of organizational life. I am particularly grateful for their inventive and playful debates to the AoMO (Art of Management and Organization) conferences organizers; to the participants in the web network Aacorn (Art, Aesthetics, Creativity, and Organizations Research Network); and to the students and scholars engaged "to do research for fun" in SCOS (Standing Conference on Organizational Symbolism), the academic network that I had the pleasure to co-found.

I am indebted to my colleagues of the University of Trento and, in particular, to my junior colleagues of the Research Unit on Communication, Organizational Learning, and Aesthetics (RUCOLA) for the research conducted together on the subject of aesthetics and art in organization. I wish also to thank my colleagues of the University of Siena in Italy, of the École polytechnique (Paris, France) and of the Copenhagen Business School and Roskilde University (Denmark) for their encouragement and support of my research on aesthetics in organization. I also owe a considerable debt to my students in Trento, Siena and several other European universities. I wish also to express my gratitude for the technical and administrative support I received for my research and teaching from the persons devoted to the organization of institutional settings, technologies and spaces. Among them all, I would like to thank especially Per-Olof Berg, Sue Jones, Alessandro Cavalli, Jean-François Chanlat, Marta Calás, Adrian Belton, Eduardo Davel, Pierre-Jean Benghozi, Kristian Kreiner, Rosemary Nixon, Gianluca Mori, Vincent Dégot, Poul Bitsch Olsen, Linda Smircich and Pasquale Gagliardi. A special thought also goes to the memory of Antonio de Lillo, Heather Höpfl and Omar Calabrese.

Finally, I am grateful to Pierre Guillet de Monthoux for the Edo Bar philosophical conversations in Riviera Ligure and Côte d'Azur, to Hugh Willmott and to Silvia Gherardi for their encouragement to write this book on organization theory and philosophical aesthetics, and to David Varley for the opportunity to do it with Routledge.

Prelude

Organizational Theory and Aesthetic Philosophies appears twenty years after *Organization and Aesthetics*, one of my books published with Sage, which was well received. In fact, this essay on the aesthetic dimension of organizational life and its study—that Sue Jones, University of Bath, in England, invited me to write for Sage—has become a point of reference for organizational aesthetic research, and has also been translated into French, Portuguese and Italian.

In French, it was for the initiative of Jean-François Chanlat, who was working at the Université Dauphine in Paris, France, and it appeared in 2004 with the Franco-Canadian publishing house Les Presses de l'Université Laval in Québec. In Portuguese, it was for the initiative of Eduardo Davel, who was working at the Université Téluq in Montreal, Canada, and was published in 2007 with the Brazilian publisher Editora Fundação Getúlio Vargas of Rio de Janeiro. In Italian it appeared some ten years later than the original publication by Sage, in 2008. It is a largely updated version that Omar Calabrese, who was working at the time at the same University of Siena where I have been teaching for fifteen years, asked me to publish with Mondadori-Università in Milan.

This book, observed Josef Chytry (2008: 61), was "saturated in the literature of philosophical aesthetics". Now, twenty years after, *Organizational Theory and Aesthetic Philosophies* documents once again my passion and taste for philosophical aesthetics, even though I am not a philosopher of aesthetics, nor an art critic and historian, but a sociologist of organization and an art photographer. This new book further illustrates my theoretical awareness that philosophy is highly relevant in organization theory and management studies. Which means, in particular, that aesthetic philosophies, as well as art history and social theories of art, are highly relevant if the organizational study is directed to understand the aesthetic dimension of organizational life. This is the principal continuity between the two books, but with a crucial difference.

Twenty years ago, in fact, with *Organization and Aesthetics*, I intended to give theoretical and methodological form to the aesthetic approach to the study of the organization; and for it, I explored, made reference and discussed aesthetic philosophy, the sociology of art, the semiotics of art and art theory. On the contrary, now, with *Organizational Theory and Aesthetic Philosophies*, I focus directly on aesthetic philosophy and art social theory, since my intent is to investigate the philosophical and epistemological roots of organizational aesthetics, art and design. The crucial difference between the two books is, therefore, that the relationship between "organization" and "aesthetics" is reversed; that is, in this new book, philosophical aesthetics constitutes the principal figure of the scenario, while the aesthetic approach constitutes its background.

Returning to the similarities that characterize these two books, in addition to my sociological taste for aesthetic philosophy, it affects something that concerns the writing process and my research practices.

Twenty years ago, when I wrote *Organization and Aesthetics*, I was reflecting on a style of organizational research that could assign aesthetic quality to both inquiring and theorizing organizational life. The book followed my article "Aesthetic Understanding of Organizational Life", which was published in the theoretical forum of the journal *Academy of Management Review* (1992) and dedicated to the new intellectual currents in organization theory, and which had been edited by Linda Smircich, Marta Calás and Gareth Morgan. In that article, I discussed the thesis of moving from the study of organizational aesthetics to an aesthetic study of the organization. When, a few years later, I wrote *Organization and Aesthetics*, my aim was to further inquire, theorize and give form to the aesthetic understanding of organization, and to characterize it in a distinctive way with respect to the various interpretative and qualitative approaches that flourished in those years in the sociology of organizations, organizational theories and management studies (Buchanan and Bryman, 2009; Clegg et al., 2006; Hatch, 2006; Strati, 1996).

Organizational Theory and Aesthetic Philosophies, too, has an essay at its origins—the chapter I wrote for the book on the philosophies and epistemologies of organization theory that Raza Mir, Hugh Willmott and Michelle Greenwood (2016) edited. In this work, I proposed to understand the philosophies, epistemologies and social theories that characterize the studies of the aesthetic dimension of organization thanks to three principal philosophical sensibilities: the hermeneutic sensibility, the aesthetic sensibility and the performative sensibility, which, in *Organizational Theory and Aesthetic Philosophies*, I further explore, describe and discuss.

At the end of that chapter, I wrote that an important future direction of organizational aesthetics research might consist in establishing a more explicit and direct dialogue between organization studies and aesthetic philosophy, art theory and social theory (Strati, 2016: 258). Something that has had few and rare examples, such as Mir, Willmott and Greenwood's *The Routledge Companion to Philosophy in Organization*

Studies mentioned above, or the collection of philosophical, sociological and anthropological essays on the aesthetics of ordinary beauty—and ordinary ugliness—in a transdisciplinary perspective edited by Janusz Przychodzen, François-Emanuël Boucher and Sylvain David (2010).

These are the origins of this book, dedicated to highlighting the philosophical basis of the study of aesthetics, art and design in the organization—that is, the diverse philosophies that constitute the theoretical ground of the study of the aesthetic side of the organization. In fact, there is not a single unique philosophy behind the organizational research of the aesthetic dimension of organizational life. As said, the book distinguishes three principal "philosophical sensibilities" amongst these philosophies: aesthetic, hermeneutic and performative philosophical sensibility. Each of them is described and critically assessed through the work of philosophers, art theorists, sociologists and social scientists who represent its main protagonists. In this way, the reader will be conducted through the variety of philosophies that constitute a reference for aesthetics, art and design in organization. From which philosophical viewpoint?

My philosophical lens concerning the aesthetic approach is grounded in the philosophical aesthetics created at the beginning of the eighteenth century, in Italian philosophy and in Simmel's sociology of the senses. These are Western philosophies that belong to European continental thought. More precisely, my philosophical point of view in writing this book is principally rooted in the "Logica poetica" of Giambattista Vico (1725) and the aesthetics of Alexander Gottlieb Baumgarten (1750–58), in the aesthetic sociology of Georg Simmel (1908), in the phenomenology of Maurice Merleau-Ponty (1947) and the existentialist and hermeneutic aesthetics of Luigi Pareyson (1954), in the hermeneutics of Hans-Georg Gadamer (1986), in the "weak thought" of Gianni Vattimo (Vattimo and Rovatti, 1983) and the "living thought" of Roberto Esposito (2010) that characterize, among other features, the Italian difference and specificity in philosophy and aesthetics.

I shall discuss these aesthetic philosophies and aesthetic social theories that characterize my philosophical lens through the various chapters of the book. Also, in this case—that is, in my "philosophical situation"—one distinctive character is emphasized: the fact that it is a plurality of aesthetic philosophies to constitute my philosophical lens, rather than a single philosophical tradition on art and aesthetics

Six "Interludes" complete the book. They are made up of photographs rather than words—as, on the contrary, has been the case with the use of the "interlude" made by John Law in his book *After Method* (2004)—and are intended to evoke and discuss visually the relationship between the philosophical aesthetics and the organizational theory that characterizes my philosophical lens. They constitute the *trait-d'union*, which represents the passage from one chapter to another, from Part I to Part II, and from Part II to the Epilogue.

Interlude is a term whose etymology "derives from the medieval Latin *inter* (between) + *ludus* (play). An interlude may be an intervening episode, an entertainment between the acts of a play, or a short musical piece put between the parts of a longer composition" (Gherardi and Strati, 2017: 104). In this book, the Interludes are constituted by my "Photopoesia" (Belli, 1982), that is, by my art photography (Hitchcock, 2005; Zannier, 1986). The six photopoems in black and white are printed each one full page to interrupt the rhythm of reading with their visual language. They are meant, in fact, to invite the reader to suspend the words-experience and instead to immerse himself/herself in the image-experience to feel its poetry and empathically live its evocative aesthetics. Photographs and words, thus, compose together the scenario of this book, and this represents another difference with *Organization and Aesthetics*.

Furthermore, art photography will represent the "leitmotiv" of my discussion of the relationship between philosophy and organizational theory. The aesthetic philosophies, as I said, comprehend such a plurality of visions, interpretations and styles of research that I felt the necessity to ground my reflections on the relevance of philosophical aesthetics on a "province" of the aesthetics—to use Alfred Schütz's (1962–64) terminology—with which I have deep familiarity. Thus, art photography will be the research field where my philosophical intuitions on aesthetics will be rooted and, by hybridizing with photography in a broad sense, art photography will also constitute a metaphor of organizational aesthetics.

The architecture of *Organizational Theory and Aesthetic Philosophies* is articulated in two parts in order to provide student and scholars in organization studies, in philosophical aesthetics, in art, in art photography and in design with an informative and agile instrument for academic research and study.

The first part of the book introduces the reader to the main themes and issues debated around art and ordinary aesthetics in everyday working life in organizations and in society. The world of art photography, of business and commercial photography, and of daily mundane photography represents the organizational and the social context of the theoretical and methodological subjects treated to depict the relevance of philosophical aesthetics in the aesthetic understanding of organizational life.

The second part of the book is dedicated to the three philosophical sensibilities—aesthetic, hermeneutic and performative—which characterize the aesthetic discourse on everyday organizational life. These philosophical sensibilities have diverse philosophical grounds and show diverse modes of aesthetic understanding of organizational life that are specifically illustrated through a selection of philosophical works and authors. Part II closes with a chapter on the relationships between these three diverse aesthetic sensibilities and the four aesthetic approaches: the "archeological approach", the "aesthetic approach", the "artistic approach" and the "empathic-logical approach".

In more detail, Part I, *Philosophy and Organizational Aesthetics*, is composed of three chapters that will introduce the reader to the core issues illustrated in the book and provide some basic information on the area of organization studies, called organizational aesthetics and its philosophical foundation.

Chapter 1, "Relevance of Philosophical Aesthetics in Organization Studies", argues for the importance of philosophical aesthetics in the study of the aesthetic dimension of work and organization. It highlights three characteristics of the organizational aesthetics: "polysemy", "mystery" and "intensity". Drawing from empirical research, the significance of the categories of the aesthetics, such as the sublime, is stressed, as well as the fact that aesthetics provides the tacit dimension of knowing in organizational life with a language that does not violate its tacit character.

Chapter 2, "Organizational Lens, Art Photography and the Creation Process", is focused on the relevant contribution of the theories of art to organizational aesthetics research, and highlights, in particular, the issue of the relationships between art practice, sensible knowledge, aesthetic philosophy and the creation process. The organizational context of the creation process is art photography. The chapter raises the issues of sensible knowing in the interaction with the digital environment, and of the corporeality of the "collective artist", which is constituted by humans, robots, organizations and institutions. The chapter argues for the relevance of philosophical aesthetics in order to grasp the materiality of the creation process through the lens of the organizational study.

Chapter 3, "Art, Everyday Aesthetics and Organizational Theory", concludes the first part of the book, underlining the philosophical foundations of the relationships between art and aesthetics in organization. The focus remains on art photography. Through the question of what makes a photograph be an art photograph, the chapter highlights the hybridizing relations between the "creation process of art" and the "creation process of aesthetics" in everyday photography. The reader, then, is led into a world, that of photography, where s/he is immersed, and that is familiar given the pervasiveness of the photographic image in contemporary society; while, at the same time, the world of photography aims also to represent a metaphor of organizational aesthetics. The last section of the chapter illustrates some main aspects of the art/aesthetics debate which are at the origins of the new philosophical movement of "Everyday Aesthetics" and shows their importance for the study of the aesthetic dimension of organizational life.

Part II, *Three Philosophical Sensibilities*, is composed of three chapters whose purpose is to illustrate and discuss the philosophical sensibilities that traverse the organizational aesthetics research. I introduced the concept of philosophical sensibility and the distinction in the aesthetic, hermeneutic and performative sensibility with my chapter "Aesthetics and

Design: An Epistemology of the Unseen" mentioned above. The aesthetic sensibility constitutes the principal distinctive character of organizational aesthetics, even if the hermeneutic and performative sensibilities are more common among the four approaches to the study of the aesthetic dimension of organizational life.

Chapter 4, "Aesthetic Philosophy and the Aesthetic Approach", begins Part II with a focus on the approach to the study of organizational life that I have introduced in organizational theories—the "aesthetic approach" (1992). The chapter will discuss the relations of the "aesthetic approach" with the philosophical and organizational themes of rationality and the sociological paradigm. This chapter also emphasizes the phenomenological and post-humanist awareness that characterizes the "aesthetic approach" and the philosophical importance of the debates concerning the post-humanist and aesthetic materiality of the corporeal relationships of all forms of life with the artifacts and the organization.

Chapter 5, "Practice and the Italian Aesthetic Philosophies", continues with a focus on the "aesthetic approach" and underlines the philosophical importance of the Italian philosophies regarding the topic of practice in the ambit of both art creation and worldly organizational creativity. The aesthetics of the practice is an important subject in the existentialist and hermeneutic aesthetics of Luigi Pareyson, which constitutes a reference for the "aesthetic approach" and for the "practice-based studies" in organizational theory. Chapter 5 also stresses that the other Italian aesthetic philosophies developed in the same period—futurism, Marxist and the phenomenological aesthetics—which opposed Crocean idealism, have investigated aesthetics in its production process, rather than just in the artwork, in continuity with the traditional interest in the "practice spheres" that has characterized Italian philosophy since the Renaissance.

Chapter 6, "Aesthetic, Hermeneutic and Performative Sensibility", highlights the principal philosophical foundations of organizational aesthetics research. It also acknowledges the wide variety of philosophies taken into due consideration in the study of aesthetics, art and design in organization. It illustrates the roots of the aesthetic discourse on organization in the thought of classic authors of philosophical aesthetics— Addison, Vico, Baumgarten and Kant—as well as in the German aesthetic sociology of Simmel, the French phenomenology of Merleau-Ponty, the Italian philosophical aesthetics of Pareyson, and the semiotics of Barthes, Calabrese and Eco. Hence, Chapter 6 (1) begins with the topic of the sensible knowledge, which constitutes social relationships of sociological relevance; (2) explores the relationship between the creation process and its interpretation, and the active involvement of the "user" in hermeneutic process; (3) highlights the relationship between performance as an aesthetic practice and Polanyi's notion of tacit dimension of knowledge and Dewey's pragmatist philosophy; and (4) illustrates the principal characteristics of the four approaches that articulate the study of organizational aesthetics, and concludes Part II by discussing their relationship with the three philosophical sensibilities.

In the Epilogue, I recapitulate the topic of the book, its treatment and its main contribution to organizational aesthetic research, and I conclude the book with a proposal to play with philosophy in the aesthetic study of organizational life.

References

Academy of Management Review (1992). Special issue on "New intellectual currents in organization and management theory: theory development forum", 17 (3). Edited by Smircich, L., Calás, M. and G. Morgan.

Baumgarten, A. G. (1750–58). *Aesthetica*, Vol. I–II. Frankfurt am Oder: Kleyb (Photostat: Olms, Hildesheim, 1986).

Belli, G. (ed.) (1982). *Antonio Strati Photopoesia*. Trento: Museo Provinciale d'Arte.

Buchanan, D. and Bryman, A. (eds.) (2009). *The Sage Handbook of Organizational Research Methods*. London: Sage.

Chytry, J. (2008). Organizational aesthetics: the artful firm and the aesthetic moment in contemporary business and management theory, *Aesthesis: International Journal of Art and Aesthetics in Management and Organizational Life*, 2 (2): 60–72, http://digitalcommons.wpi.edu/aesthesis/23.

Clegg, S. R., Hardy, C., Lawrence, T. B., and Nord, W. R. (eds.) (2006). *The Sage Handbook of Organization Studies*. 2nd edn. London: Sage.

Esposito, R. (2010). *Pensiero vivente. Origine e attualità della filosofia italiana*. Torino: Einaudi. (English trans.: *Living Thought. The Origins and Actuality of Italian Philosophy*. Stanford, CA: Stanford University Press, 2012).

Gadamer, H. G. (1986). *The Relevance of the Beautiful and Other Essays*. Cambridge: Cambridge University Press.

Gherardi, S. and Strati, A. (2017). Talking about competence: that "something" which exceeds the speaking subject, in Sandberg, J., Rouleau, L., Langley, A., and Tsoukas H. (eds.), *Skillful Performance: Enacting Capabilities, Knowledge, Competence, and Expertise in Organizations*. Oxford: Oxford University Press, pp. 103–124.

Hatch, M. J. (2006). *Organization Theory: Modern, Symbolic, and Postmodern Perspectives*. With A. L. Cunliffe. Oxford: Oxford University Press.

Hitchcock, B. (2005). When Land met Adams, in Crist, S. (ed.), *The Polaroid Book: Selections from the Polaroid Collections of Photography*. Köln: Taschen, pp. 1–6.

Law, J. (2004). *After Method: Mess in Social Science Research*. London: Routledge.

Merleau-Ponty, M. (1947). *Le Primat de la perception et ses conséquences philosophiques*. Grenoble: Cynara. (English trans.: *The Primacy of Perception, and Other Essays on Phenomenological Psychology, the Philosophy of Art, History, and Politics*. Evanston, IL: Northwestern University Press, 1964).

Mir, R., Willmott, H. and Greenwood, M. (eds.) (2016). *The Routledge Companion to Philosophy in Organization Studies*. London: Routledge.

Pareyson, L. (1954). *Estetica. Teoria della formatività*. Torino: Edizioni di "Filosofia". Reprinted 1988, Milano: Bompiani. (Partial English trans.: Pareyson, L.,

Existence, Interpretation, Freedom: Selected Writings. Ed. Bubbio, P. D. Aurora, CO: The Davies Group, 2009).

Przychodzen, J., Boucher, F. E. and David, S. (eds.) (2010). *L'esthétique du beau ordinaire dans une perspective transdisciplinaire. Ni du gouffre ni du ciel.* Paris: l'Harmattan.

Schütz, A. (1962–64). *Collected Papers I–II. The Problem of Social Reality.* The Hague: Nijhoff.

Simmel, G. (1908). *Soziologie: Untersuchungen über die Formen der Vergesellschaftung.* Leipzig: Dunker & Humblot. (English trans.: *Sociology: Inquiries into the Construction of Social Forms*, Vol. I–II. Ed. Blasi, A. J., Jacobs A. K. and M. Kanjireathinkal. Leiden: Brill, 2009).

Strati, A. (1992). Aesthetic understanding of organizational life, *Academy of Management Review*, 17 (3): 568–581.

Strati, A. (1996). *Sociologia dell'organizzazione: paradigmi teorici e metodi di ricerca.* Roma: NIS-Carocci. (English trans.: *Theory and Method in Organization Studies: Paradigms and Choices.* London: Sage, 2000).

Strati, A. (2016). Aesthetics and design: an epistemology of the unseen, in Mir, R., Willmott, H. and Greenwood, M. (eds.), *The Routledge Companion to Philosophy in Organization Studies.* London: Routledge, pp. 251–259.

Vattimo, G. and Rovatti, P. A. (eds.) (1983). *Il pensiero debole.* Milano: Feltrinelli. (English trans.: Vattimo, G. and Rovatti, P. A. (eds.), *Weak Thought.* Ed. Carravetta, P. Albany: State University of New York Press, 2012).

Vico, G. (1725). *Principi di una scienza nuova.* Napoli: Mosca. 3rd edn. 1744. (English trans.: *The New Science of Giambattista Vico.* Ed. Bergin, T. G. and M. H. Fisch. Ithaca, NY: Cornell University Press, 1968).

Zannier, I. (1986). *Storia della fotografia italiana.* Bari: Laterza.

Part I
Philosophy and Organizational Aesthetics

1 Relevance of Philosophical Aesthetics in Organization Studies

Part I, *Philosophy and Organizational Aesthetics*, is dedicated to introducing the reader to the core issues illustrated and discussed in this book, and also, at the same time, to my style of researching, theorizing and communicating on the aesthetics of organization.

Part I is composed of three chapters. The first chapter aims to argue for the importance of philosophical aesthetics in the study of the aesthetic dimension of work and organization. The second chapter focuses on the organizational study of the creation process. The third chapter discusses the relationship between art and ordinary beauty in the understanding of organizational aesthetics.

Two Interludes create a symbolic bridge between the three chapters—a bridge that connects and interrupts, at the same time, the flow of the written words using art photography. My principal intent with these Interludes is to point out the different organizational knowledge that we can acquire through written language, on one hand, and visual language on the other hand. All the "different media of non-verbal representation", writes the American philosopher Susanne K. Langer (1942: 96–97), are often indicated as distinct "languages"—and this is a "loose terminology"—but their main difference with the verbal and written language, that is, the "language", is that

> [T]he meanings given through language are successively understood, and gathered into a whole by the process called discourse; the meanings of all other symbolic elements that compose a larger, articulate symbol are understood only through the meaning of the whole, through their relations within the total structure. Their very functioning as symbols depends on the fact that they are involved in a simultaneous, integral presentation. This kind of semantic may be called "presentational symbolism", to characterize its essential distinction from discursive symbolism, or "language" proper.

Photography, we shall see, constitutes both a metaphor of organizational aesthetics and the field study of my argument for the relevance of philosophical aesthetics in organizational theories.

The importance of the aesthetic philosophy in researching organization constitutes the leitmotiv of this book. This is therefore the principal subject of Chapter 1, where I shall illustrate how it has been that, in doing empirical research on organizational cultures, I gave form to my aesthetic approach to understand organization thanks to the aesthetic philosophies.

1.1 Polysemy, Mystery, Intensity

The relevance of philosophical aesthetics in organization theory and management studies became evident in my research from the very beginning of my study of the aesthetic dimension of organization. My "discovery" of the sociological relevance of the aesthetic side of organizational life happened during a research study on the organizational culture of three departments—art, mathematics and education—of one of the oldest Italian universities (Strati, 1990). Aesthetics emerged as an important dimension in the work to be done, individually and collectively, and was also able to influence the organizational settings and the power relations of the department. Moreover, the empirical research showed that aesthetics as an organizational dimension of these departments was characterized by polysemy, mystery and intensity:

1. Polysemy emerged as an important characteristic because aesthetics referred to organizational interactions and events that were very different, such as, for instance, the elegance of a mathematical demonstration, the ugliness of the hierarchical expressions flaunting power in the department organizational life or the nostalgia of past work relationships and work atmospheres which were intellectually fascinating.
2. Mystery emerged as another important characteristic because the beauty of the construction of a statistical data table, or of the study of a painting, or of the creation of a mathematical formula, was not self-evident and self-explaining. These beauties required intuition, socialization, learning process, symbolic understanding and metaphorical thinking—that is, characteristics which are distinctive of the specific working practices in organizations conducted, in one case, as a social scientist of the education department; and in another case, as an art historian of the art department; and in a third case, as a mathematician of the department of mathematics.
3. Intensity emerged as an equally relevant characteristic because the relevance of aesthetics varied enormously, according to my fieldwork results:

    (a) In the department of mathematics, aesthetics was in great consideration and influenced the practices of the department. The

beauty was in "doing pure mathematics" and the pure mathematicians were dominating the departmental organizational
cultures and dynamics.

(b) In the art department, aesthetics was situated in and circumscribed to the artwork at study. Art historians were not seeing
themselves and their colleagues dedicated to creation and beauty,
such as the pure mathematicians did. They were considering their
research study as the production of knowledge about works of
beauty.

(c) In the department of education, aesthetics was a "sin" *tout court*,
given that the organizational culture was inspired by the *ethos*
of doing useful things for specific communities and the society in
general.

Now, the question is: why did my sociological research need to create
a dialogue with philosophical aesthetics? Because, in order to reach the
research results mentioned above and "discover" the sociological relevance of aesthetics for understanding organizational cultures, philosophy does not seem to be necessary. There was, of course, my sensibility
towards philosophical theories and epistemological debates, which was
rooted in sociology and social theory. There was also my sensibility
towards the arts and the research in the arts made by art historians, critics and artists, which was grounded in my conceptual art photography.
But how my dialogue with the aesthetic philosophies began is better illustrated by the field research process itself.

Two of "my situations" that have come into being during my empirical
research can explain why I felt the need for a dialogue between the sociology of organization and philosophical studies. The first highlights the
issue of acquiring organizational knowledge, while the second highlights
the question of judging the organizational experience. These two issues
have been fundamental; they gave to my aesthetic approach to the study
of organizational life a distinctive form.

I shall illustrate them in Chapter 1, just after pointing out that they
both originated from within my field inquiry—that is, from the specific
and concrete research situation I was in. Specific and concrete in the sense
that the Italian existentialist and hermeneutic philosopher Luigi Pareyson
expresses through the following considerations:

I have *this* body, *these* relatives, *these* friends, *this* homeland, *this*
job, *these* relations with others and other things: that is I have a very
definite position in the universe, a specific place in the world. In a
word: a situation, or better, *my* situation. I cannot regard my situation as one among many others, any of which I could have been given
at random. My situation is my [. . .] "incarnation": without it, I, as
a single person, would not exist. The bonds that connect me to my

situation are very tight, and above all, they are essential to me: they are not links of "features", but of "essence".

(1943; Eng. trans. 2009: 42)

1.2 Tacit Dimension of Knowing and Aesthetics

My first situation was created when an internationally well-known Italian mathematician told me that a "beautiful result is often one in which the author demonstrates more than he says" (Strati, 2008; reprint 2012: 136). This consideration captured my attention, also because of my typification of mathematicians' work. The philosopher and sociologist Alfred Schütz pointed out that our process of acquiring knowledge derives only in part from our direct experience. A large part of our knowledge originates, in fact, in our social heritage.

> It consists of a set of systems of relevant typifications, of typical solutions for typical practical and theoretical problems, of typical precepts for typical behavior.
>
> (Schütz, 1962: 348)

According to my social heritage, I was used to assuming that, in the exact world of mathematics, everything was in the demonstration, that is, that the scientific formalization represented by the mathematical demonstration would say *all* it has to be said. The fact that a mathematician could demonstrate "more than" what s/he actually says was therefore an unexpected research's surprise.

This also resonates with something that I noticed in other work settings, such as in the sawmills, where the work practices were finalized to sawing a tree to produce boards for the furniture industry: even though the production standards were in principle well specified, the outcome was never scientifically predictable. This was due to the state of the wood and the state of the saw, as well as to the technology of the work process and the ability of the people to work.

The "scientific aura" of the mathematical demonstration pushed me to deepen the epistemological debate in the sciences and, in doing it, I found inspiring the research in the field of the philosophy of science conducted by the Hungarian philosopher Michael Polanyi. With his research, Polanyi highlighted the distinction between two dimensions of knowing:

1. the explicit dimension, constituted by the knowledge that is formalized in scientific terms, and
2. the tacit dimension, that is, the knowledge that is not expressed formally and scientifically.

Both dimensions constitute our personal knowledge, but the tacit dimension is of crucial importance. To stress this point, Polanyi made explicit reference to the rules of art, which

> can be useful, but they do not determine the practice of an art; they are maxims, which can serve as a guide to an art only if they can be integrated into the practical knowledge of the art. They cannot replace this knowledge.
>
> (1958: 50)

My typification of the mathematical world was neglecting the tacit dimension of the mathematicians' personal knowledge, while, on the opposite dimension, the personal knowledge of a mathematical result was "something" richer than the mere scientific comprehension of the theorem demonstration. But there was something more to grasp in the words of the famous mathematician: in the department, the mathematicians were aware of the fact that there is some kind of beauty when an author demonstrates more than s/he says.

For me, the fact of understanding that in the world of mathematics, the explicit dimension of knowledge—formalized and scientific—has to face the mystery, due to tacit knowledge, that characterizes the aesthetic practice of knowledge, has profoundly influenced my aesthetic approach to the study of daily work practices in organization.

This was "my situation" when Polanyi's philosophical distinction between the tacit dimension—the practice of an art—and the explicit dimension of knowledge—the rules of an art—became one of my arguments in favor of the aesthetic approach to the study of social practice in organizational settings, and also in polemic against the cognitivist approach to the study of organization (Strati, 2003; reprint 2012: 30–32).

Thereafter, I even stressed something more, that is, that the aesthetic approach is able to provide the tacit dimension of knowing with a language—poetic, artistic, through metaphors. The aesthetic language is in fact able to express the organizational experience without violating its tacit character because it does not seek to transform the tacit dimension into explicit knowledge.

This argument clearly expressed the difference and the distance of the aesthetic study of the organization from the organizational approaches and epistemologies which, on the contrary, were seeing the tacit knowledge as translatable in the explicit, such as the cognitivist approach and the rationalist and positivist study of organization have been attempting to do.

1.3 The Sublime and the Categories of Aesthetics

My second situation that shows how immediate my search for philosophy has been during my field study in the three Italian departments always occurred in the department of mathematics. This one was, in fact, the context where the aesthetic dimension of work and organization emerged with an intensity that was not foreseen, and this beautiful surprise was intriguing. During an interview, another famous Italian mathematician told me that the act of giving a mathematical problem to be solved to the mathematics community—an act done by a very well-known colleague—was something "sublime", and he emphasized his comment with a wide movement of his right arm.

How to understand sublime? This question denotes my situation in which, in order to deepen the aesthetic quality of the sublime, I decided to move from the original frame of the sublime used, given by the context of sociological research, to that of the investigation of how the sublime was treated in the aesthetic philosophies. Through this shift from sociological field research to philosophy, I had the sensation of achieving a better understanding of what both the word and the gesture accompanying it meant. As philosophical aesthetic category, in fact, sublime connects the beauty to the nobility of spirit, to dignity, to high-minded moral rectitude (Bodei, 1995).

This was the philosophical interpretation of sublime that I preferred among the various philosophical ways to understand this aesthetic category. I felt it respondent and appropriate to the sentiments I experienced in the field study. I had the impression that the shift from the ordinary language of the interview to philosophy configured the sublime used in a new shape that was respectful of both the departmental context and the sociological research context.

From then, the philosophical debate around the aesthetic categories, in general, became part of my research style. "Beautiful" lost its status as an umbrella concept depicting art and aesthetics in organization and translated itself into an aesthetic category. Other categories of aesthetics, such as the "sacred", the "picturesque", the "tragic", the "ugly", the "comic" and the "graceful", as well as the "agogic" aesthetic categories that concern rhythm, had emerged from my empirical studies, and all of them shaped, through their philosophical background, my aesthetic understanding of the organizational settings at study (Strati, 1999: 184–188). That is, they contributed to sophisticate my approach through "fragments" of their own long philosophical history.

Thus, on one side, the categories of aesthetics studied belong to the normal language used in organizational life, and they are explored in the context of the organization to comprehend, as far as possible, in the dialogue with the organizational actors, what sense they can have in their daily working context and what implications they can have for understanding the practices in organizations. On the other side, the aesthetic categories are seen also in the complex heritage they have acquired in philosophical debates, disputes, controversies and fashions.

The dialogue between the aesthetic category used in the context of the organizational research study and the same aesthetic category used in the context of the philosophical aesthetics debate is thus a dialogue between "fragments of knowing". The fragments of organizational knowledge acquired during the research evoke, in fact, fragments of philosophical knowledge that are appropriate to shed a new light on the category of aesthetics that emerged in the study of organizational life.

"My situation", in which the sublime emerged during the research, clearly illustrates what can consist of the dialogue between fragments of knowing. Even though sublime, such as other aesthetic categories, does not have roots in the sociology of organization, nor in organizational theories, this adjective:

- qualifies aesthetically as an organizational action addressed to the collectivity of the organizational actors and to the community of the mathematicians in general;
- engages both the verbal and the corporeal languages;
- assumes, at the same time, an ordinary and an extraordinary level in the communication process activated by the mathematician and addressed towards the organizational scholar: ordinary because it is used in terms of natural organizational language, and extraordinary because it enhances mystery in the aesthetic quality of the organizational action;
- is characterized by a debate in philosophy and theories of art that begins with the writings attributed to Longinus (1995) in ancient Greece, the considerations developed in modern aesthetic philosophies by Joseph Addison (1712), Edmund Burke (1757) and Immanuel Kant (1790), and the reflections realized in the context of postmodern aesthetic philosophy by Jean-François Lyotard (1991);
- evokes the polysemy of the aesthetic category, that is, of a plurality of meanings, which can also even be at odds with each other.

The crucial point in the aesthetic study of organization is that an aesthetic category emerges from organizational research like it happened with the sublime. That is, a category of aesthetics has been suggested

- from the organizational actors—as it is, for example, in the case of the relation of Norwegian seafarers with the seascapes illustrated by Kathy Mack (2007);
- from the researcher, such as in the study of the students' engagement in university education described by Alexander Kofinas (2018).

Thus, by doing aesthetic research, the aesthetic category of kitsch can characterize both the aesthetic side of organizational life observed and the experience of research lived (Linstead, 2002; Kostera, 1997). In another organization, the rhythm, that is, the agogic aesthetic category, can represent the aesthetics of collective action, such as observed in the case study of a military assault team (Piras, 2007). An organizational event can be disgusting (Pelzer, 2002), just as certain odors that belong to the routine of work can be, such as Patricia Martin (2002) has described in her research on residences for elderly people.

I conclude this section on the categories of aesthetics and the aesthetic study of organizational life by stressing that the dialogue established between organizational theories and philosophical aesthetics occurs *through fragments*: fragments of organizational life as well as fragments of organization theory evoke fragments of philosophy, that is, fragments of the rich and renewed philosophical debates that emphasize the polysemy and the mystery of aesthetics.

I want to clarify what is meant here by "fragment". Art can give us an appropriate image with a legend surrounding the modernist architecture of Antoni Gaudí. It is said, in fact, that the great Catalan architect asked the craftsman who had prepared the crystal for the door of a building in Barcelona to let it fall to the ground and, once the crystal had broken up, to patch those fragments of crystal with wrought iron and thus prepare the door of the house.

The fragment, as we can see—intuitively, of course—has very little in common with the systematic indication that instead evokes the image of *ad hoc* cropping. The boundaries of the fragments are not "delimited"; they are "inter-rupted", writes Omar Calabrese (1987: 77–78), as revealed by its etymological origins in the Latin *frangere*.

These boundaries are formed by chance and not by logical analysis, as is also the case in organizational studies, in which the researcher "finds" fragments of organizational life, "invents" fragments of organizational knowledge and "gives form" to fragments of organizational theory. Fragments that *take form in the interaction between different competences*, such as that of the architect Gaudí and that of the craftsman, and between individuals and artifacts, including so much taste and inventiveness, as hierarchical and power relations, as well as the presumable conflict of feelings and aesthetic judgments that lead to processes of destruction— the beautifully prepared crystal—and of organizational construction, that is to say, the building's door.

This constitutes an important element of the organizational scholar's awareness, as I shall further discuss in the next section, where the inter-relationships that occur between organizational aesthetics research and aesthetic philosophies are illustrated in the context of a more global discourse.

1.4 Philosophy and the Aesthetic Study of Organization

Nowadays there is a more accentuated attention among organizational scholars towards the importance of philosophy and social theory in organization studies. However, it has to be pointed out that the philo-sophical sensibility does not characterize all the researches and studies conducted to understand the aesthetic side of organizational life. Said differently, philosophical aesthetics do not constitute either the common ground or the deep roots of organizational aesthetics research. The relevance of philosophical aesthetics became more and more evident in the literature on the study of organizational aesthetics the last three decades, but it is expressed explicitly only in a part of the writings on the aesthetics of organization.

Nevertheless, it can not be claimed that the philosophical sensibility divides the organizational aesthetics researchers into the two broad camps delineated by Raza Mir, Hugh Willmott and Michelle Greenwood (2016: 1–2) in their introduction to *The Routledge Companion to Philosophy in Organization Studies*.

> First there are those who would rather not engage with what they regard as irrelevant or tiresome abstractions. For them, the only priority is that of "application", of consensus building, of paradigmatic unity and incremental advancement. [. . .] Turning to the second camp, their number includes those who see the foundations of organizational theory as yet to be charted terrain, worthy of philosophical examination. This philosophical examination has often been variously undertaken from a philosophy of science orientation (examining the ontological, epistemological and methodological orientation of various organizational theories and practices), a sociopolitical standpoint (evaluating the ideological underpinning of the field with respect to a variety of subjectivities), or some combination of these orientations.

To provide an example of the first camp, Mir, Willmott and Greenwood indicate Jeffrey Pfeffer's (1993) and Lex Donaldson's (1995) works, while John Hassard and Denis Pym's (1990) or Gareth Morgan's (1997) books are representative of the second camp. I mention these examples because they evoke the paradigmatic *querelle* that followed the crisis of the dominance of the rationalistic and positivistic paradigm in organization theory and management studies, and in social sciences more generally. And, in fact, the separation in these two camps does not occur in the study of organizational aesthetics, mainly because this area of research study has its origins in the crisis of the rationalistic and positivistic paradigm and breathes the atmosphere of the paradigmatic conflicts, as we shall see in Chapter 4.

Furthermore, it is almost exclusively due to the academic work of this area of research that the aesthetic philosophies reached some relevance in organizational theories, the sociology of organization and management studies. This is a first consideration to take in due account, because it denotes, on one side, the absence of aesthetic references in a large part of the organizational theories, and, on the other side, the limited persuasiveness of the organizational aesthetics discourse among the organizational theories.

Thus, we can depict the general features of the relationship between organization theory and aesthetic philosophy along the following points:

1. It is principally through the aesthetic discourse on organization that has established a dialogue between organizational theories and management studies, on one side, and philosophical aesthetics and art theories on the other side.
2. Even in the area of research study dedicated to the aesthetic side of organization, philosophical aesthetics is not always considered as relevant.
3. The disinterest towards philosophy, however, does not denote a choice against philosophical argumentations within the organizational aesthetics research.
4. When considered, aesthetic philosophy may also represent only a mere ritual act that does not imply a dialogue between organizational theories and philosophy of aesthetics.
5. The attention towards the aesthetic philosophies and art theory is just one of the various different forms to approach the aesthetic dimension of organizational life.

These five considerations delineate a panorama of the relationships between organizational theories and aesthetic philosophies which emphasize the variety of research styles that contribute to the configuration and the identity of an area of study in social sciences. In my eyes, they also evoke an image of democracy in doing social research and give strength to the irreducible differences in researching organization—*différance* in Derrida's (1967) terms—that has been a fundamental characteristic of the approaches to the study of organization which are characterized by an aesthetic lens (Strati, 2014).

In a way, this fundamental image of difference in researching organizational aesthetics is in tune with the Italian philosophy of "weak thought" (Vattimo, 1983), which accompanied my aesthetic approach since its beginning (Strati, 1992: 580) and stressed its distance and opposition against the search for strong paradigms in organizational theory, sociology of organization and management studies. In the polemic against the strong paradigms based in strong metaphysics, the weak thought emphasizes difference, finitude—"*the transcendental [. . .] is nothing less than transience*" (Vattimo, 1983; Eng. trans. 2012: 47; emphasis in the original)—and the everyday life of research practices.

Concluding Remarks

The first chapter of this book illustrates how it happened that my aesthetic study of work and organizational life intertwined with philosophy.

It has occurred since I "discovered" the aesthetic side of organization during my empirical study conducted in three departments of a prestigious and ancient Italian university. From its origins, thus, and thereafter, philosophical aesthetics and philosophy *tout court* became a "resounding wall" of my empirical study.

This is also the form in which to take in due account philosophical research and theory. A form, that is, which is grounded in the empirical study of organizational aesthetics. Two of "my situations"—to use Pareyson's terms (1943)—that emerged during the field study have been discussed in this chapter: (1) the organizational issue of the tacit dimension of knowing in work practices in organizations, and (2) the organizational aesthetic judgment that evokes a category of aesthetics.

These two situations have been of crucial importance in the configuration of my aesthetic approach to the study of organizational life. On the one hand, my attention to the micro-social practices in work and organizational contexts (Gherardi and Strati, 2012) emphasized the close link between aesthetic knowing and the tacit dimension of personal knowledge. On the other hand, at the same time, my attention to the "natural" mundane language used in the organizational communication emphasized the close link between the aesthetic judgments used in the everyday organizational life and the philosophical debate regarding the categories of aesthetics.

However, as I observe in the chapter, the dialogue between organizational theories and aesthetic philosophies is not always considered relevant in the organization studies and, in particular, in the organizational aesthetics research. On the contrary, this chapter—and all of this book— is meant to encourage the organizational scholar to engage in a dialogue with philosophical aesthetics, aesthetic social theory and the theory of art. But this is without arguing for a new "strong" theory on organizational aesthetics, because, as I clarify in the last section of the chapter, my philosophical viewpoint is keen towards the Italian philosophy of the weak thought.

In the introduction to the English translation of the book that Gianni Vattimo and Pier Aldo Rovatti edited on the philosophy of weak thought (1983), Peter Carravetta writes:

> If there is no possibility of turning back the clock on account of our finitude, and we no longer believe in the (by now presumptuous) value of making *tabula rasa* of all we inherited in order to seek some 'new' foundation or beginning, then our condition is that of dealing with the amass of *existing interpretations* which we can summon or even invent to make sense of the world. However, these interpretations will be marked by the gesture of appropriation and thus inevitably of distortion, or twisting (*Verwindung*), we might even say of misreading. This requires recognition of the fact that some of these versions have become authoritative (archives, canons, traditions) and

others have been marginalized (minority discourse, the wretched of the earth, the 'slaves') or forgotten (erasures, 'dead metaphors', suppressed voices).

(Carravetta, 2012: 4–5)

This is not "a question of *theoretical* weakness, but of *practical* weakness", Franco Crespi observes (1983; Eng. trans. 2012: 264) with reference to Heidegger, Nietzsche and Wittgenstein, and points out that the

rigorous recognition of the unsayable as the limit of the sayable means maintaining a tension between the sayable and the unsayable which finds its high point and 'appropriate' attitude in *being silent* [*tacere*].

(Crespi,1983; Eng. trans. 2012: 256)

The tension between the sayable and the unsayable bring us to *Interlude I: Poetry as manifesto N. 2*. As said in the Introduction of the book, the Interludes are meant to interrupt the flow of words and invite the reader to abandon it—if s/he wants—in order to immerse himself or herself in the visual world of a photograph, thus making a shift from written text language to the visual language of photography.

References

Addison, J. (1712). On the pleasures of the imagination, *The Spectator*, in Addison, J. and Steele, R. (eds.), *Selections from the Tatler and Spectator*. Ed. Ross, A. London: Penguin, 1982.

Bodei, R. (1995). *Le forme del bello*. Bologna: Il Mulino.

Burke, E. (1757). *A Philosophical Enquiry into the Origin of Our Ideas of the Sublime and the Beautiful*. Ed. Phillips, A. Oxford: Oxford University Press.

Calabrese, O. (1987). *L'età neobarocca*. Bari: Laterza.

Carravetta, P. (2012). What is 'Weak thought'? The original theses and context of *il pensiero debole*, in Vattimo, G. and Rovatti, P. A. (eds.), *Weak Thought*. Ed. Carravetta, P. Albany: State University of New York Press, pp. 1–38.

Crespi, F. (1983). Assenza di fondamento e progetto reale, in Vattimo, G. and Rovatti, P. A. (eds.) (1983). *Il pensiero debole*. Milano: Feltrinelli. (English trans.: Absence of foundation and social project, in Vattimo, G. and Rovatti, P. A. (eds.), *Weak Thought*. Ed. Carravetta, P. Albany: State University of New York Press, 2012, pp. 253–267).

Derrida, J. (1967). *L'écriture et la différence*. Paris: Éditions du Seuil. (English trans.: *Writing and Difference*. Chicago: University of Chicago Press, 1978).

Donaldson, L. (1995). *American Anti-management Theories of Organization: A Critique of Paradigm Proliferation*. Cambridge: Cambridge University Press.

Gherardi, S. and Strati, A. (2012). *Learning and Knowing in Practice-based Studies*. Cheltenham: Edward Elgar.

Hassard, J. and Pym, D. (1990). *The Theory and Philosophy of Organizations: Critical Issues and New Perspectives*. London: Routledge.

Kant, I. (1790). Kritik der Urteilskraft, in Kant, I. (ed.), *Werke in zwölf Bänden*, Vol. X. Ed. Weischedel, W. Frankfurt am Main: Suhrkamp, 1968. (English trans.: *The Critique of Judgement*. Ed. Meredith, J. C. Oxford: Oxford University Press, 1952).

Kofinas, A. (2018). Managing the sublime aesthetic when communicating an assessment regime: the Burkean Pendulum, *Management Learning*, 49 (2): 204–221.

Kostera, M. (1997). The Kitsch-organization, *Studies in Culture, Organization and Societies*, 3 (3): 163–177.

Langer, S. K. (1942). *Philosophy in a New Key: A Study in the Symbolism of Reason, Rite, and Art*. 4th edn. 1963. Cambridge, MA: Harvard University Press.

Linstead, S. (2002). Organizational kitsch, *Organization*, 9 (4): 657–682.

Longinus (1995). *On the Sublime*. Ed. Russell, D. Cambridge, MA: Harvard University Press.

Lyotard, J. F. (1991). *Leçons sur l'Analytique du sublime*. Paris: Éditions Galilée. (English trans.: *Lessons on the Analytic of the Sublime*. Stanford, CA: Stanford University Press, 1994).

Mack, K. S. (2007). Senses of Seascapes: aesthetics and the passion for knowledge, *Organization*, 14 (3): 373–390.

Martin, P. Y. (2002). Sensations, bodies, and the 'spirit of a place': aesthetics in residential organizations for the elderly, *Human Relations*, 55 (7): 861–885.

Mir, R., Willmott, H. and Greenwood, M. (2016). Introduction: philosophy in organization studies—life, knowledge and disruption, in Mir, R., Willmott, H. and Greenwood, M. (eds.), *The Routledge Companion to Philosophy in Organization Studies*. London: Routledge, pp. 1–11.

Morgan, G. (1997). *Images of Organization*. New edn. Thousand Oaks, CA: Sage.

Pareyson, L. (1943). *Studi sull'esistenzialismo*. Firenze: Sansoni. (Partial English trans.: Pareyson, L., *Existence, Interpretation, Freedom: Selected Writings*. Ed. Bubbio, P. D. Aurora, CO: The Davies Group, 2009).

Pelzer, P. (2002). Disgust and organization, *Human Relations*, 55 (7): 841–860.

Pfeffer, J. (1993). Barriers to the advance of organizational science: paradigm development as a dependent variable, *Academy of Management Review*, 18 (4): 599–620.

Piras, E. M. (2007). Il ritmo dell'organizzare, in Strati, A. (ed.), *La ricerca qualitativa nelle organizzazioni: la dimensione estetica*. Roma: Carocci, pp. 43–54.

Polanyi, M. (1958). *Personal Knowledge: Towards a Post-critical Philosophy*. 2nd edn. 1962. London: Routledge and Kegan Paul.

Schütz, A. (1962). *Collected Papers I: The Problem of Social Reality*. The Hague: Nijhoff.

Strati, A. (1990). Aesthetics and organizational skill, in Turner, B. A. (ed.), *Organizational Symbolism*. Berlin: de Gruyter, pp. 207–222.

Strati, A. (1992). Aesthetic understanding of organizational life, *Academy of Management Review*, 17 (3): 568–581.

Strati, A. (1999). *Organization and Aesthetics*. London: Sage.

Strati, A. (2003). Knowing in practice: aesthetic understanding and tacit knowledge, in Nicolini, D., Gherardi, S. and Yanow, D. (eds.), *Knowing in Organizations: A Practice-based Approach*. Armonck: M.E. Sharpe, pp. 53–75. Reprinted in Gherardi, S. and Strati, A. (2012). *Learning and Knowing in Practice-based Studies*. Cheltenham: Edward Elgar, pp. 16–38.

Strati, A. (2008). Aesthetics in the study of organizational life, in Barry, D. and Hansen, H. (eds.), *The Sage Handbook of New Approaches in Management and Organization.* London: Sage, pp. 229–238. Reprinted in Gherardi, S. and Strati, A. (2012). *Learning and Knowing in Practice-based Studies.* Cheltenham: Edward Elgar, pp. 132–148.

Strati, A. (2014). The social negotiation of aesthetics and organisational democracy, in Murphy, P. and de La Fuente, E. (eds.), *Aesthetic Capitalism.* Leiden: Brill, pp. 105–127.

Vattimo, G. (1983). Dialettica, differenza, pensiero debole, in Vattimo, G. and Rovatti, P. A. (eds.) (1983). *Il pensiero debole.* Milano: Feltrinelli (English trans.: Dialectis, difference, weak thought, in Vattimo, G. and Rovatti, P. A. (eds.), *Weak Thought.* Ed. Carravetta, P. Albany: State University of New York Press, 2012, pp. 39–52).

Vattimo, G. and Rovatti, P. A. (eds.) (1983). *Il pensiero debole.* Milano: Feltrinelli. (English trans.: Dialectics, difference, weak thought, in Vattimo, G. and Rovatti, P. A. (eds.), *Weak Thought.* Ed. Carravetta, P. Albany: State University of New York Press, 2012).

Interlude I: Poetry as manifesto N. 2, 2018

le Leica M, HDR, software Adobe Lightroom

2 Organizational Lens, Art Photography and the Creation Process

Interlude I is a photopoem that began with a photograph I took in a little square of the Parisian historic district of Butte aux Cailles, in the 13th arrondissement. It happened the day after the ISIS's massacre at the Bataclan theater, and at cafés and restaurants during the night of Friday, 13 November 2015, which was claimed by the Islamic State as retaliation for French airstrikes. The text of this graffiti on the wooden wall below the windows of a bistro says something that, after this terrible terrorist attack—where 130 people were killed and another 413 injured—gave me relief: *LA POÉSIE EST UN LUXE/DE PREMIÈRE NÉCESSITÉ*, that is POETRY IS A LUXURY/OF FIRST NECESSITY.

It sounded to me as a manifesto against the murderous attack and the somberness that was inevitably dominating the Parisian atmosphere of those days. It was a manifesto in favor of poetry that was strengthened by the portrait of the young woman on the other side of the wooden wall—which, with her gaze and her green t-shirt, looked sensual—and by the lamp, the bottles and the tools that stood above the words and the portrait, behind the two windows of the bistro.

In this chapter I will describe the process of creating this photopoem and the influence that some "fragments" of the debates in philosophy, art criticism and semiology have had on my artistic practices. The reader, if s/he wants, can take an active part in these reflections using the evocative form of knowledge, imagination and empathic understanding.

2.1 Let's Give a Chance to the Walls

Graffiti, nowadays, is an established artistic tradition that is able to problematize the arts in quotidian life and in public social contexts. Walls, trains and stations are decorated with words, images and colors that illustrate how ordinary beauty and ordinary ugliness may have an influence on our everyday life and our aesthetic taste. These are walls that can be those of the organization we are working in, trains that can be those that take us to work and stations that are part of our quotidian landscape to go to work. And they are the walls that are those of the Parisian square where I took the photograph.

2.1.1 *Imaginary Participant Art Photography*

If s/he had been at my place in front of that graffiti that day, would the reader have felt relief reading those words? In that case, what photograph would the reader have taken? With what framing? Highlighting what, in particular? In which style? According to what aesthetic judgment?

I pose these questions because the reader, if s/he wants, can immerse himself/herself in the situation that *Interlude I* shows and evokes, and s/he can act—and not just think through the resources of the logic analysis— as if s/he were there, and—imaginatively—smell the atmosphere and the odors, scrutinize the lights and the shadows, touch the graffiti's surface, listen to the voices, the noises and silences, and judge—aesthetically— according to his/her taste, what photograph to take.

The reader, probably, has already had both a direct experience of graffiti on a wooden wall in a square or in a street and an indirect experience of it through films, books and videos. Probably, s/he has also had direct experience of taking photographs of walls. Curtis L. Carter remarks that photography, in our contemporary globalized society,

> having moved beyond its status as autonomous art, it is free to explore other ways of contributing to the aesthetics of everyday life. [. . .] Thanks to digital imaging, virtually every cell phone is able to take and instantly transmit photographs on the internet, TV and social media networks across the world and into every aspect of everyday life.
>
> (2014: 95)

Art photography, in fact, comments Thomas Leddy (2014: 61), should not be depicted in philosophy "as taking us to a separate world (a world of Platonic Forms, for example) but as continuous with and interconnected with the various forms of photography associated with everyday life".

So, in the context of this philosophical and technological change of status of contemporary photography, the reader can imagine himself or herself exploring from what angle to frame the picture, the few steps to walk and the small movements to do to reach the preferred position, the decision to make to take the photograph. Obviously, all this is happening just in the reader's imagination. S/he sees, smells, moves, touches, hears, perceives— that is, s/he experiences and appreciates aesthetically rather than just by means of logic and rationality. S/he is photographing the graffiti by drawing on the evocative process of knowing. A photograph is taken by activating— imaginatively—the sensory faculties and the aesthetic judgment.

This is due, therefore to the aesthetic knowing and doing, rather than to mere cognition, such as we do in aesthetic research when we use the "imaginary participant observation" (Strati, 1999: 11–18; 2003, reprinted 2012: 20–23; 2009, reprinted 2012: 204–206) to prepare the design of the empirical research—to be realized, thus, physically and virtually—to identify the principal research questions that will lead the field study or to re-live the organizational interaction observed in order to re-examine it with all our perceptive faculties.

The reader, in fact, probably did not look on this graffiti of Butte aux Cailles, at least not in the exact moment I photographed it exploring its signs, colors, lights and shadows. I must also add that s/he has not even seen the final "photopoem"—a color photograph that is characterized by the style of my conceptual photographic research, which is named "Photopoesia".

What I want to stress is that "what" the reader has seen in *Interlude I* is, in fact, something else. It is the Routledge typographical print of my photopoem, rather than my photopoem, that is, an image printed in black and white which constitutes—according to the Italian designer Giovanni Anceschi (1992: 171)—an illustration that "creates the evocation of the object", that is, of the photopoem—which is in color—but also of the graffiti—which is also in color—and which, at the same time, "realizes an interpretation" of them.

In other words, the reader saw neither the origin of my photopoem, that is, how the graffiti of La Butte aux Cailles looked, nor the final artifact, but just a printed translation of it that, in Anceschi's terms, reifies my photograph in a new artifact.

Most importantly, s/he has not witnessed the process of creation of the photopoem, an important process because it characterizes in a distinctive way every work of art, or "every corpus of works built consistently"— such as both the graffiti and the photopoem are. As the Italian semiologist Omar Calabrese (2006: VII) notes, this is a process which

> inevitably constitutes the theory of itself, because—given the individuality deriving from its aesthetic character—it puts in scene, in a more or less hidden way, the principles that are at its foundation.

2.1.2 *Art Practices and the Creation Process*

As regards *Interlude I*, for instance, the reader did not see my various attempts to create this image. The aesthetic quality of the printing press beautifully conceals in itself the aesthetics of these attempts as well as all the organizational dynamics and processes that construct the concrete creation situations of this photopoem.

For instance: Where did I end up? When was it done? "How can an artist finish with a work", writes Pierre-Michel Menger (2006: 41), "if we admit that Picasso's dictum—'The most difficult thing is to know when to stop'—can be applied generally?" How to grasp quality and meaning of the work of art that is said to be "unfinished"?

What should be emphasized is that the situation of creative invention is that of striving to an end that, even if it is impossible to specify and plan, is in a sense directing the process. Uncertainty and variability of that process are both the motor of the invention engine and the obstacle to an easy and straightforward decision-making process.

(Menger, 2006: 63)

The question is, in fact, affirms Howard Becker (2006: 25), essentially of "choice", a word he "would make central to a sociological analysis of artistic work". But not just with reference to the varying versions of an artwork that "are treated as variants from which the one 'authentic' work must be extracted" (Becker, 2006: 22).

That is, it is impossible, in principle, for sociologists or anyone else to speak of the "work itself" because there is no such thing. There are only the many occasions on which a work appears or is performed or read or viewed, each of which can be different from all the others. [. . .] This is not merely a philosophical conundrum or a sociological caprice. If the artwork is fundamentally indeterminate, people will have problems dealing with it. They will not be sure when it exists and when it doesn't, won't know what its form and nature are, won't be able to talk about it (after all, which version are we discussing?). They (and therefore we) can only distinguish the "work itself" by invoking some convention.

(Becker, 2006: 23)

Conventions in the sociology of organizations and organization theory may be indicated as norms, agreements, shared values and organizational cultures. Becker's "Principle of the Fundamental Indeterminacy of the Artwork" (2006: 22–23), and Menger's view of the process of creative invention as a purposeful moving "towards an unspecified end", well illustrate the arguments that I like to emphasize for organizational research by using the term of awareness of the creation process.

The awareness that the process which characterizes the realization of a work of art is essential for understanding it aesthetically and philosophically is important from an organizational theory point of view, as well as from a sociological and from the other social sciences viewpoints, such as the semiotic one. As often happens in the art practices, "the singular characterization—the difference more than the identity—becomes almost a *sine qua non*, or is nonetheless constitutive of the intentions of those who produce an artifact", observes Omar Calabrese (2006: IX), "even from the general epistemological point of view of semiotics the focus on the process is not only legitimate but desirable".

2.1.3 Which One Was the Subject of My Photopoem?

The young lady in a green t-shirt in the graffiti has had a particular importance for the photopoem in *Interlude I*: she acted as a *commentator*, a figure that founds its origins in the theory of Renaissance painting by Leon Battista Alberti (1435). The *commentator* looks at the scene on behalf of the spectator and not only creates, but constitutes a symbolic bridge with the spectator who watches the graffiti. At the same time, the *commentator* belongs to the represented scene in the graffiti. In doing so, observes Omar Calabrese (2006: 33), it configures "a character that attends to what the picture gives to see, and follows the Aristotelian rules of spatial, temporal and action unity" in order to tell the spectator "what and how to watch (perhaps emphasizing this function with the addition of indicative gestures)".

I realized only later on the simple, essential importance of the young lady in green t-shirt as *commentator*, as well as that of the wooden wall.

Regarding the *commentator*-young lady, it is apparent how the walls aesthetically resound aspects and moments of quotidian life inside and outside organizations. With her gesture of looking on the words of the graffiti—*LA POÉSIE EST UN LUXE/DE PREMIÈRE NÉCESSITÉ*, that is poetry is a luxury/of first necessity—we are invited to pay attention to the "word", to its symbolism.

To the point, the exact words of poetry as a luxury, but a luxury which is of first necessity, gave to me a sentiment of relief that was physically perceived, corporeal, while their meaning resonated with my photopoetic research in art photography and their symbolism evoked my cultural belief in the political character of art.

Also, at the same time, with her gesture, the young lady in green t-shirt underlines to us the fact that "the walls guard the word", as notices the historian Emmanuelle Loyer (2018: 6) in an article in the newspaper *Le Monde*. Since 1789, the walls of Paris took part in the material construction of the public space through urban inscriptions that conformed to the following three logics: (1) the official information policy; (2) the informal and sometimes subversive—such as during May 1968—writing, i.e., graffiti and ephemeral prints; (3) the technical vector for fame, i.e., advertising. Nowadays, while institutional information prefers other ways, like the digital one, amid the invasion of the city realized by advertising, also remains the

> untamed urban graffiti. Before being partially institutionalized as heritage under the term "street art", they spring in their freshness as a state of society, but also a state of the language.
>
> (Loyer, 2018: 6)

As regards the wooden wall, it is well-known, notes the French philosopher and semiotician Roland Barthes (2002: 711), that what "makes a

graffiti is the wall, the table, the bottom"—in a word, its background—
that "exists fully, as an object that has already lived". Thus, it is neither
the inscription, nor the message, but the wall that constitutes the graffiti,
thanks to the fact that this background *"is not clean"* and therefore it is
not appropriate for the thought—unlike, therefore, the white sheet used
by the mathematician or the philosopher—but "very peculiar to all that
remains—art, laziness, impulse, sensuality, irony, taste: all that the intellect can feel as many aesthetic disasters" (Barthes, 2002: 711).

Walls, tables and bottoms, observes the Italian historian and critic of
photography Roberta Valtorta, while commenting on the art photography of Aaron Siskind, Salvatore Mancini, David Robinson and Leland
Rice, are surfaces which

> already live by a specific material texture, compact or porous,
> smooth, tormented, determined by their natural or historical destiny;
> and they live of colors (stains, traces, chromatic discontinuity of mat-
> ter): thus, they are already written, drawn, painted. The graffiti is
> really a "supplement".
>
> (2005: 33)

Thus, which one was the subject of my photopoem? The graffiti-supplement,
the wooden wall that "made" the graffiti, the symbolism of the written
words *LA POÉSIE EST UN LUXE/DE PREMIÈRE NÉCESSITÉ*, or
the hybridization of all of them?

In a sense, I would say, none of them. When I first took the photograph, in order to eventually create a photopoem, while photographing
with my digital Leica M, my focus was on the aroused feelings I was
experiencing, since "to photograph feelings" is what characterizes distinctively my aesthetic research in photography. My attention was thus
emotionally focused on the sentiment of relief that the graffiti aroused in
all my body, that is, on something that was behind the lens of the Leica
rather than in front of the camera.

This feeling, thus, was my principal subject, the "figure" of the photographic scene. The graffiti and the wooden wall were just constituting
the background of it. Focusing on a sentiment, according to Leon Battista
Alberti (1435), implies a motion of the soul, rather than a static translation, and it implies also that, emphasizes Omar Calabrese (2006: 39),
besides

> the definition of to look on as an "active cognitive act", we will have
> to add that of "forming a passionate act" (forming because it is not
> an exclusive element of the representation of passions). On the other
> hand, the dictionary itself indicates looks of this nature: "stern gaze",
> "seductive gaze", "hate-laden gaze", "intriguing gaze", "ambiguous
> gaze", and so on.

But, is it this sentiment of relief that we see, looking at *Interlude I*?

When I framed the image, I did it in a way that the photopoem comprehended not only the written text and the lady in green, but also the two windows and the bistro's tools and lamp. This aesthetic choice was due to avoid that, in order to grasp the sentiment of relief—the "figure" of my photopoem—I could just let in the shadow, the feeling of sadness of these days and the mourning for the massacre that was in the Parisian atmosphere. Both relief and sadness had to be a presence in the photopoem: relief as the principal figure, sadness as its perceptible ground. So I framed the photograph as if a graveyard cross was sculpted in the wooden wall as a constituent element of the graffiti's background and, later on, I elaborated this form electronically in order to make its presence slight, hardly to be noticed.

2.2 No Detail Is Insignificant in Art Photography

The aesthetic dynamic between the sentiment of relief and the sentiment of sadness in framing the photopoem in *Interlude I* detached my art photography from the art of the graffiti. This had constituted a fundamental change: with my photopoem, I was including in the graffiti aesthetic sentiments that were not necessarily a component of its aesthetics.

On the other hand, I was not taking photographs to make a mere representation of the graffiti aesthetics. Rather, on the contrary, I was reinventing the aesthetics of the graffiti of La Butte aux Cailles in my dialogue:

- on one side, with the aesthetics of daily life of the graffiti in the Parisian square, and with the recent philosophical current of "Everyday Aesthetics" (*Aisthesis. Pratiche, linguaggi e saperi dell'estetico*, 2014; Formis, 2010; Friberg and Vasquez, 2017; Przychodzen, Boucher, David, 2010; Saito, 2007; Yuedi and Carter, 2014); and,
- on the other side, with the aesthetic style of my photopoesia and the recent art debate that poses photography at the center of theories of art (Cotton, 2004; Fried, 2008; Soulages and Tamisier, 2012; Valtorta, 2004).

Roberta Valtorta observes that a change

> of sensibility occurred in contemporary photography when the theoretical debate pointed out that photographic practice is based on the overcoming of the artistic moment in favor of the aesthetic one, and by its nature takes into account, therefore, not so much of the work as the process that determines it and the intentions that drive it. Thus, moving away from the representation, the photograph seems to free itself from the compulsory search for meaning and becomes

action, implementing an approach to the world which is not only of a visual type, but involves all the senses in a relational way.

(2005: 156)

Also, as David Bate points out (2015), it is the engagement of the arts outside art—that is, in the society and in the organizational contexts— which characterizes the debates on why and how photography acquired a new centrality in art, a centrality that the photography never had before. Referring to the lecture that the French philosopher Jacques Rancière gave in 2002, in Paris, at the National Centre of Photography—which has now ceased its activities—Bate emphasizes the tensions and dynamics between art and the worlds outside art.

> In his lecture Rancière introduced three different categories of interaction between what he calls the "aesthetic regime of art" with non-art images: the naked image, the ostensive image and the metamorphic image. A naked image is one not intended as art, but which ends up in art because of its document-like qualities [. . .]. The ostensive image is one that refers to something that is not itself, as often in conceptual art. The metamorphic image is one that refers to commercial or media imagery, filtered back into art with difference. These categories, which we could clearly name as document, conceptual and postmodern (or allegory), are taken up where relevant, their associated strategies noted as a means to open up a space for visual dissensus (not consensus). The new centrality of the photographic image in art recognizes the necessity of such engagements of art outside itself. Photography is a pervasive social practice linked to all social types of image use and thus porous to changing definitions and practices. Such interactions are now crucial to what we consider art to be and what photography performs within it.
>
> (2015: 11)

2.2.1 A Movement in the Non-Representational Sphere

What one can see in *Interlude I* is not a representation but "a momentum", suggests Martin Engler (2012: 13), "a movement in the non-representational sphere which cannot be captured—somewhere between development and exposure, between chance and contamination". There is a common ground between the graffiti and my photograph, which is crucial, since, through the two diverse art languages, there was an attempt to create a manifesto in favor of poetry in everyday life. *LA POÉSIE EST UN LUXE/DE PREMIÈRE NÉCESSITÉ*, therefore, did not become just a mere cognitive message, eight words that bear a logic analytic meaning. This, unfortunately, is exactly what often happens in research on the organizational field: we do a video interview, and then we analyze what is said—the words, their logic—and we forget the visual aesthetics, and the aesthetics of the sound, images and words that, in other words, are one with the logical and cognitive meaning of the interview.

In fact, the manifesto in favor of poetry did not become a mere cognitive pretext, first of all because of its aesthetic materiality, and second because the main characteristic of photography consists of operating exclusively as a visual language. And, since the materiality of the wooden wall was showing its difference from the materiality of the windows, of the texts, of the portrait and of the tools of the bistro, and that, moreover, these diverse materialities all together were rendering complex the interpretation of the graffiti—mainly because of the different textures, and of the different lights and shadows—I chose to take five pictures framed in the same identical way, but each one with a different exposure of the lights and the shadows:

1. in the first one, I emphasized the thickness of the sign and the black and green colors of the graffiti;
2. in the second one, the wooden texture of the wall;
3. in the third one, the opaque transparency of the window pane;
4. in the fourth one, the lights and shadows of the artifacts behind the windows; and
5. in the fifth one, the reflections of the sun on the wooden wall.

I want to point out that these files were also due to the "phenomenological doubt" which is intrinsic to the photographic practice. The "act of photography"—writes the Czech phenomenologist philosopher Vilém Flusser (1983; Eng. trans. 2000: 38)—is that of phenomenological doubt, "to the extent that it attempts to approach phenomena from any number of viewpoints" through a "jump-start pursuit".

> The act of photography is divided into a sequence of leaps in which photographers overcome the invisible hurdles of individual time-and-space categories. If they are confronted by one of these hurdles (e.g. on the borderline between close-up and long shot), they hesitate and are faced with the decision about how to set the camera. (In the case of fully automatic cameras this leap, this quantum nature of photography, has become totally invisible—the leaps take place within the micro-electronic "nervous system" of the camera.) This type of jump-start pursuit is called "doubt".
>
> (Flusser, 1983; Eng. trans. 2000: 37–38)

2.2.2 Details Embody Present Mode of Being

Beyond all things, it was in fact impossible "to separate things from their way of appearing", as observed Maurice Merleau-Ponty (2002; Eng. trans. 2004: 70) in the talks he gave on French radio in 1948. When I am before a table, he continues, "I perceive" the table and "I do not withdraw my interest from the particular *way*" (2002; Eng. trans. 2004: 70) that this table has of performing. Rather, on the opposite, I explore and emphasize the details of that performance.

> No detail is insignificant: the grain, the shape of the feet, the colour and age of the wood, as well as the scratches or graffiti which show that age. The meaning, "table", will only interest me insofar as it arises out of all the "details" which embody its present mode of being. If I accept the tutelage of perception, I find I am ready to understand the work of art. For it too is a totality of flesh in which meaning is not free, so to speak, but bound, a prisoner of all the signs, or details, which reveal it to me.
>
> (Merleau-Ponty, 2002; Eng. trans. 2004: 70–71)

Thus, I employed the digital high dynamic range (HDR) photographic technique provided by the Adobe Photoshop Lightroom software (Evening, 2015) to merge the five photographs to obtain a wide dynamic range of luminosity of the final photograph. This style of making photography was used in art and professional photography since the beginning of the photographic medium, and it was generally surrounded by a halo of mystery. The actual capabilities of the digital manipulation through dedicated software are eliminating, nowadays, the mystery which has characterized the aesthetics of this photographic practice, and which consisted in these steps:

1. taking a number of photographs with the camera, in a first moment, without being sure of how the merged photograph would look at the end of the process, and therefore experiencing the aesthetic mystery of the final photographic result;
2. merging the "negatives" by using the enlarger in the darkroom, in the case of the technological environment of the analogic photography, or merging the "files" by employing a computer and the chosen dedicated software, in the environment of digital photography. The merging of the photographs thus happens in a second moment that is distinct for time, technology and space from the moment of taking the photographs;
3. manipulating the merged photograph through the techniques of the traditional analogic photography or through the digital software. In fact, it is not sufficient to combine the photographs to obtain the desired final image, and several attempts are needed to modify the "combined photograph" in order to give the final shape sought to the dynamic range of luminosity.

The disappearance (1) of these principal steps, (2) of the use of a variety of technological equipment and of organizational working spaces, and (3) of the sequence of different working times regarding each photographic practice, produced a deep transformation of the aesthetics of the use of the HDR technique in photography. This disappearance has not just been due to the continuous change in photographic technology—something that is clearly important, given that it creates a symbolic landscape for art photography. At the same time, it has been due to the continuous change in photographic aesthetics, as illustrated by the philosophical debates on art photography:

> Given the radical phases of its development thus far, through the stages of painterly photographs, modernist "pure photography", photojournalism, photography as a means of social commentary, and photo-conceptualism, we may expect that photography and the changes in its objecthood will continue to develop alongside new developments in technology and the ongoing evolutions of understanding in other spheres of culture—philosophical, economic and political.
>
> (Carter, 2014: 94)

However, technological transformation in art photography remains the main aspect generally considered. Rafael Conception, for example, underlines the radical nature of technological transformation in the introduction of the second edition of his manual on HDR for photographers:

> When I wrote the first version of this book, I really set out to debunk the entire idea that HDR was this overly complex dark art that few could really master. The fact of the matter is that making an HDR file is actually pretty easy: capture a set of images, jiggle a couple of sliders, and export. You're done.
>
> (2014: 13)

And the producers of software programs for photography are echoing this image to create an easy way to take HDR photography, making HDR a *de facto* standard for taking photographs, even using smartphones:

> HDR (high dynamic range) helps you get great shots in high-contrast situations. iPhone takes three photos in rapid succession at different exposures—and blends them together. The resulting photo has better detail in the bright and midtone areas.
>
> (Apple Inc., 2018)

HDR is used by default thanks to software employed by the smartphone, and it has to be deactivated manually in case its "being always in-use" is not desired. Thus, there is no aesthetic mystery anymore, but just an almost unseen and implicit standard to take photographs of higher quality in the everyday use of the aesthetics of photography. However, this leads us to a philosophical view of this technological improvement in the everyday aesthetics of art photography, as I shall illustrate in the next section.

2.3 Perception and the Materiality of the Image's Virtual Body

After having emphasized the organizational processes that constitute the "humus", that is, the interactive environment where the creation process finds its "situation" and develops, let me recapitulate the main aspects of this creative process:

- The graffiti had a vivid aesthetic influence on me, capturing my attention, arousing my sentiment of relief, and inspiring my art photography.
- Deciding to take a photograph in order to make a photopoem, I immersed my aesthetic action and my aesthetic knowing in the dialectics between the aesthetics of the graffiti and my photopoetic research.
- My photographs—that were not yet my "photopoem"—were constituted by attempts to include novel aesthetic sentiments and emotions into the photographed graffiti.
- My photographs were also, at the same time, analytical inquiry and aesthetic interpretation of details regarding the graffiti's aesthetics and materiality in view of the creation of a unique photopoem.
- The technological environment of the two "art facts"—that is, one of the graffiti that existed already, and the other of the photopoem that instead was still in its creation process, and, thus, literally did not exist yet—were highly diverse "in nature", given that the graffiti was immersed in the environment of physical materiality, while the photopoem was immersed in that of virtual materiality.

In fact, to be precise, what I did at the beginning of the photopoetic process was not to take five photographs, but to do something profoundly different: that is, to create five slightly diverse "files", one from the other, with my digital camera. This clarification is necessary because, as Sylvia Wolf writes, in the virtual environment, the materiality of the photographic process takes on a specific form:

> In digital photography, the construction of a likeness is based on code and algorithms. Information from the physical world that starts with a transmission of light is received by sensors in a digital camera and converted into data that is stored as zeros and ones in a computer memory. Unlike the grain that photographic film is made up of, a digital image is comprised of picture elements that are independent, discrete, tiny squares. Each pixel, as these units of information

are called can be individually altered, molded, and modulated in an infinite variety of ways.

(Wolf, 2010: 26)

The principal aspect that is similar for both the digital photography and the analogic traditional photography we have known for almost two centuries is that they are both based on the transmission of light. The principal characteristic that, on the contrary, distinguishes the film of analogic photography from the file of digital photography, is that the latter requires interaction with the "gaze" of the people who look at it to translate it into a photograph. In his *Aesthetics of the Virtual*, Roberto Diodato (2005; Eng. trans. 2012: 1) writes that a digital photograph constitutes a "virtual body", that is

> the self-phenomenalization of an algorithm in binary format arising in its interaction with a user-consumer. It is a function of writing that, in its sensible appearance, at the same time exposes and conceals the translation project through which it is constituted in its computational operations. As apparition of a grammar, such a language-image [*immagine-linguaggio*] implies a peculiar spectrality that affects the visible-invisible relation and structures the modality of its fruition. From this point of view, the digital image [. . .] is a genetic-relational form that belongs to a multiple system of translation. The digital image is not, one could say, properly "image" but image-body [*corpo-immagine*], since it is made of tidy sequences of binary units, or, in other words, strings of characters that develop at various levels of a syntax that constructs the coincidence between these strings and their sensible appearances, which currently are mostly sonorous or visual but in general perceptible.

Now we can understand how the evocation of my sentiment of relief in seeing this graffiti was then aesthetically investigated and reinvented photographically through metamorphosis and translation. "The bond linking emotion and imagery", writes Timothy Druckrey (1993: 33), "has been a continuing presence in the history of photography"; and the digital photographs rendered on the screen

> are based on the reciprocity between language and desire. The computer's ability to create an image from sequences of letters forming an algorithm would seem to be an exercise in processing and randomness. Yet the opposite occurs. Emerging from the clock cycles and the resolution developing in the screen image, images are produced that evolve toward representation. There is an inversion of tradition in which images are broken into constituents.

Digital photography questions the issue of representation and interrogates the conditions for a poetics that is grounded in information. So, the virtual environment of my "photopoesia" made the practice of my art photography involved in "a more dialectical vision and perception, a deeper reciprocity that sees exist together the real sensible and ourselves" (Valtorta, 2005: 156), and where authorship belongs to the artist and the robot (Bertrand Dorléac and Neutres, 2018), and to the organization.

2.3.1 The Collective Artist: Art Photographer, Information Engineer, Photographic Industry and Public

What I have described from within the process of creating a photographic artwork is, indeed, crossed, supported and even opposed by organizational actions that are often considered only marginal, while, on the contrary, they are crucial. I want to illustrate this point thoroughly for reasons of clarity:

- The wooden wall, the windows, as well as the bistro's instruments are the products of organizational action, the realization of organizational design, the choice due to organizational taste. The white color of the wooden wall, the look of the bottles and lamps, the transparency of the glass of the windows exhibit a complex mix of a plurality of organizational aesthetics. But also, the kind of wood, glass and metal and the chemical composition of colors, represent aesthetic choices that have been made in organizational settings and that belong to diverse organizational aesthetics.
- The black color of the texts and of the lines drawing the young lady's portrait, as well as the green color of the t-shirt of the woman, show the organizational work done in order to produce them according to the organization's aesthetic choices.
- The brushes and spray cans for coloring, that is, the instruments employed to paint the graffiti, too, are due to organizational work and aesthetics. We did not see them in action, but, despite it, we cannot assume that their specific characteristics are not of importance, nor that they have little influence on the realization of the graffiti.
- The eventual instrument ad hoc to serve as a mask for coloring, expressly realized for signing the graffiti in the same style we can also see in other Parisian graffiti, might be an artisanal realization, but the materials with which it has been made are probably produced by some industrial organization.
- My Leica M, which is a professional digital camera, is due to organizational work that traverses this photographic company to involve other organizations producing glass for the lens, special metals for the hard components, software dedicated for its use, leather for the

containers of camera and lens, as well as research laboratories for innovating, centers for marketing, shops for selling, web site design dedicated to organizational communication, photography meetings to exhibit the new products, art photographers for testing innovative products—and illustrate them in tutorials or write a book on them— and also amateurs, professional photographers and social communities of fans. From the organizational design of the photographic camera until the web galleries dedicated to its capabilities and moving further towards the prosumers' communities, we can see, in part, and in part hypothesize, the negotiation processes of a rather large variety of diverse individual and organizational aesthetics.

- The Adobe photographic software I used to manipulate the five photographic files in order to create a single file is able, in the interaction with my looking at it, to become a virtual body; thus, a photograph responding to my aesthetic research style is an organizational product, resulting from research both in information engineering and in art photography, and which is promoted through tutorials on the web, in videos and books, and at photographic meetings, besides in fans' and users' communities.

- The typographic structures of Routledge and/or of the companies that have printed this book are according to aesthetic canons regarding the quality of the print in black and white which, it can be assumed, have been established through negotiation processes in the publishing house.

- The digital environment of the Internet to send the digital photopoem via e-mail and exchange information on it has been socially constructed and reconstructed through organizational actions, networks and communities that have also been inspired by specific organizational aesthetics. However, it should be noted that the aesthetic choices operating in the technological world of the Internet have no influence on the aesthetic quality of the photopoem, because, as the French philosophers Gilles Deleuze and Félix Guattari (1980) observed, the image in cyberspace is devoid of substance, since it does not have "a form that is given *a priori*" (Buydens, 2003: 62).

To have taken the photographs and to have manipulated them in order to create the photopoem in *Interlude I* of this book has been, therefore, a creation process immersed in a complex set of organizational actions and practices.

What I want to emphasize at this point is that both photopoem and Interlude are not the result of an individual creative act that is bounded to art photography, but, instead, that they are the result of a process which is due to the aesthetic contamination of various individual, collective and organizational tastes. In other terms, my artistic conceptual research in photography and its photopoetic works are in a continuous dialogue and negotiation with the aesthetics of other art photography researches that are significant for my photopoesia; with the aesthetics which are dominant or just prevailing in the photographic industries; with the aesthetics of a graffiti and with the aesthetics of its background, the wooden wall; and also, with the typographic aesthetic standards relative to the quality of the print of images.

Thus, not only is the author of the photopoem in *Interlude I* the "collective artist" I have just begun to delineate, but also the aesthetics of this artwork printed in *Interlude I* is a *collective aesthetics*. In fact, my art photography research style, my Photopoesia, has had to deal with the interactive capabilities of the programs of photographic software through which I have used the digital camera and the computer. These software programs provided me with a wide range of aesthetic choices and of information on how to adopt them. These aesthetic choices were not my creation, just as my photographic aesthetics was not their creation.

I have been activating the software range of aesthetic choices, just as these choices have been activating my aesthetic intuition, my art mastery, my imagination. I have included, transgressed, challenged, contrasted and denied the aesthetic choices suggested, recommended and provided by the photographic software programs. I did so both when taking the photograph with the camera, and all along with my manipulation of the digital photographs using the computer.

However, the interactions between my photographic aesthetics and the aesthetics of the software programs dedicated to photography did not foresee that the software had been operating independently from my aesthetic decisions, as an artist-robot which has emancipated itself and co-creates thanks to its artistic artificial imagination. Rather, the process of creation has hybridized the aesthetics of photopoesia with those of software programs dedicated to photography. After all, the computer itself is a machine to create hybrids, observes Laurence Bertrand Dorléac:

> If an artist looks to the new techniques to see new forms, the machinery with which s/he almost merges questions his/her "authority", to the point that we could speak of a collective work: artist/engineer/robot/viewer. And if the dialogue between the artists and the robots (computers) began since a good fifty years, it has recently gained complexity. We must think of the new qualities of the works, starting with their "common" dimension. The artist is allied with the robot and the engineer (when s/he is not him/herself), but also with the public more and more active.
>
> (2018: 31)

2.3.2 Which One Is the Original?

The photopoem published in *Interlude I* is entitled *Poetry as manifesto N. 2* and is dated 2018. This is because it exists as a previous version of this photopoem—*Poetry as manifesto. The Day After November 13*—realized in 2015 to be the third of three photopoems (Strati, 2017) that have appeared in the Special Issue of *Culture and Organization* (2017), a memorial publication dedicated to Heather Höpfl's academic work.

These two photopoems are slightly different, and a close comparison of the two diverse typographical prints—the journal's one, and the book's one—might let the differences emerge that exist between the two versions of *Poetry as manifesto*. So, what is the original photopoem?, one could ask. Both are original, can be the only answer, for each of them belongs to a specific and peculiar creation process.

This is my aesthetic understanding, even when I appreciate the originals and copies of the work of art, as in the case of the "Wedding Feast at Cana" (*Le nozze di Cana*), which once again stimulated the theoretical debate on this *topos* in the history of art.

The oil on canvas realized by the late Renaissance Italian artist Paolo Caliari, called "Veronese", in 1563 is a very large painting, about 7 m × 10 m, because it was intended to decorate the refectory of the church of San Giorgio Maggiore in Venice. But it decorated the refectory only for about two centuries, that is, until Napoleon's French Revolutionary Army took it as spoils during the "Italian campaigns" of 1797. So, this great oil on canvas was exhibited at the Louvre Museum in Paris, where it is still located in the *salle de la Joconde* opposite the "Gioconda" of Leonardo da Vinci.

Thus, *Le nozze di Cana* never returned to decorate the refectory of the church of San Giorgio Maggiore. Nevertheless, since 2007, the refectory has been decorated by Veronese's *Nozze di Cana*. In fact, there exists a second "version"—in my terms—of Veronese's oil on canvas, of the same size, thanks to

- the aesthetic and technological innovations of digital photography;
- the work of Adam Lowe, the director of "Factum Arte", a company dedicated to the development of digital technology in relation to the conservation of cultural heritage;
- the passionate initiative of Pasquale Gagliardi, one of the pioneers of the study of the aesthetic side of organization (Gagliardi, 1990) and for several years the head of the Italian Senate foundation, the "Fondazione Cini"; and
- the agreement between the Fondazione Cini and the Louvre in Paris.

The debate on the relationship between the "original" and its "copied version" has a long tradition in the theories of art and aesthetic philosophies, from the copy of the sculptures to be exposed in public places, to the "false originals" that are counterfeited but sometimes also signed by the same artist who made the original. More recently, the debate has also affected facsimile, as it is called, in a bad way, the digital version of Veronese by Lowe or the 1:1 scale photographic reproduction of the *Cappella Sistina* located in Japan (Settis, 2007).

The long tradition of this debate underlines its relevance for aesthetic philosophies, the sociology of art, semiology and theories of art, because the topics covered range from the aura of the work of art and its aesthetic appreciation, to the ethical issues posed by the diffusion of a "cultural policy of the facsimile" policy amongst cultural institutions and cultural industry (Clair, 2011; Latour and Lowe, 2011).

In my aesthetic understanding, the point is that oil painting and digital facsimile belong to two diverse creation processes, separated by more than four centuries of aesthetic culture, aesthetic negotiation and aesthetic history, distinguished by the different materiality of oil on canvas and digital photography on canvas; and distanced by their being situated, one in the organizational context of the museum, the other in the refectory of the church—a refectory that, in turn, was subject to changes in appearance and in use, along these four centuries.

Furthermore, a paradox concerns exactly the "original" of these two works of art. The *Nozze di Cana*, which is now in the refectory, reproduces the *Nozze di Cana* that continues to remain in the Louvre—which is exactly the opposite of the origins of this great Veronese painting.

My aesthetic considerations concerning the works of art of Veronese and of Lowe and Factum Arte resonate in the following annotations regarding the two photopoetic versions of *Poetry as manifesto*.

The two creation processes have the first part in common, since the photographs I realized with my Leica M are constituted by the same identical digital files. But, I pointed out, the photographs do not coincide with the photopoem, and once the photographs are taken, the photopoem has yet to be made. Moreover, since the photographs are constituted by digital files, and also all the aesthetics of the digital environment are due to algorithms in interaction with the art photographer, it is nonsense to raise the question of the original photopoem: all photopoems are original and unique digital files.

The difference between the two photopoems, instead, can be explored. It is due to the process of manipulation through the photographic software programs used on the computer. The elaboration of these files with the computer software has been, in fact, highly different, because of the following:

- The manipulation took place in different times, 2015 for the case of the journal and 2018 in the case of the book, which circumscribe and evoke two different artistic "situations", according to Pareyson's existentialist philosophy (1943).
- The symbolism, also, of each photopoem is diverse. The first one published in the journal memorial special issue emphasized the common ground I have shared with Heather Höpfl in organizational research.

The second one that appears in this book emphasizes, instead, the topic of the creation process as a hybridization of art, aesthetic philosophy and organizational theory.

- The philosophical aesthetics is more explicitly relevant in the creation process of the book version of *Poetry as manifesto*. In particular, the reader can notice, by looking at the photopoem, the importance of the considerations expressed by Roland Barthes (2002)—it is the wall that makes the graffiti—and by Roberta Valtorta (2005)—the material texture of the wall is so rich in elements that the graffiti becomes just a supplement.

The two photopoetic versions of *Poetry as manifesto* respond, in one word, to their specific creation processes, which have been characterized by specific interactions between "fragments" of aesthetic philosophies, the semiology of art, the philosophy of art photography, and "fragments" of the organizational theories, as I argued in Chapter 1.

It is, however, the *commentator*—the young lady in the green t-shirt—which constitutes the "bridge", according to semiologist Omar Calabrese (2006), that strongly connects both versions of the photopoem. The young lady in green, in fact, with her gesture, underlines the written text *LA POÉSIE EST UN LUXE/DE PREMIÈRE NÉCESSITÉ*; and these eight words, in their materiality of graffiti, have resounded inside me, on one side, the intent to constitute a "manifesto", and on the other, the fact of having a poetic touch, that is, two aspects that I had caught in some writings by Heather Höpfl. For example, she observed—in the chapter she wrote for a book on philosophical aesthetics (Höpfl, 2008: 21)—that the time when the aesthetics of organization "has come to prominence has coincided with an increasing metrification of organizational processes and performance" and with "an emphasis on the text to the exclusion of the body". The study of the aesthetic dimension of organizational life, she continued (Höpfl, 2008: 21), represents a resistance against:

- Crude utilitarian theories of organizations and organizational behavior
- A world reduced to simple statistical measures
- One dimensional accounts of organizational life and simple "case-studies"
- An absence of the senses and embodied experience
- A culture of performance measurement and monitoring
- Matrix structures and other definitional simplicities
- Naive change strategies
- An absence of compassion
- Rationality privileged in theories of organizing

- A view of organizations in which "people skills" are only relevant to the extent that they support organizational objectives
- A commitment to continuous improvement which implies a loss of contact with the moment

Concluding Remarks

To conclude Chapter 2, I will ask: Which photographs did the reader take by means of his/her imaginative participant art photography? Which attempts did s/he imagine before the final artwork? In which technological environment of art photography? In what dialogue with philosophy, art theory, aesthetic social theory, and organizational approaches? In co-operation with which co-authors? Furthermore, how many different versions of *Poetry as manifesto* were made in his/her imagination? And, thus, what about the question of which one is the original?

In fact, by illustrating the creation process of my photopoem in *Interlude I*, my intent has been exactly to reflect on these interrogatives, and this has also been the sense of deepening the details concerning the two different creation processes that have realized the two versions of the photopoem *Poetry as manifesto*.

The point I have been making was that of the relevance of the aesthetic philosophies for a work practice that is inspired to produce creativity and art. This relevance is due, first of all, to the indirect, often unseen, pervasiveness of philosophical aesthetics in everyday life, and art photography, as well as digital photography *tout court*, which shows it in an incontrovertible way, as we have seen in this chapter (Carter, 2014; Diodato, 2005; Wolf, 2010). This relevance is also due to the direct and aware choice of the art photographer, who creates a dialogue between fragments of the creative process and fragments of aesthetic philosophies.

Thus, we have seen how far the process of creating a photograph which resonates with an artistic research in photography can bring into light its theoretical framework; how intrinsically diverse is the virtual environment of digital photography from the previous traditional "analogic" one as well as from the typographic representation of it; and how closely connected are the experiential flux of the creation process and the artwork realized.

Each version of the photopoem had its "situation", concrete, material and inherently philosophical. Each creation process showed (1) the hybridization of aesthetics that characterized each version of the photopoem, (2) the negotiation processes conducted at the aesthetic level, and (3) the organizational interactions between art photographer, photographic industry and information engineering. The latter delineates the world of art photography as "organization without walls" (Strati, 1995, 1996, Eng. trans. 2000: 24–26), a concept of the organization that emphasizes the elusiveness of the organization and its constant process of organizing and disorganizing.

I will say more about the concept of "organization without walls" in the next chapter. Now, if we think of photography as if it were a metaphor of everyday aesthetics in social life, we will grasp the visible and invisible traits and situations of art and aesthetics in organizational life. I shall also discuss this subject in the next chapter. Before passing to it, however, the rhythm of the words will be interrupted and distracted by the visual language of the photopoem in *Interlude II*.

References

Aisthesis. Pratiche, linguaggi e saperi dell'estetico (2014). Special Issue on "Everyday objects", 7 (1). Edited by Matteucci, G., Di Stefano, E. and A. Mecacci.

Alberti, L. B. (1435). *De Pictura*. Bari: Laterza, 1964. (English trans.: *On Painting. A New Translation and Critical Edition*. Ed. Sinisgalli, R. New York: Cambridge University Press, 2011).

Anceschi, G. (1992). *L'oggetto della raffigurazione*. Milano: Etaslibri.

Apple Inc. (2018). iPhone User Guide for iOS 11. iBooks, https://itunes.apple.com/it/book/iphone-user-guide-for-ios-11-3/id1263310224?mt=11.

Barthes, R. (2002). *Oeuvres complètes, tome 5: Livres, textes, entretiens, 1977–1980*. Ed. Marty, E. Paris: Éditions du Seuil.

Bate, D. (2015). *Art Photography*. London: Tate Publishing.

Becker, H. S. (2006). The work itself, in Becker, H. S., Faulkner, R. R., and Kirshenblatt-Gimblett, B. (eds.), *Art from Start to Finish*. Chicago: The University of Chicago Press, pp. 21–30.

Bertrand Dorléac, L. (2018). Pourquoi avoir peur des robots?, in Bertrand Dorléac, L. and Neutres, J. (eds.), *Artistes & Robots*. Paris: Réunion des musées nationaux—Grand Palais, pp. 14–35.

Bertrand Dorléac, L. and Neutres, J. (eds.) (2018). *Artistes & Robots*. Paris: Réunion des musées nationaux—Grand Palais.

Buydens, M. (2003). La forme dévorée. Pour une approche deleuzienne d'Internet, in Lenain, T. (ed.), *L'image. Deleuze, Foucault, Lyotard*. Paris: Librairie Philosophique J. Vrin, pp. 41–63.

Calabrese, O. (2006). *Come si legge un'opera d'arte*. Milano: Mondadori Università.

Carter, C. L. (2014). Art photography and everyday life, in Yuedi, L. and Carter, C. L. (eds.), *Aesthetics of Everyday Life: East and West*. Newcastle upon Tyne: Cambridge Scholars Publishing, pp. 80–95.

Clair, J. (2011). *L'inverno della cultura*. Milano: Skira.

Conception, R. (2014). *The HDR Book: Unlocking the Pros' Hottest Postprocessing Techniques*. 2nd edn. San Francisco, CA: Peachpit—Pearson Education.

Cotton, C. (2004). *The Photograph as Contemporary Art*. London: Thames & Hudson.

Culture and Organization (2017). Special issue "Professor Heather Höpfl, 1948–2014: eine gedenkschrift". Edited by Brewis, J., Meisenbach, R., Rippin, A., Risberg, A., Sayers, J. and D. Sköld.

Deleuze, G. and Guattari, F. (1980). *Mille plateaux: capitalisme et schizophénie*. Paris: Éditions de Minuit. (English trans.: *A Thousand Plateaus: Capitalism and Schizophrenia.* Ed. Massumi, B. Minneapolis: University of Minnesota Press, 1987).

Diodato, R. (2005). *Estetica del virtuale.* Milano: Bruno Mondadori. (English trans.: *Aesthetics of the Virtual.* Albany: State University of New York Press, 2012).

Druckrey, T. (1993). Revisioning technology, in Druckrey, T. (ed.), *Iterations: The New Image.* Cambridge, MA: The MIT Press, pp. 17–39.

Engler, M. (2012). Abstract worlds—Painting in the light of photography, in Engler, M. (ed.), *Malerei in Fotografie/Painting in Photography.* Berlin: Kehrer Verlag, pp. 8–13.

Evening, M. (2015). HDR Photomerges in Lightroom CC/Lightroom 6—YouTube. Video 6', www.youtube.com/watch?v=0eVxeAYjFX4.

Flusser, V. (1983). *Für eine Philosophie der Fotografie.* Berlin: European Photography Andreas Müller-Pohle. (English trans.: *Towards a Philosophy of Photography.* London: Reaktion Books, 2000).

Formis, B. (2010). *Esthétique de la vie ordinaire.* Paris: Presses Universitaires de France.

Friberg, C. and Vasquez, R. (eds.) (2017). *Experiencing the Everyday.* Copenhagen: NSU Press/Aarhus University Press.

Fried, M. (2008). *Why Photography Matters as Art as Never Before.* New Haven, CT: Yale University Press.

Gagliardi, P. (ed.) (1990). *Symbols and Artifacts: Views of the Corporate Landscape.* Berlin: de Gruyter.

Höpfl, H. (2008). Aesthetics and management, in Palmer, C. and Torevell, D. (eds.), *The Turn to Aesthetics: An Interdisciplinary Exchange of Ideas in Applied and Philosophical Aesthetics.* Liverpool: Liverpool Hope University Press, pp. 17–27.

Latour, B. and Lowe, A. (2011). The migration of the aura, or how to explore the original through its facsimiles, in Bartscherer, T. and Coover R. (eds.), *Switching Codes: Thinking Through Digital Technology in the Humanities and the Arts.* Chicago: University of Chicago Press, pp. 275–298.

Leddy, T. (2014). Everyday aesthetics and photography, *Aisthesis. Pratiche, linguaggi e saperi dell'estetico*, 7 (1): 45–62.

Loyer, E. (2018). Les murs gardent la parole, *Le Monde Week-End: Idées*, Saturday 14 April, p. 6.

Menger, P. M. (2006). Profiles of the unfinished: Rodin's work and the varieties of incompleteness, in Becker, H. S., Faulkner, R. R., and Kirshenblatt-Gimblett, B. (eds.), *Art from Start to Finish.* Chicago: The University of Chicago Press, pp. 31–68.

Merleau-Ponty, M. (2002). *Causeries 1948.* Paris: Éditions du Seuil. (English trans.: *The World of Perception.* New York: Routledge, 2004).

Pareyson, L. (1943). *Studi sull'esistenzialismo.* Firenze: Sansoni. (Partial English trans.: Pareyson, L., *Existence, Interpretation, Freedom: Selected Writings.* Ed. Bubbio, P. D. Aurora, CO: The Davies Group, 2009).

Przychodzen, J., Boucher, F. E. and David, S. (eds.) (2010). *L'esthétique du beau ordinaire dans une perspective transdisciplinaire. Ni du gouffre ni du ciel.* Paris: l'Harmattan.

Saito, Y. (2007). *Everyday Aesthetics.* Oxford: Oxford University Press.

Settis, S. (2007). Copie da copione, *Il Sole 24 ORE*, 23rd September, www.ilsole24ore.com/art/arteconomy/2007-09-27.

Soulages, F. and Tamisier, M. (eds.) (2012). *Photographie Contemporaine & Art Contemporain*. Paris: Klincksieck.

Strati, A. (1995). Aesthetics and organizations without walls, *Studies in Cultures, Organizations and Societies*, 1 (1): 83–105.

Strati, A. (1996). *Sociologia dell'organizzazione: paradigmi teorici e metodi di ricerca*. Roma: NIS-Carocci. (English trans.: *Theory and Method in Organization Studies: Paradigms and Choices*. London: Sage, 2000).

Strati, A. (1999). *Organization and Aesthetics*. London: Sage.

Strati, A. (2003). Knowing in practice: aesthetic understanding and tacit knowledge, in Nicolini, D., Gherardi, S. and Yanow, D. (eds.), *Knowing in Organizations: A Practice-based Approach*. Armonck: M.E. Sharpe, pp. 53–75. Reprinted in Gherardi, S. and Strati, A. (2012). *Learning and Knowing in Practice-based Studies*. Cheltenham: Edward Elgar, pp. 16–38.

Strati, A. (2009). "Do you do beautiful things?": aesthetics and art in qualitative methods of organization studies, in Buchanan, D. and Bryman A. (eds.), *The Sage Handbook of Organizational Research Methods*. London: Sage, pp. 230–245. Reprinted in Gherardi, S. and Strati, A. (2012). *Learning and Knowing in Practice-based Studies*. Cheltenham: Edward Elgar, pp. 194–209.

Strati, A. (2017). Heather's poetic touch alive in our memory, *Culture and Organization*, 23 (2): 149–156.

Valtorta, R. (ed.) (2004). *È contemporanea la fotografia?* Milano: Lupetti—Editori di Comunicazione.

Valtorta, R. (2005). *Volti della fotografia. Scritti sulla trasformazione di un'arte contemporanea*. Milano: Skira editore.

Wolf, S. (2010). *The Digital Eye: Photographic Art in the Electronic Age*. New York: Prestel.

Yuedi, L. and Carter, C. L. (eds.) (2014). *Aesthetics of Everyday Life: East and West*. Newcastle upon Tyne: Cambridge Scholars Publishing.

Interlude II: Designing the bottle to own its water, 2016

le smartphone HTC, software Adobe Photoshop

3 Art, Everyday Aesthetics and Organizational Theory

Interlude II introduces the themes that shall be treated in Chapter 3, which continue to refer to the aesthetic philosophy, the creation process and the organization studies, that is, to the principal subjects discussed in Part I of the book. The photopoem shown in it has the title *Designing the bottle to own its water*, and was made in 2016, three years after the photograph that is at its origin. The subject of both the photopoem illustrated in the Interlude and the photograph taken to be included in my PowerPoint presentation at a conference on Kierkegaard in Copenhagen, which I will discuss later, has been the relationship between the design and the organizational aesthetics: How can we understand the relationship between design, art, organizational creation and organizational communication? How can we approach the design of mundane artifacts in accordance with the aesthetic study of organizational life?

These are the interrogatives that are at the basis of this chapter, which is structured into three sections. In the first section, I will focus on the world of photography and of art photography, both as an empirical study of my aesthetic approach and as a metaphor of organizational aesthetics. In the second section, I will discuss the topic of "art as a problem" and of the influence of the philosophical distinction between art and aesthetics on the study of organizational life. In the third and final section, I shall illustrate the importance of the aesthetics of everyday life in the recent Eastern and Western philosophical aesthetics and in organizational theories.

3.1 Photography as a Metaphor of Organizational Aesthetics

I took the picture that is at the origin of the photopoem *Designing the bottle to own its water*, which constitutes *Interlude II*, while I was attending a conference organized in Copenhagen to celebrate the Danish philosopher Søren Kierkegaard, two centuries since his birth in 1813.

The conference, held at the Copenhagen Business School in October 2013, was on "The Uses and Abuses of Kierkegaard: Lessons for Integrating Humanities in Future Business Education" and was organized by the Department of Management, Politics and Philosophy, Copenhagen Business School, and The Søren Kierkegaard Research Centre at the University of Copenhagen. Philosophers and scholars of organization presented research and theoretical studies on various uses, distortions and "abuses" of the philosophy of Kierkegaard. They did it generally in English, but sometimes in German as well. For three days, we were seated in a beautiful amphitheater hall with a small screen right in front of us projecting PowerPoint presentations. Thus, we could look at the colleagues who were presenting and, at the same time, at the texts, the images and sometimes the videos projected on the screen. From our position, we could also see the two doors on the sides of the screen, through which, occasionally, natural light entered, giving the feeling that behind those doors there was sunlight.

I had been invited to discuss uses and abuses of Kierkegaard's philosophy of existentialism in research on organizational aesthetics, and I had to present it on the third day, almost at the end of the conference. I cannot remember exactly when, but during the second day of the conference, I realized that a bottle of still mineral water was always with me, along with my notes, my pencil and my laptop computer.

That bottle was signed by the Copenhagen Business School (CBS). I was drinking, therefore, CBS still mineral water, although the Copenhagen Business School is not an organization that produces drinking water. From a cognitive point of view, it was clear to me that CBS's signature only indicated the low-priced distribution and marketing of water. But, on an aesthetic level, I had the feeling of living in an organizational culture in which CBS was everywhere during those three days, signing everything, even the still mineral water I drank.

So, since I did not have my professional cameras with me, I used my smartphone to take a photograph to include in the presentation of my PowerPoint the following day. This was a file, to be precise, rather than an analogue photograph, as I pointed out in my discussion on *Interlude I* in the second section of the previous chapter. "Electronic images", in fact—observes Sylvia Wolf (2010: 26)—"can be displayed on a computer or projected, made as photographic prints, or transmitted via the Internet". Furthermore, comments Roberta Valtorta, photography is increasingly losing its autonomy as a creative form:

> photography acts today on a media platform on which many image technologies move, resulting in an extremely mobile and varied production, with considerable loss of specificity of the individual mediums: as a specific field of work, it therefore tends to no longer exist by itself. It exists naturally as a professional and popular practice, but increasingly loses its autonomy as a specific and *self-sufficient* creative form, a condition for which it had long struggled since the nineteenth century.

(2004: 9)

3.1.1 Photography and Everyday Aesthetics

Some considerations can give an adequate image of the organizational context of the creation of the digital file that is at the origins of the photopoem *Designing the bottle to own its water*. These considerations bring into light the materiality of my situation, that is:

- the written words of the label of the plastic bottle containing still mineral water, which were saying "CBS—Copenhagen Business School";
- the drawings always of the label of the bottle, the conference notebook and the conference pen on which the bottle lies, the transparency of the plastic texture of the bottle, the artificial lights reflected on the plastic, a few drops of water, the emptiness of the bottle of water, the word "distance" I wrote on the notebook and that I underlined, circumscribing it with an oval (and that can be recognized—not without difficulty—in the lower left corner of the photopoem);
- my body sitting for a rather long time to attend the sessions of the conference;
- the absence of my professional camera;
- the photographic opportunity offered by my HTC smartphone;
- the Microsoft PowerPoint software and my laptop computer.

This material situation illustrates the organizational setting that provided me with the opportunity to take a photograph with just a silent click of the smartphone and, thus, to be able to complete my PowerPoint presentation with some vivid aesthetic feelings experienced during the conference. All this happened in the time frame of a few minutes. In this way, my sentiments regarding the organizational control I experienced, as well as my sociological reflections on the aesthetics of organizational design, have had the chance to be expressed and communicated "aesthetically", in words, but also in a visual form. This was mainly due to the digital environment and to the "globalizing character" of the computer because of its capacity to align procedures and significations of the visual image beyond their differences:

> In photographic, graphic, television and film studios, in editorial offices, in agencies, as in homes and schools, but also in the studies of those operators we call artists, and in every place of our life, only one medium is always present to unify the way we communicate and produce images (and certainly not only these): the computer, capable of aligning the procedures and the sense of different types of visual representation and invention.
>
> (Valtorta, 2004: 9)

This was due, in the case of *Interlude II*, to the peculiarities of the digital photograph, that is, to its "virtual body" (Diodato, 2005) which, even though is just a mere file, maintains the aesthetic characters that are specific to photography and interrogates the aesthetic philosophies with regard to photography and art photography. In fact, as states the French artist and art theoretician Jean-Louis Boissier, director of the "Aesthetics of New Media Lab" at Paris University, one cannot merely assert that there is "a global digital art. It is extremely simplistic, it prevents from grasping the cultural and political complexity of the artistic production since it is the world that becomes digital" (2016: 37).

And, returning to the aesthetics of the photograph I took during the Kierkegaard conference in Copenhagen, the other point I want to make is that its creation process refers in any case to just a mundane situation of work in organizational life. Thomas Leddy stresses the relevance of the aesthetics of photography in everyday life. He does it even with regard to the mundane use of "selfies":

> But what about amateur photography, which plays such an impor-
> tant role in our everyday aesthetic lives? Take, for example, the
> recent fascination with "selfies": pictures taken of oneself usually by
> smartphone and shared in social media. Can amateur photography
> give us aesthetic experiences? Is the "selfie" or other types of ama-
> teur photo aesthetic? It might be argued that the aesthetic here is
> narcissistic and shallow. Nonetheless, those who take these pictures
> of themselves pose the subject and manipulate the image to enhance
> certain desired qualities.
>
> (2014: 48)

Moreover, the aesthetic qualities of selfies are due to a complex mundane photographic practice, since the selfie is intrinsically inseparable from its intended or desired communication and operates in the digital photographic environment of making and sharing the image (Tifentale, 2018). On the other hand, "the simple process of taking a selfie engages a philosophy of skin", observe Janet Borgerson and Jonathan Schroeder (2018: 110). This could shed a new light on contemporary discourses in social sciences, marketing studies and organizational theories regarding

- the rich photographic history of the aestheticization of the human body, thanks also to the continuous innovative techniques of communication which are used within branding and marketing; and
- "the 'mixing' of evolving human forms, such as the cyborg, as well as surgically, technologically, or digitally transformed beings. Related discussions encompass the cyborgian 'mixing' of human skin and machine skin, as well as transgender 'mixing' of 'female skin' and 'male skin'" (Borgerson and Schroeder, 2018: 118).

In any case, in support of the aesthetic qualities of the amateur photos, Leddy observes (2014: 48), one can also just refer to "the ways in which curators select such photos for exhibition in museums, thus bringing out their art-like qualities and foregrounding other aesthetic features". However, we must always keep in mind that in art photography, there is a tradition of research related to selfies, as happens in the case of Jean Pigozzi's "ME & CO" selfie project (*Leica Fotografie International Magazine*, 2017). Pigozzi began his project at Harvard in 1974, with selfies taken with actress Faye Dunaway, and continued this project until the present, with selfies of small or medium dimensions realized with musicians like Lady Gaga, film directors like Sergio Leone, and artists like Maurizio Cattelan and Andy Warhol.

The wide range of uses and "abuses" of digital photography—to resonate also with the humor inherent in the Kierkegaard conference title—urges us to consider how, nowadays, it would be difficult—even though stimulating—"to try to imagine a world without photographs", as observes Sylvia Wolf (2010: 24),

> especially given today's glut of visual images. And yet before 1826, when French inventor Joseph Nicéphore Niépce made the first known photograph—a fuzzy view of rooftops seen from the window of his study—the only imagery of people, still lives, and landscapes were described in words or artists' renderings, often with remarkable precision, but nonetheless interpreted with language, pigment, graphite, or ink.

The invention of the photograph, in fact, which dates less than two centuries, constituted "a historical event as equally decisive as the invention of writing", points out Vilém Flusser (1983; Eng. trans. 2000: 17–18) in his essay *Towards a Philosophy of Photography*. With writing—Flusser continues (1983; Eng. trans. 2000: 18)—"history in the narrower sense begins as a struggle against idolatry", while with photography, the "post-history" begins "as a struggle against textolatry".

In writing these considerations, Flusser raises a polemic against the relationships between the subject and the religion, the ideology and the science, if they are "determined by magic and ritual" (von Amelunxen, 2000: 91). If, therefore, the "history" begins as a polemic against the act of faithfulness to the image, the "post-history" begins as a criticism against the faithfulness to the text.

At the same time, due consideration must be given to the fact that the post-history that begins with photography is aesthetically characterized by contradictions, paradoxes and ambiguities that resonate in the aesthetic conflict, in aesthetic competition and in aesthetic negotiation between organizations. First of all, this is because photography "evokes predatory metaphors", as William Mitchell (1992: 56) stresses:

> a picture is "taken", the photographer operates in a ruthlessly competitive economy of image hunting and gathering. Photographs are

trophies—won by skill and cunning and luck, by being in the right place at the right time, and by knowing how to aim and when to shoot. Form is out there to be discovered, then impressed on matter by means of a swift, automatic process.

This is the ambiguous aesthetics of photography, while we are immersed in a world of photographic categories when we are doing our work or enjoying our free time in the organizational contexts. Our existence has been transformed by the aesthetic philosophies of photography in general, and of art photography in particular, and we are dealing with a new existential revolution that sheds new lights and new shadows on the "question of freedom" in the contemporary society and in the contemporary organizational life. Therefore, writes Vilém Flusser, the philosophy of photography is a necessity in order to raise the photographic practice to

the level of consciousness, and this is again because this practice gives rise to a model of freedom in the post-industrial context in general A philosophy of photography must reveal the fact that there is no place for human freedom within the area of automated, programmed and programming apparatuses, in order finally to show a way in which it is nevertheless possible to open up a space for freedom.

(1983; Eng. trans. 2000: 81–82)

In our contemporary societies dominated by the "apparatuses", the philosophy of photography has the task and the responsibility to reflect on the possibility and on the meaning of freedom. This is the motive explaining why a philosophy is necessary. Indeed, this reflection constitutes "the only form of revolution left open to us" (Flusser, 1983; Eng. trans. 2000: 82). This is also because photographs, in "their all-pervasiveness, they now occupy our universe and fill our psyches" (Wolf, 2010: 51), rather than simply being visual representations of aspects of our daily life in the organizational contexts and in society.

3.1.2 Phenomenological Doubt as Photographic Practice

"At the beginning there was the digital file", it could be affirmed without fear of contradiction as regards to the photopoem *Designing the bottle to own its water* in *Interlude II*. The distinction between the photopoem, which constitutes the art photograph realized, on one hand, and the photograph taken, that is, at the origin of this photopoem, on the other hand, has been illustrated in Chapter 2 with the description and the discussion of the creation process of the image that composes *Interlude I*. I shall not describe in detail, therefore, this distinction with regard to *Designing the bottle to own its water*. I want instead to underline that the digital file of the photograph I took was also due to the "phenomenological doubt"—the attempt to approach phenomena from any number of points of view through a jump-start search—that is intrinsic to photographic practice, as pointed out by Vilém Flusser (1983; Eng. trans. 2000: 38). I also found an echo of Flusser's phenomenological doubt in some reflections on photography made by Richard Shusterman, the American pragmatist philosopher who proposes a philosophy of body consciousness and of "somaesthetics" (2008).

Shusterman (2012: 68–69) observes that "the photograph and its aesthetic perception are only part of a larger complex of elements that constitutes photography as an activity and as an art" and that the aesthetics of the somatic skills of the photographer should be philosophically explored because taking "a photographic shot, like any action we perform, always involves some bodily action" and requires somatic competence. With caution, Shusterman warns (2012: 74) that the fact of highlighting an overlooked aspect of the art of photography does not imply erecting that aspect "into the distinctive, defining essence of that art, if it indeed has one".

Said differently, in my eyes, Flusser and Shusterman both stress the performative dimension of making a photograph, the first one according to phenomenologist aesthetics, the second one according to pragmatist aesthetics. The point they make is important since the practice of photographing and its performative dimension represent neglected areas of study in the aesthetic philosophy of photography. The performative process that concerns the photographic art is occluded by the *reduction of the photography to the photograph*, as it happens in organizational theories when organizational life is reduced to the organization as an ontological entity. But the origins of art photography are also in the art of theater, as remarked Roland Barthes (1980), that is, in an art where the artistic performance and the practice of the embodied skills are essential.

If one imagines the theatrical performance, one can see the importance of the action, of the learning, and of the experiencing of the body of the photographer while s/he is taking and/or making a photograph. One can see—even just through imagination and the evocative process of knowing that I have illustrated in the first section of Chapter 2—how far the aesthetic judgments inherent in the photographic phenomenological doubt and the somaesthetics intrinsic to the somatic skill are important, both in performing the art of photography and in its study. Also, one can see the art photographer, the business and commercial photographer, and the amateur photographer united by the fact that they all make aesthetics in the contemporary world of organizations in which we live. And thus, one can also grasp the significance of the metaphor of organizational aesthetics as photography.

Metaphors have been largely used in organizational theories:

• as a criterion for systematizing the organizational literature (Morgan, 1986) with the metaphors of the organization as machine, organism, brain, culture, politics, psychic prison, flux and transformation, and domination;

- as a cognitive operation able to create an interaction between organization studies and communication theory (Putnam, Phillips and Chapman, 1996; Putnam and Boys, 2006) with the metaphors of communication in organization as conduit, lens, linkage, performance, symbol, voice, discourse and contradiction;
- as a symbolic understanding of the emotional organizational life with the metaphor of organization as a theater (Mangham and Overington, 1987);
- as an aesthetic lens through which to study the organizational life with the metaphor of organization as hypertext (Strati, 1996, Eng. trans. 2000: 68–75).

The metaphor is a way to imagine and understand the world, as well as a way to act and to communicate in it, which belongs to philosophical aesthetics. Metaphor, image and fantasy, in fact, constitute the three pillars of the mythical thought described by the Neapolitan philosopher Giambattista Vico (1725) in his *logica poetica*, that is, his "poetic logic" that represents a fierce controversy against the analytic and rational logic for knowing the world. The metaphor poses in interaction—through fantasy, intuition and imagination—two different worlds, and highlights some aspects and leaves in the shadow other aspects.

The interaction that the metaphor of organizational aesthetics as photography suggests between the world of photography and the world of organizational theories requires the simultaneous awareness of both these worlds in order to operate "translations" between these two contexts on the basis of their acknowledged autonomy, difference and distance. Organizational theory does not coincide, in fact, with photography, but we can deepen our understanding of the aesthetic dimension of organizational life through the translations that we are able to invent and establish between the two contexts.

Thanks to the metaphor of photography, in fact, a critical reading of the aesthetic study of organization can be carried out that is based on intuitions as well as on conceptualizations where the comprehension of organizational aesthetics is stimulated by analogy, by paradox, by contrast and contradiction. However, it is important to be aware that through the metaphor of organizational aesthetics as photography, only certain characteristics of the aesthetic dimension of organizational life are highlighted, while other characteristics remain left in the shadows.

In any case, the use of this metaphor gives the scholar freedom to fantasize about the aesthetic side of organization in an innovative way, changing perspective, and in the awareness that the talent of the metaphorical operation—as Umberto Eco warns us (2002: 38)—"cannot be taken to loan from others, and therefore it is a matter not of mere imitation but of invention".

What can we appreciate of the metaphor of organizational aesthetics as photography?

1. first of all, the instance that a philosophy is necessary in order to explore aesthetically the aesthetic dimension of organizational life;
2. second, that we act, learn and communicate aesthetically in organization and in the study of organizational life, because we are anyway immersed in an organizational world where, as the metaphor brings into light, we all can take photographs, and occasionally make art photographs, at the same time that we all are exposed to marketing and branding through photographs;
3. third, that when we are inquiring organizational aesthetics, we have a philosophical task, that of exploring the aesthetic possibilities for freedom of people at work in organizational contexts, as well as in society at large. Said in other terms, we have the social scientist responsibility of inventing and constructing the philosophical fundaments of the aesthetic citizenship in organization;
4. fourth, that the photographic phenomenological doubt has to be taken in due account while studying the organizational creation process of an artwork or the organizational creation process of ordinary beauty—or ugliness—in the quotidian life in contemporary societies;
5. fifth, that the virtual body—of the image, as we have seen in Chapter 1—that we create in our interaction with the digital environment poses the issue of the aesthetic characteristics of the materiality of our "situation" while we are doing aesthetics in the daily work in the organization, as well as while we are aesthetically studying organization and society.

These are aspects that the photographic metaphor of organizational aesthetics brings into light with reference, in particular, to the aesthetic study of organization. This is my favorite way to explore the insights and the intuitions that the photographic metaphor can provide. I could have limited, therefore, this metaphor to the organizational aesthetics research, but I preferred to contextualize its capacity for evocative knowledge in the wider aesthetic ambience of organizational life *tout court* in order to let this metaphor be grounded in the hybridizing organizational processes that position the organizational scholar in a multiplicity of identities, which can all be operating at the same time: to be user of commercial photography while we experiment with art photography and, at the same time, sending selfies to family or friends.

Let us see now, in the next section, how significant this metaphor is for understanding a crucial debate in the aesthetic study of organization: art *versus* aesthetics/aesthetics *versus* art.

3.2 Philosophy of Art, That's the Problem

The aesthetic philosophy of photography as art represents a polemic against textolatry, in Flusser's terms, and, as well, it constitutes "a criticism of functionalism in all its anthropological, scientific, political and aesthetic aspects" (Flusser, 1983; Eng. trans. 2000: 78). However, this philosophical awareness of the aesthetics of photography has escaped the photographers' consciousness, but with one exception, affirms Flusser (1983; Eng. trans. 2000: 84): that of the experimental art photographers, who attempt "to place, within the image, information that is not predicted within the program of the camera". These art photographers

> are conscious that *image, apparatus, program* and *information* are the basic problems that they have to come to terms with. They are in fact consciously attempting to create unpredictable information, i.e. to release themselves from the camera, and to place within the image something that is not in its program. They know they are playing against the camera.
>
> (Flusser, 1983; Eng. trans. 2000: 81)

Yet even the experimental art photographers are *unaware of the extent of their practice*. They are not conscious that "they are attempting to address the question of freedom in the context of apparatus in general", that they are trying to provide an answer through aesthetics to the issue of the "human freedom within the area of automated, programmed and programming apparatuses" (Flusser, 1983; Eng. trans. 2000: 81).

3.2.1 Making Strange: Altered Photographs and Art Photography

Playing against the camera, experimenting against the predictable information, placing within the photograph something that is not intended by the programming "apparatus" was what I did to transform the photograph taken during the Kierkegaard conference into the photopoem *Designing the bottle to own its water*, which constitutes *Interlude II*. The diversity between the two images consists, in fact, in my digital manipulation of the photograph taken with the camera of my HTC smartphone and, of course, in their organizational communication:

- The smartphone photograph was a faint color with a dominant magenta. It was inserted as it was in the PowerPoint presentation. Only its perspective was slightly modified to fit the default format of the slides of the PowerPoint software. It has been seen projected on the screens of some conferences and workshops, but without a title.

- The photopoem is the result of my digital manipulation with Adobe Photoshop of the smartphone photograph. First, I transformed the color photograph into an image in black and white. Thus, I changed dramatically the perspective of the bottle. My desire was to "make strange" the textural materiality of the plastic bottle in order to create a sense

  - of space and of wide volume;
  - of lights that illuminate, traversing dynamically, this space;
  - of water bubbles that decorate the superficies of the bottle;
  - of bas-reliefs—the drawings of the label of the bottle, the word "distance" and the oval circumscribing it on the notebook; and
  - of a blurred and therefore almost illegible text—that of CBS— but strongly imprinted on the label of the bottle and with a stroke capable of evoking rails that move in all directions.

- I also wanted to give strength to the overall tone of the gray in order to obtain a sense of drama, and I superimposed slightly different versions of the digital file to give form to a sort of movement and to an illusion of flux and mystery. Unlike the photograph, the photopoem had a title, *Designing the bottle to own its water*.

Anyhow, as I have stressed in Chapter 2, what the reader can look at in *Interlude II* is neither the photograph projected on the conference screen, nor the photopoem, but the Routledge typographic print of the latter. In other words, the reader cannot aesthetically appreciate either the first or the second image, but a third image. Three photographic pictures constitute the pillars of the creative process and of the organizational process which produced, as the final result, the photopoem in *Interlude II*. But what has been crucial, in order to obtain it, has been the aesthetic transformation of the photograph taken with the smartphone into the photopoem.

The aesthetic transformation is intrinsic to photography since its invention, as discussed with regards to the photographic phenomenological doubt in the previous section. The transformation of a photograph also belongs to the "process of transcription" that is inherent to the photographic image, and which Umberto Eco emphasizes in the following way:

> The theory of the photo as an *analogue* of reality has been abandoned, even by those who once upheld it—we know that it is necessary to be trained to recognize the photographic image. We know that the image which takes shape on celluloid is analogous to the retinal image but not to that which we perceive. We know that sensory phenomena are *transcribed*, in the photographic emulsion, in such a way that even if there is a causal link with the real phenomena, the

graphic images formed can be considered as wholly arbitrary with respect to these phenomena. Of course, there are various grades of arbitrariness and motivation, and this point will have to be dealt with a greater length. But it is still true that, to differing degrees, *every image is born of a series of successive transcriptions.*

(1982: 33)

The other aspect of the aesthetic transformation of the photograph calls into question the aesthetic philosophies of the photographer who, points out Diarmuid Costello (2018: 146), if s/he operates in the digital environment, can digitally create these transcriptions by intervening "strictly *photographically*" and "in any of the stages that are necessary for the production of an image that can be visually appreciated".

Experimental and/or artistic techniques for altering photographs, observes Curtis Carter (2014: 88), are illustrated and discussed in "photographic journals of the 1890s", and can be traced back to the 1880s, when Eadweard Muybridge and Étienne Jules Marey "focused attention on the aesthetic features of both human and animal behaviour in everyday life". In the contemporary digital environment of art photography, experimental techniques for "making strange" familiar artifacts, such as famous paintings or photographs, are, for instance, the "googlegrams"—a term that resonates with Man Ray's "rayograms" during the 1930s or Ugo Mulas's "photograms" during the 1970s—created by the Catalan art photographer Joan Fontcuberta.

Googlegrams are digital photographs constructed through a freeware program dedicated to photomosaics out of pictures found on the Internet by using Google's Image Search. Through this technique, "Googlegramme Niépce, 2005", which represents a photographic icon—that of Joseph Nicéphore Niépce's study—was constructed out of 10,000 pictures found on the Internet by using a function responding to the word "photo" in English, French and Spanish (Fontcuberta, 2008: 80–81). "Googlegram 9: Homeless, 2005" was constructed out of another 10,000 pictures found on the Internet by using a function responding to the names of the twenty-five richest people in the world (Valtorta, 2014: 27).

The "making strange" of familiar artifacts, i.e., the icon of the Niépce's study and the conventional image of the Fontcuberta's homeless, or of familiar and ordinary artifacts such as my bottle of water, highlights the "image that doubts", writes Dominique Baqué (2004: 24), because the art photography of the banal constitutes a counterpoint of the "self-assured image, indexed on a stable, intelligible, rationalizable world", and is, on the contrary, "constantly infiltrated by anxiety—that of the sense, that of the subject, that of the work—as it admits to being rebellious to all certainty, to any affirmation threatened by dogmatism".

The creation of altered images "can also be found in more documentary photographs", writes Barbara Savedoff (2000: 5), since "photographs do not simply record", but

> transform their subject. They have the power to make even the most familiar objects appear strange, the most chaotic events appear structured, or the most mundane items appear burdened with meaning. Photographs seem to reveal to us things that cannot be seen with our eyes alone.
>
> (2000: 2)

In fact, the status of the photographic image in general, but especially of the photograph that we have known before the digital revolution—and that is called "analog" after "the process of creating a likeness of a subject" (Wolf, 2010: 26)—is due to a previous revolution that Walter Benjamin (1931; 1935) identified in the mechanical nature of its reproduction. For which the photograph is still generally seen "as having a special connection with reality and an independence of the photographer's intentions", to the point that even "a blurred and indistinct photograph is seen as having this special link, and as having a documentary value unavailable to painting" (Savedoff, 2000: 193). Furthermore, writes William Mitchell (1992: 222), photography "has established a powerful orthodoxy" of visual expression and communication, and "if one accepts the Foucauldian thesis" that

> modern science reversed the scholastic view of an assertion's authority as something derived from its author and substituted the notion that matters of fact are impersonal things, then it becomes obvious that the impersonal process of photography answered to a dominant conception of what the coinage of communication should be.

In contrast, Victor Burgin (2008: 260) maintains that the "object of the 'play' that is the *work* of art" and of art photography "is to render a proposition that is barely plausible in terms of the historical real irrefutable in the register of form". In any case, William Mitchell affirms (1992: 222–223), since digital images "have a much less standardized production processes" than the analogue photographs, and that these processes are intrinsically "less subject to institutional policing of uniformity", that they "can stand in a wider variety of intentional relationships to the objects that they depict" and are open for resistance and subversion against the dominance of conventional aesthetics. Because,

> they can be used to yield new forms of understanding, but they can also disturb and disorient by blurring comfortable boundaries and by encouraging transgression of rules on which we have come to rely.

Digital imaging technology can provide openings for principled resistance to established social and cultural practices, and at the same time it can create possibilities for cynical subversion of those practices.

(Mitchell, 1992: 223)

3.2.2 Art Photography and the Organization Without Walls

We have seen that an ordinary smartphone photograph of a plastic bottle of water has been at the origin of the photopoem *Designing the bottle to own its water*. This digital photograph with which the creation process of an art photograph began, however, was not an "art" photograph. Nor was the slide composed with this smartphone photograph for my Power-Point presentation at the conference an artwork, even though the original photograph has been altered through photographic digital manipulation in order to adapt to the predefined PowerPoint format. The photopoem that constitutes *Interlude II* is instead art photography. Why?

This interrogative is important—not in order to define what is art in photography, but in order to catch the paradoxes, the ambiguities and the blurred confines that characterize the distinction and the separation between art and everyday aesthetics in the social world of photography. This is, in fact, a crucial issue that also resonates in the aesthetic study of organization, showing how far photography operates as a metaphor of organizational aesthetics in contemporary societies. In fact, if we consider the use of photographs in our daily life in society, we can

- notice the great variety of forms through which photography can be present in our daily work and in our organizational contexts, from the printed reproductions displayed on the walls to the digital "virtual bodies" displayed on the screens of computers, tablets, smartphones and other professional devices;
- plausibly imagine having colleagues who manifest passion and commitment for art photography, and who make, for example, street photography, landscape photography or portrait photography, if not abstract conceptual photography;
- also see ourselves visiting a museum or a photographic gallery for an exhibition of art photographs, browsing an art photography book or a photographic magazine in a bookstore, or attending a workshop dedicated to art photography;
- take for granted that a talented photographer who practices commercial and business photography has exhibitions of his/her more artistic photographic research.

We are not surprised, in other terms, by the fact that art photography:

- is not clearly separated from our quotidian life;
- does not constitute an organization formally structured;

- is, instead, a collective social phenomenon, which is precarious, unstable and ephemeral in many respects; and
- looks paradoxically quite the opposite, if one thinks of the photographic industries, the museum's departments of photography, the photographic courses in universities and schools, the photographic art collections, the photographic publishing houses or the art photography market.

Therefore, how is it that an analogue or digital photograph enters the context of such a collective social phenomenon, thus acquiring the "aura" and the "status" of art photograph?

On one hand, the artistic canons of photography are subject to continuous collective processes of negotiation, and no official repository of the art photography canons exists. On the other hand, a photograph can enter the collective social phenomenon of art photography, even without having an author, as I learned during my aesthetic ethnography conducted at the end of the 1980s on art photography in Europe (Strati, 1995).

I discussed in Chapter 2 the issue of the authorship of the art photograph. I have emphasized its aspect of "collective artist", that is, an *auteur* which is formed by art photographer, information engineer, photographic industry and the public. I want to add the authorless, the anonymous, the "absence" of the author into the image of the collective artist that creates an art photograph, such as we include the silence and the absence of voice in the study of organizational communication and in the formation of organizational discourse.

An authorless photograph can also be art and can contribute to the social legitimation of photography as an art form. The legitimation of photography as art—which at the time of my research was still far from being consolidated, as it became later on—was, in fact, the symbolic artifact to be socially constructed through the interactions between:

- "collective artist";
- organizations such as museums, galleries, photographic schools and photographic companies;
- photographic paper and film, digital devices and photographic software, cameras, enlargers, projectors and the large variety of other equipment, i.e., lamps, cases, tripods, batteries, books, CDs and online photographic tuition programs;
- institutions like the public administrations and state departments;
- communities of prosumers—that is, of consumers who are at the same time producers, since they interact, for example, with companies that produce photographic software and photographic materials on the characteristics of these photographic products—and amateurs.

In order to give an answer to the question of how a photograph becomes an art photograph, I imagined the collective social phenomenon of art photography *as an organization* which, instead of being a formal organization, was a "bizarre" organization, one that did not have fixed formal boundaries, nor an above and below, but a series of relations and interactions that constantly interweave. The concept of the texture of organizing (Gherardi and Strati, 1990; *Journal of Management Studies*, 1990; Strati, 1996; Eng. trans. 2000: 75–82), which emerged in the organizational theories during the crisis of the dominance of the rationalist and positivist paradigm in the social sciences, was at the basis of my reflections, because of the evocative power of the notion of "connecting in acting" (Cooper and Fox, 1990). But it did not suffice. I felt it was needed to give more strength to the image of the organization. Thus, I proposed a novel concept, and I coined the name of "organization without walls" (Strati, 1995) to depict an organization where the continuous process of organizing and disorganizing consists of the following (Strati, 1996; Eng. trans. 2000: 25):

- specific forms of initiation, "which develop sentiments of belonging", and particular rites of passage, "which actuate upward and downward mobility among positions of power, command, prestige and reputation";
- distinctive aggregations and subdivisions, internal hierarchies and characteristic forms of control over the members;
- shared "organizational myths, heroes and sacred places";
- shared "meanings of organizational actions for the individuals, organizations and institutions that, through processes of multiple membership and reciprocal influence", give life and sense to the organization without walls.

And I indicated an image of the organization without walls, the Greco-Roman arena of the Colosseum, which has arches that separate the outside from the inside but does not have doors or windows.

> Nevertheless the image of the colosseum is that of a robust structure comprising a threshold that must be crossed to join the organization. This threshold is the encounter between curators and photographers and is distinguished by the artistic talent for photography displayed by both. Once inside there are other thresholds to cross, but all based on the same event, the encounter between the promoters and the *auteurs*, which mirrors the essentiality of the architectural motifs that the colosseum repeats to its interiors.
>
> (Strati, 1995: 99)

This is how a photograph transforms itself in a work of art, by entering the Colosseum, that is, by passing through the rites of passage that symbolize the unequal distribution of power within the organization without walls between the "collective artist" and the community of the curators of photography collections, of museum photographic departments, of photographic galleries, as well as the community of art photography critics, historians, semiologists and philosophers.

At the same time, the interrogative regarding how a photograph becomes a photographic artwork highlights how far photography can be a philosophical subject which is particularly suitable for examining the aesthetics of everyday life in organization and in society at large. Photography has, by now, largely enjoyed its legitimation as an autonomous art, in fact, and at the same time,

> photography's successes in serving media industries in advertising, medicine, propaganda and virtually every aspect of contemporary life have become the core of our image-driven society. What has changed with respect to art photography is that some art photographers create their work with no intentional boundaries between the activities of everyday life and their works.
>
> (Carter, 2014: 95)

It "should be no surprise", comments Curtis L. Carter (2014: 95), "to find photography testing these boundaries while maintaining its place among the arts".

3.3 Art and Aesthetics in Eastern and Western Recent Philosophy

The considerations made about photography as a creation process in art photography and as a daily expression of aesthetic appreciation in the organization and in society illustrate the sense of my study of the aesthetic dimension of organizational life. In my approach, in fact, art is considered to be important for the aesthetic understanding of organization, but at the same time, is seen as *only* an essential and vital aspect of the organizational aesthetics *among* the others, rather than constituting the principal focus of the aesthetic organizational research.

I shall further illustrate this issue in Part II of the book. Here, I want to underline that the reference I am making (1) to photography in society, (2) to art photography, and (3) to the philosophy of photography—besides my artistic passion as an art photographer—is intended to provide the reader with an image of organizational aesthetics where s/he can see himself/herself fully immersed, and of a metaphor for understanding the polysemy, the mystery and the intensity of the aesthetic dimension of organizational life.

The separation and the autonomy of the photograph in *itself* from its "collective *auteur*" evoke the separation of the organization from its subject—human, non-human, post-human. This separation and this autonomy can even represent the aesthetic photographic style that characterizes distinctively the way a photograph should be made. I have observed it with regards to the oldest photographic organization still active in the world (Strati, 1999: 139–155)—the "Fratelli Alinari", founded in 1852 by Leopoldo Alinari in Florence and dedicated above all to the documentation of the Italian artistic heritage. This style that provides an aura of an objective view and a rigorous aesthetic composition to the art photographs of this Italian photographic company has been transmitted from generations to generations of photographers that have been working in this organization. This is a style which, while it is making highly recognizable the photographic art created and communicated by this Italian company, renders paradoxically invisible, anonymous and even absent its "collective *auteur*".

Now, what happens to organizational aesthetics is that it is often considered to be coinciding with art in the organizational contexts and that the term "organizational aesthetics" means merely 'art of the organization' or the 'art displayed and/or in use in the organization'. But, even if, without any doubt, art is so influent and pervasive in organizational life, art is, however, just an aspect of the aesthetic dimension of organization. As well as—it's important to stress—if the creation process is essential to art in the various organizational contexts, the creation process is also essential to the mundane and non-artistic practices in organizations (Gherardi and Strati, 2012; Hjorth et al., 2018; Meisiek and Barry, 2014; *Organization Studies*, 2018; Paris, 2007; Sternberg and Krauss, 2014).

This implies that, in my aesthetic approach to the study of organizational life, the philosophy of art represents just one aspect of the aesthetics of everyday life and in the organization—even though, as one can see also in this book, I consider art to be essential to the aesthetic discourse on organization. On the contrary, during the last three centuries or so, the philosophy of art has assumed a central, dominant and pervasive position in the philosophical aesthetics. But—fortunately—this constitutes one of the fundamental problems debated in philosophical aesthetics and, also, in the recent philosophy of "Everyday Aesthetics".

3.3.1 Everyday Aesthetics and the Aesthetics of Living

With the philosophy of "Everyday Aesthetics", a recent philosophical movement in the aesthetic philosophies, the conceptualization of the relationship between "aesthetics", on one side, and "art" on the other side, emerges as a crucial philosophical issue. As just said, this is a debate that is open and vital in the organizational aesthetics research (Guillet de Monthoux and Strati, 2008), and that has been pointed out with particular attention also in the past and in philosophies apparently quite different between them—such as, for instance, the pragmatism of the American philosopher John Dewey (1934/1987) and the existentialist hermeneutics of the Italian philosopher Luigi Pareyson (1954). Because the aesthetic experience, writes Diané Collinson (1992: 114), "in spite of its close relationship with beauty and with art, need not to be of art nor of the beautiful", and "need not be defined either in terms of art or in terms of beauty, even though it may be closely connected with both".

The philosophy of "Everyday Aesthetics" also has a number of aspects and topics that are in common with the description of photography and of art photography that I am depicting in this first part of the book, also in terms of a metaphor of organizational aesthetics. In observing the relationships between art photography and photography in society, it has been unavoidable to notice that—as Crispin Sartwell (2003: 761) emphasizes with regards to the new philosophical area of "Everyday Aesthetics"—the "realm of the aesthetics extends well beyond the realm of what are commonly conceived to be the fine arts", as well as the fact that "art emerges from a range of non-art activities and experiences". But, what is the focus of the philosophy of "Everyday Aesthetics"?

Liu Yuedi and Curtis L. Carter introduce the collection of essays published in the volume dedicated to the international features of the philosophy of "Everyday Aesthetics" with the following statement:

> As a recent trend of aesthetics worldwide, the aesthetics of everyday life rejects a narrow, art-centred methodology for aesthetics, and points to the continuities between aesthetic/artistic experience and everyday experience. Following this development, the subject matter of aesthetics and aesthetic engagements ceases to be merely about artworks or nature with a focus on a narrowly construed canonical set of aesthetic properties. The notion of aesthetic experience has also been expanded to accommodate a wider range of human experiences.
>
> (2014: VII)

They also stress something that sounds rather novel in the philosophy of aesthetics: the aesthetic analysis "has extended to all areas of living world" under the influence of the philosophy of "Everyday Aesthetics", and, thanks to "these developments, it is not difficult to see that the aesthetics of everyday life is beginning to prosper in both western and eastern aesthetics" (Yuedi and Carter, 2014: VII).

Never before, in fact, has the philosophy of aesthetics been considered to be a worldwide philosophical trend which is able to develop, at the same time, in both the Eastern cultures and the Western cultures. Usually, the separation between East and West in the philosophical aesthetics has been quite rigorous, and an invisible wall has always been circumscribing the traditional philosophical distinction between the Anglo-Saxon "analytical aesthetics" (Gaut and Lopes, 2001) and the French, German, or Italian "continental aesthetics" (Cazeaux, 2000). In both the different aesthetic traditions of the Western and the Eastern philosophies, observes

Yuriko Saito (2007: 55), this separation has been recognized in the influence of aesthetics:

> In the Western tradition, Plato was the first to acknowledge this power of the aesthetic, without which his advocacy for censoring arts would not make sense. In the non-Western tradition, we see Confucius as someone who also recognized the way in which both human beings and the society at large are molded by the proper observance of rites and rituals, which consist not only of appropriate behavior but also of music, attire, recitation, and the like.

Eastern—or non-Western—philosophical aesthetics has, however, some characteristics that shed a specific particular light to its contribution to the debates in the new area of the philosophy of "Everyday Aesthetics" (*Contemporary Aesthetics*, 2018). The notion of aesthetics only came from France to Japan during the Meiji period, that is, during the second half of the nineteenth century, remarks Natalia Teplova (2010: 202); this was at the time of the great contacts with foreign cultures, as was the arrival of Zen from China. Also, the origins of "*wabi*", which refers to the sentiment of satisfaction of the simple life without ornaments or material artificiality, and of "*sabi*", which regards the feelings of melancholy and nostalgia, are in the Chinese culture and have been adapted to the Japanese culture. The term "*bigaku*" or "aesthetics"

> is created (or rather translated from French) by Nakae Chōmin in 1833 and it is always from the eighties of the nineteenth century that the first lectures on aesthetics are given at the University of Tokyo. No text of Japanese origin is then used. In addition, it is often foreigners who are invited to deliver speeches.
>
> (Teplova, 2010: 207)

On the other hand, no lexical equivalent of "aesthetics" exists in classical Chinese, observes Anna Ghiglione (2010: 185), also since the term

> "*meixue*"—literally, "the study of beauty"—used in modern Chinese, is a relatively recent neologism. It was first introduced into the Japanese lexicon before being adopted in China, and this only at the beginning of the twentieth century. The development in East Asia of a new interest in the aesthetic approach is due to the influence of the Western world.

Thus, what aesthetics is the Chinese one? Sor-Hoon Tan (1999) stresses that Chinese aesthetics cannot be confined to art and, on the contrary, must be seen as experience, as John Dewey and Richard Shusterman have emphasized with their philosophical pragmatism. Gu Feng and Dai

Wenjing (2017) also outline a series of differences that distinguish Chinese aesthetics from Western aesthetics. First of all, in Chinese aesthetics, perception is not opposed to rationality. "Contrary to the western aesthetics that is based on perception but strays away from it and makes perception and rationality one opposed to each other", they write (2017: 130), the Chinese aesthetics "is based on perception and sticks to it, turning into a genuine study of perception and an aesthetics that integrates perception with rationality". Another distinctive character that Feng and Wenjing underline is that the aesthetics

> in China pursues "Shen Yun", while that in the West pursues "essence". "Shen Yun" is hard to define. [. . .] "Shen" means the beauty in the appearance or air, and "Yun" refers to the beauty in the lingering charm. Whether used to refer to the beauty of nature, man or art, "Shen Yun" means the inner vitality, spirit and implication of an aesthetical object.
>
> (2017: 127–128)

What looks interesting, for it echoes the topic of the tacit dimension of knowledge in organization treated in Chapter 1, is that the "thing that cannot be described by words" but which has—continue Feng and Wenjing (2017: 128)—the capacity to attract so much "is the so-called 'Shen Yun'. Since their aesthetics upholds 'Yi Xiang', Chinese prefer to use their eyes instead of brain when appreciating beauty". Compared to the Western tradition which, even if it is rooted in sensation, deviates from it in order to reach the superior level of rationality, Chinese aesthetics "originates from the sensation and adheres to it all the time" (Feng and Wenjing, 2017: 125). All the non-Western aesthetics can be seen to be deeply influenced from this distinctive characteristic, and the "aesthetics of the everyday life" can be transformed and assume a slightly diverse and novel connotation, that of the "living aesthetics". Liu Yuedi and Curtis L. Carter stress this interesting "translation" of everyday life in "living":

> Since Eastern aesthetics is traditionally concerned with the art of living, Eastern philosophers may prefer to use the term "living Aesthetics" or "Aesthetics of Living". "Everyday life" tends to designate only an aspect of human existence, while "the Art of Living" acknowledges the presence of the aesthetics throughout human experiences. This amounts to saying that there is a deep-rooted tradition of living aesthetics in the East. Whether it is Chinese literati art or folk art, Japanese chado or gardening, or Korean porcelain or folk painting, all are part of the artistic expression of living aesthetics.
>
> (2014: VIII–XIX)

Important sources of the "art of living" in East Asian cultures are the Chinese Confucian aesthetics, the Taoist aesthetics and, later on, also the Indian Zen aesthetics. These are roots that date back to Lao Zi and Confucius, that is, five or six centuries before Christ. Along this line, therefore—that is, of the "living aesthetics", of the "art of living" and of the idea of "artful life" of the Chinese classical aesthetics—the Eastern aesthetics contributes to the configuration of the recent philosophical trend of the "Everyday Aesthetics".

3.3.2 Philosophy of Everyday Aesthetics and the Aesthetics of Organization

Everyday aesthetics also denotes "a current movement within the field of philosophy of art", comments Crispin Sartwell (2003: 761), "which rejects or puts into question distinctions such as those between fine and popular art, art and craft, and aesthetic and non-aesthetic experiences". Said differently, on one side, the philosophy of "Everyday Aesthetics" refers to the aesthetic experience of the ordinary beauty of non-art objects and non-art events, such as those of the daily working life in the organizational contexts, and, on the other side, this philosophy problematizes the art dimension of the social practices in contemporary societies (*Aisthesis. Pratiche, linguaggi e saperi dell'estetico*, 2014; Friberg and Vasquez, 2017; Mandoki, 2007; Saito, 2007).

The roots of this new philosophical movement can be found in the pragmatist philosophical aesthetics (Dewey, 1934/1987; Shusterman, 1992) and in the phenomenological and hermeneutic traditions of continental philosophy, in particular with the series of lectures on the origin of the work of art given in 1935 and 1936 by Martin Heidegger (1971). They can also be found in the analytic Anglo-American tradition, even though its influent and pervasive art-centered philosophy were a main cause of neglecting daily aesthetics until recent years.

> Heidegger distinguishes between authenticity and non-authenticity in art in his calling for a return to everyday life, and while Dewey seeks to find art in the stream of experience, the followers of Wittgenstein prefer to understand art in terms of social institutions, such as the art world. Apart from their differences, it seems that Heidegger's phenomenology, Wittgenstein's analytic philosophy and Dewey's pragmatism are in some respects sympathetic to everyday life aesthetics.
> (Yuedi and Carter, 2014: XII)

In some way, the philosophical polemics on what is aesthetics and on what is art that has characterized philosophical aesthetics in the last three centuries are also still vital and relevant in the debates regarding the new philosophical movement of "Everyday Aesthetics". This makes this movement intrinsically "heterogeneous, since it follows different traditions (continental, pragmatist, and analytical) and defends contradictory accounts of some core practical and theoretical issues", comments Dan Eugen Ratiu (2017: 23–24); a "weak" version and a "strong" version of aesthetics of everyday life also can be identified (Ratiu, 2013).

The philosophy of "Everyday Aesthetics", in fact, does not depict just one single approach. The enlargement of the scope of aesthetics regards, for instance, the aesthetic legitimacy gained by nature and the urban environment as occasions for aesthetic pleasure in the context of the conceptual frame of "aesthetic engagement" and of the "embeddedness of the appreciator" in the environment (Berleant, 2010). Arnold Berleant also refers to the arts to illustrate the relevance of the "aesthetic engagement". He reports the interest of John Cage in the aleatoric music during the 1950s to give an important example of experimental and innovative approaches of arts that created a "progressive broadening in the scope of aesthetic inquiry and away from the conventional venues of art" (2014: 6). An analogous development, observes Berleant, is

> the idea of relational aesthetics developed by the French critic Nicolas Bourriaud. Applied to the work of a number of contemporary artists, relational aesthetics recognizes that their art creates a social space, a context for human relationships. The art work then becomes an occasion for human interactions and the audience is turned into a community.
>
> (2014: 8)

Together with Bourriaud's "relational aesthetics" (2001), Berleant also refers to the "social aesthetics"—where aesthetics and ethics merge to produce social criticism (Murphy and de la Fuente, 2014)—and to the "political aesthetics" which aim to take, in due account, uses and control of sensibility through the notion of the "distribution of the sensible" proposed by the French philosopher Jacques Rancière (2000).

"Aesthetic engagement" is one of the approaches that Allen Carlson (2014) considers in his overview of the new philosophical area of "Everyday Aesthetics". Among the other approaches to understand the "aesthetic appreciation of everyday life" (2014: 51) are the following:

- In the "classic formalism" approach, aesthetic appreciation is directed toward the formal combination of lines, colors and shapes, that is, toward the "significant form". Many artists adopt the formalist approach in order to translate into formalist beauty the squalid or the unattractive or even the ugly in everyday life, as does the art photographer Edward Burtynsky, with his beautiful landscapes of devastated industrial contexts.

- In the "aesthetization" approach, the aesthetic appreciation of everyday life is subject to manipulation. Aesthetization is also due to:

  - the "artification" (*Contemporary Aesthetics*, 2012), that is, the "process of processes"—since it combines displacement, recategorization, redefinition of time, dissemination, patronage and so on—through which, observes Natalie Heinich and Roberta Shapiro (2012), ordinary events, artifacts and activities are transformed into art-like components of everyday life. This happens, to give an example, with urban art—such as the graffiti discussed in Chapter 2—that occupies spaces that are not art spaces, and translates them in an operator of the social transformation or in an analytic spy of the dominant societal values (Colacicco, 2016). Also, as Shapiro and Heinich observe (2012), the issues of de-artification and of the obstacles against artification must be taken in due consideration;

  - the "rituralization" of everyday mundane social practices, such as those that elevate "having a comforting cup of tea to a complex ritual" (Carlson, 2014: 54), and in a "ceremonious" social event (Saito, 2007; Teplova, 2010) through their isolation from the experiential flow of the daily activities.

- In the "pleasurable and enjoyable sensation" approach, pleasure is obtained through the senses of sight, hearing, smell, taste and touch in the daily life that is ordinarily experienced.

- In the "mental state and cognitive resources" approach, the aesthetic appreciation is directed towards the cognitive level (Carlson, 2000). For instance, points out Carlson (2014: 61), an "appropriate appreciation of work such as Jackson Pollock's *One (#31) (1950)* requires that we experience it as a painting and moreover as an action painting within the general school of 1950s American Abstract Expressionism, and therefore that we appreciate it in light of knowledge about painting in general, and 1950s American Abstract Expressionism and action painting in particular".

New aesthetic categories characterize the philosophy of everyday aesthetics, observes Elisabetta Di Stefano (2017): the "extraordinary/ordinary", the "aura/atmosphere", and the "luxury/décor". In fact, from the intent to identify different aesthetic categories to be combined, and sometimes to contrast, with traditional ones—such as the aesthetic category of sublime discussed in Chapter 1—"the need arises to resort to a method of investigation through couples", observes Elisabetta Di Stefano (2017: 63). Namely, these categories are as follows:

- The aesthetic category of "extraordinary/ordinary" highlights the beauty, but also the paradox and the contradiction of the aesthetic dimension of the everyday, in which the special moments that interrupt everyday life—the extraordinary—follow the moments in which the aesthetic dimension of the ordinary returns.

- The aesthetic category of "aura/atmosphere" relates the aesthetic dimension of the aura (Benjamin, 1935) with that of the atmosphere developed by the new German phenomenology (Böhme, 1993), which highlights, for instance, the seductive atmospheres radiated by ordinary artifacts and mundane events in the aesthetic capitalism (Biehl-Missal and Saren, 2012; Böhme, 2003; Murphy and de la Fuente, 2014).

- The aesthetic category of "luxury/decoration" emphasizes the aesthetic dynamics for which the aestheticization of "the real has transformed luxury into a mode of living and feeling that aspires to the 'extraordinary in the ordinary' through the mundane reconfiguration of the aura" (Di Stefano, 2017: 84). This happens with furniture or fashion, areas in which luxury is tinged with artistry and raises the question of tact (Naukkarinen, 2014), that is, of the style and acting with decorum.

We can conclude this final section of this chapter dedicated to the topic of art, everyday aesthetics and organizational theory with the following note written by Yuriko Saito (2007: 243), because she argues in it that the philosophy of "Everyday Aesthetics" is a subject to be pursued for a number of reasons:

> First, exploring everyday aesthetics remedies a deficiency in the mainstream art-based philosophical aesthetics by being truthful to the diverse dimensions of our aesthetic life, which is not confined to the artworld and other art-like objects and activities. Secondly, by analyzing various ways in which we interact with everyday objects and phenomena aesthetically, we can enrich the content of the aesthetics discourse. Finally, even the seemingly trivial, insignificant everyday aesthetic attitudes and judgements often wield surprising power that can determine the quality of life, the state of the world, or social and cultural ethos in the most literal manner. For most of us, engagement with everyday objects and environments far exceeds interactions with art, both in frequency and in regularity, rendering the former's effect on every aspect of life immeasurable.

Concluding Remarks

At the beginning of Part I, the relationship between philosophy and organizational aesthetics was discussed in terms of the relevance of philosophical aesthetics in the study of the aesthetic dimension of organizational life. My intent was to ground the relevance of philosophy, first of all, in the context of doing aesthetic field research, but also in the context of the theoretical and methodological construction of the aesthetic understanding of organization.

The emphasis on the aesthetic empirical study characterized also the illustration and the discussion of the relationship between art photography and the creation process, between art and everyday aesthetics in photography, between the art photographer's freedom and his/her work practice, between the philosophy of photography and the aesthetic study of organization.

Some of these issues are also visually raised—with a delicate and poetic touch—by Agnès Varda and JR (2017) in their documentary film *Visages Villages/Faces Places*. They travel through French villages, they meet the people who live there, they photograph them and paste the black and white images made in huge dimensions on the walls of their houses, on their company containers, on train cars, on the rocks at the sea. At a certain point, JR takes some photographs of Agnès Varda's feet and, with the help of their team, makes a very large black and white print and pastes this art photograph on a wagon. One of the workers, looking at the photograph above the wagon, asks Agnès Varda:

"Why to put toes on trains? Is there a point, or is it . . .?"
"The point is the power of imagination",

answers Agnès Varda. And she continues specifying that

"we're given ourselves the freedom, JR and I, to imagine things, and ask people if we can express our imagination on their turf. But our idea has always been to be with people, at work. Hence the group photos. So we want to have an exchange with you, and also try out our own quirky ideas. We enjoy it, and we hope you do too".

The two Interludes resonate with Varda and JR's work. They have had the sense to provide some principal clues in order to reach an aesthetic understanding of the creation process, of its "collective *auteur*", and of its influence and pervasiveness in terms of aesthetic invention, of aesthetic negotiation and of aesthetic appreciation in our contemporary organizational contexts. The Interludes have constituted the bridge that has connected the first chapter, dedicated to the relevance of philosophy in organizational research, with the second chapter, dedicated to photography and the creation process; and with the third chapter where the everyday aesthetics and the ordinary beauty constituted the "object of reflection intrinsically traversed by tensions and conflicts" (Przychodzen,

2010: 33). It is "the end of 'aesthetics' as a specific discipline or value", writes Peter Carravetta (2017: 32), and

> the aesthetizicing (or anaesthetizicing) of all cultural interactions that demand that everything and everyone be (potentially) admitted into the process. In this perspective, hybridism, *mestizaje*, creolization will find greater spaces or channels for expression and growth. Because at bottom, change is the norm, stability the exception, chance and error are probabilities built into any plan or system.

A main "shift", therefore, writes Peter Murphy (2014: 52), has "occurred in the past two centuries", beginning with the existentialist philosophy of Søren Kierkegaard, and this was "the transformation of art into aesthetics", into the "aesthetic capitalism", and also into the aesthetics of daily working life in organization. These are the principal topics that I have discussed in Chapter 3.

I want now to conclude this chapter and Part I with an important consideration: organizational aesthetics is an area of the organization studies that is receiving attention from philosophy (Di Stefano, 2017; Murphy and de la Fuente, 2014; Przychodzen, 2010; Ratiu, 2017; Saito, 2007). This attention is still timid and comes directly from the research areas in philosophical aesthetics which recently developed from diverse perspectives, an interest in the daily aesthetics that were previously neglected because of the influence of the art-centered aesthetic theory. In fact, Dan Eugen Ratiu (2017: 23) writes that "the growing scholarly interest in the aesthetic dimension of daily life in organizations has fueled the development of a new field of study, 'organizational aesthetics', which departs from the positivist and rationalist paradigms". Exactly: while, as we have seen in these three chapters of Part I of the book, "art" has been the problem for aesthetic philosophies, "rationality" has been the problem for organizational theories. We will see this in Chapter 4, which begins Part II, dedicated to the aesthetic, hermeneutic and performative philosophical sensibilities of organizational aesthetics research.

But, before passing to the problem of rationality and of its relationships with the philosophical sensibilities which influence organizational aesthetics research, as a ritual, the flow of the words will be interrupted and distracted with the rhythm of the visual language in *Interlude III: Homage to Gaspare Traversi*.

References

Aisthesis. Pratiche, linguaggi e saperi dell'estetico (2014). Special Issue on "Everyday objects", 7 (1). Edited by Matteucci, G., Di Stefano, E. and A. Mecacci.

Amelunxen, von, H. (2000). Afterword, in Flusser, V., *Towards a Philosophy of Photography*. London: Reaktion Books.

Baqué, D. (2004). *Photographie plasticienne, l'extrême contemporain.* Paris: Éditions du Regard.

Barthes, R. (1980). *La chambre claire: Note sur la photographie.* Paris: Éditions du Seuil. (English trans.: *Camera Lucida: Reflections on Photography.* Trans. Howard, R., New York: Hill and Wang, 1981).

Benjamin, W. (1931). Kleine Geschichte der Photographie, in Benjamin, W. (ed.), *Schriften.* Frankfurt am Main: Suhrkamp Verlag, 1955. (English trans.: A short history of photography, *Screen,* 1972, 13 (1): 5–26).

Benjamin, W. (1935). Das Kunstwerk im Zeitalter seiner technischen Reproduzierbarkeit, in Benjamin, W. (ed.), *Schriften.* Frankfurt am Main: Suhrkamp Verlag, 1955. (English trans.: The work of art in the age of mechanical reproduction, in *Illuminations.* Ed. Arendt, H. New York: Schocken Books, 1969, pp. 217–251).

Berleant, A. (2010). *Sensibility and Sense: The Aesthetic Transformation of the Human World.* Exeter: Imprint Academic.

Berleant, A. (2014). Transformation in art and aesthetics, in Yuedi, L. and Carter, C. L. (eds.), *Aesthetics of Everyday Life: East and West.* Newcastle upon Tyne: Cambridge Scholars Publishing, pp. 2–13.

Biehl-Missal, B. and Saren, M. (2012). Atmospheres of seduction: a critique of aesthetic marketing practices, *Journal of Macromarketing,* 32 (2): 168–180.

Böhme, G. (1993). Atmosphere as the fundamental concepts of new aesthetics, *Thesis Eleven,* 36 (1): 113–126.

Böhme, G. (2003). Contribution to the critique of the aesthetic economy, *Thesis Eleven,* 73 (1): 71–82.

Boissier, J. L. (2016). *L'écran comme mobile.* Genève: Mamco, Musée d'art moderne et contemporain.

Borgerson, J. and Schroeder, J. (2018). Making skin visible: how consumer culture imagery commodifies identity, *Body & Society,* 24 (1–2): 103–136.

Bourriaud, N. (2001). *Esthétique relationnelle.* Dijon: Les presses du réel.

Burgin, V. (2008). *Components of a Practice.* Milano: Skira.

Carlson, A. (2000). *Aesthetics and the Environment: The Appreciation of Nature, Art and Architecture.* London: Routledge.

Carlson, A. (2014). The dilemma of everyday aesthetics, in Yuedi, L. and Carter, C. L. (eds.), *Aesthetics of Everyday Life: East and West.* Newcastle upon Tyne: Cambridge Scholars Publishing, pp. 48–64.

Carravetta, P. (2017). After all: critical theory and the geography of culture at the end of the postmodern age, in Perez, R. (ed.), *Agorapoetics: Poetics after Postmodernism.* Aurora, Colorado: The Davies Group, Publishers, pp. 2–35.

Carter, C. L. (2014). Art photography and everyday life, in Yuedi, L. and Carter, C. L. (eds.), *Aesthetics of Everyday Life: East and West.* Newcastle upon Tyne: Cambridge Scholars Publishing, pp. 80–95.

Cazeaux, C. (ed.) (2000). *The Continental Aesthetics Reader.* London: Routledge.

Colacicco, M. (2016). La street art come pratica di riconoscimento e appaesamento degli spazi sociali urbani. Il caso di Torpignattara a Roma, *Cambio. Rivista sulle trasformazioni sociali,* 6 (11): 49–63.

Collinson, D. (1992). Aesthetic experience, in Hanfling, O. (ed.), *Philosophical Aesthetics: An Introduction.* Oxford: Blackwell, pp. 111–178.

Contemporary Aesthetics (2012). Special Issue on "Artification", Special Vol. 4. Edited by Naukkarinen, O. and Y. Saito, www.contempaesthetics.org/

Contemporary Aesthetics (2018). Special Issue on "Aesthetic consciousness in East Asia", Special Vol. 6. Edited by J. Min, www.contempaesthetics.org/

Cooper, R. and Fox, S. (1990). The "texture" of organizing, *Journal of Management Studies*, 27 (6): 575–582.

Costello, D. (2018). *On Photography: A Philosophical Inquiry*. London and New York: Routledge.

Dewey, J. (1934/1987). *Art as Experience—The Later Works, 1925–1953*. Vol. 10: 1934. Ed. Boydston, J. A. Carbondale: Southern Illinois University Press.

Diodato, R. (2005). *Estetica del virtuale*. Milano: Bruno Mondadori. (English trans.: *Aesthetics of the Virtual*. Albany: State University of New York Press, 2012).

Di Stefano, E. (2017). *Che cos'è l'estetica quotidiana*. Roma: Carocci.

Eco, U. (1982). Critique of the image, in Burgin, V. (ed.), *Thinking Photography*. London: Macmillan, pp. 32–38.

Eco, U. (2002). Averroè e la metafora, in Centro Comunicazione e Marketing (ed.), *I dieci anni di Scienze della comunicazione*. Siena: Università degli Studi di Siena, pp. 37–112.

Feng, G. and Wenjing, D. (2017). What is the aesthetics in China?, *Aisthesis. Pratiche, linguaggi e saperi dell'estetico*, 10 (2): 125–134.

Flusser, V. (1983). *Für eine Philosophie der Fotografie*. Berlin: European Photography Andreas Müller-Pohle. (English trans.: *Towards a Philosophy of Photography*. London: Reaktion Books, 2000).

Fontcuberta, J. (2008). *Joan Fontcuberta*. Tours: Actes Sud.

Friberg, C. and Vasquez, R. (eds.) (2017). *Experiencing the Everyday*. Copenhagen: NSU Press/Aarhus University Press.

Gaut, B., and Lopes, D. McIver (eds.) (2001). *The Routledge Companion to Aesthetics*. London: Routledge.

Gherardi, S. and Strati, A. (1990). The "texture" of organizing in an Italian university department, *Journal of Management Studies*, 27 (6): 605–618.

Gherardi, S. and Strati, A. (2012). *Learning and Knowing in Practice-based Studies*. Cheltenham: Edward Elgar.

Ghiglione, A. (2010). La place du beau dans la pensée chinoise ancienne: le ritualisme confucéen et la critique moïste (Ve-IIIe s. av. J. C.), in Przychodzen, J., Boucher, F. E. and David, S. (eds.), *L'esthétique du beau ordinaire dans une perspective transdisciplinaire. Ni du gouffre ni du ciel*. Paris: l'Harmattan, pp. 185–200.

Guillet de Monthoux, P. and Strati, A. (2008). "Ponte dei Sospiri": bridging art and aesthetics in organizational memories, *Aesthesis. International Journal of Art and Aesthetics in Management and Organizational Life*, 2 (1): 3–7.

Heidegger, M. (1971). The origin of the work of art, in Heidegger, M. (ed.), *Poetry, Language, Thought*. Trans. Hofstadter, A. New York: Harper and Row, pp. 15–88.

Heinich, N. and Shapiro, R. (eds.) (2012). *De l'artification. Enquêtes sur le passage à l'art*. Paris: EHESS.

Hjorth, D., Strati, A., Drakopoulou Dodd, S., and Weik, E. (2018). Organizational creativity, play and entrepreneurship: introduction and framing, *Organization Studies*, 39 (2–3): 155–168.

Journal of Management Studies (1990). Special issue on "The texture of organizing", 27 (6). Edited by Fineman, S. and D. Hosking.

Leddy, T. (2014). Everyday aesthetics and photography, *Aisthesis. Pratiche, linguaggi e saperi dell'estetico*, 7 (1): 45–62.

Leica Fotografie International Magazine (2017). Johnny Pigozzi, 6: 18–31.

Mandoki, K. (2007). *Everyday Aesthetics: Prosaics, the Play of Culture and Social Identities*. Aldershot: Ashgate. Reprinted 2017, New York: Routledge.

Mangham, I. L., Overington, M. A. (1987). *Organizations as Theatre*. Chichester: Wiley.

Meisiek, S. and Barry, D. (2014). The science of making management an art, *Scandinavian Journal of Management*, 30 (1): 134–141.

Mitchell, W. J. (1992). *The Reconfigured Eye: Visual Truth in the Post-Photographic Era*. Cambridge, MA: The MIT Press.

Morgan, G. (1986). *Images of Organization*. Thousand Oaks, CA: Sage.

Murphy, P. (2014). The aesthetic spirit of modern capitalism, in Murphy, P. and de La Fuente, E. (eds.), *Aesthetic Capitalism*. Leiden: Brill, pp. 47–62.

Murphy, P. and de La Fuente, E. (2014). Introduction: aesthetic capitalism, in Murphy, P. and de La Fuente, E. (eds.), *Aesthetic Capitalism*. Leiden: Brill, pp. 1–9.

Naukkarinen, O. (2014). Everyday aesthetic practices, ethics and tact, *Aisthesis. Pratiche, linguaggi e saperi dell'estetico*, 7 (1): 23–44.

Organization Studies (2018). Special Issue on "Organizational creativity, play and entrepreneurship", 39 (2–3). Edited by Hjorth, D., Strati, A., Drakopoulou Dodd, S., and E. Weik.

Pareyson, L. (1954). *Estetica: Teoria della formatività*. Torino: Edizioni di "Filosofia". Reprinted 1988, Milano: Bompiani. (Partial English trans.: Pareyson, L., *Existence, Interpretation, Freedom: Selected Writings*. Ed. Bubbio, P. D. Aurora, CO: The Davies Group, 2009).

Paris, T. (2007). Organization, processes and structures of creation, *Focuses on Cultural Topics*, 5: 2–16.

Przychodzen, J. (with Boucher, F. E. and David, S.) (2010). Le beau ordinaire, une nouvelle catégorie esthétique?, in Przychodzen, J., Boucher, F. E. and David, S. (eds.), *L'esthétique du beau ordinaire dans une perspective transdisciplinaire. Ni du gouffre ni du ciel*. Paris: l'Harmattan, pp. 11–33.

Putnam, L. L. and Boys, S. (2006). Revisiting metaphors of organizational communication, in Clegg, S. R., Hardy, C., Lawrence, T. B. and Nord, W. R. (eds.), *The Sage Handbook of Organization Studies*. 2nd edn. London: Sage, pp. 541–576.

Putnam, L. L., Phillips, N. and Chapman, P. (1996). Metaphors of communication and organization, in Clegg, S. R., Hardy, C. and Nord, W. R. (eds.), *Handbook of Organization Studies*. London: Sage, pp. 375–408.

Rancière, J. (2000). *Le partage du sensible. Esthétique et politique*. Paris: La fabrique éditions. (English trans.: *The Politics of Aesthetics*. London: Continuum, 2004).

Ratiu, D. E. (2013). Remapping the realm of aesthetics: on recent controversies about the aesthetic and aesthetic experience in everyday life, *Estetika: The Central European Journal of Aesthetics*, L/VI (1): 3–26.

Ratiu, D. E. (2017). Everyday aesthetic experience: explorations by a practical aesthetics, in Friberg, C. and Vasquez, R. (eds.), *Experiencing the Everyday*. Copenhagen: NSU Press/Aarhus University Press, pp. 22–52.

Saito, Y. (2007). *Everyday Aesthetics*. Oxford: Oxford University Press.

Sartwell, C. (2003). Aesthetics of the everyday, in Levinson, J. (ed.), *The Oxford Handbook of Aesthetics*. Oxford: Oxford University Press, pp. 761–770.

Savedoff, B. E. (2000). *Transforming Images: How Photography Complicates the Picture*. Ithaca, NY: Cornell University Press.

Shapiro, R. and Heinich, N. (2012). When is artification? *Contemporary Aesthetics*, Special Vol. 4, www.contempaesthetics.org/

Shusterman, R. (1992). *Pragmatist Aesthetics*. Oxford: Blackwell.

Shusterman, R. (2008). *Body Consciousness: A Philosophy of Mindfulness and Somaesthetics*. Cambridge: Cambridge University Press.

Shusterman, R. (2012). Photography as performative process, *The Journal of Aesthetics and Art Criticism*, 70 (1): 67–77.

Sternberg, R. and Krauss, G. (2014). *Handbook of Research on Entrepreneurship and Creativity*. Cheltenham: Edward Elgar.

Strati, A. (1995). Aesthetics and organizations without walls, *Studies in Cultures, Organizations and Societies*, 1 (1): 83–105.

Strati, A. (1996). *Sociologia dell'organizzazione: paradigmi teorici e metodi di ricerca*. Roma: NIS-Carocci. (English trans.: *Theory and Method in Organization Studies: Paradigms and Choices*. London: Sage, 2000).

Strati, A. (1999). *Organization and Aesthetics*. London: Sage.

Tan, S. H. (1999). Experience as art, *Asian Philosophy*, 9 (2): 107–122.

Teplova, N. (2010). L'historicité du "beau ordinaire" au Japon, in Przychodzen, J., Boucher, F. E. and David, S. (eds.), *L'esthétique du beau ordinaire dans une perspective transdisciplinaire. Ni du gouffre ni du ciel*. Paris: l'Harmattan, pp. 201–210.

Tifentale, A. (2018). The selfie: more and less than a self-portrait, in Neumüller, M. (ed.), *Routledge Companion to Photography and Visual Culture*. London: Routledge, pp. 44–58.

Valtorta, R. (ed.) (2004). *È contemporanea la fotografia?* Milano: Lupetti—Editori di Comunicazione.

Valtorta, R. (ed.) (2014). *2004–2014. Opere e progetti del Museo di Fotografia Contemporanea*. Milano: SilvanaEditoriale.

Varda, A., and JR (2017). *Visages Villages/Faces Places*, Documentary Film, 1h32'.

Vico, G. (1725). *Principi di una scienza nuova*. Napoli: Mosca. 3rd edn. 1744. (English trans.: *The New Science of Giambattista Vico*. Ed. Bergin, T. G. and M. H. Fisch. Ithaca, NY: Cornell University Press, 1968).

Wolf, S. (2010). *The Digital Eye: Photographic Art in the Electronic Age*. New York: Prestel.

Yuedi, L. and Carter, C. L. (2014). Introduction, in Yuedi, L. and Carter, C. L. (eds.), *Aesthetics of Everyday Life: East and West*. Newcastle upon Tyne: Cambridge Scholars Publishing, pp. VII–XVII.

Interlude III: Homage to Gaspare Traversi, 2017

file internet PD Wikimedia Commons, software Adobe Photoshop

Part II

Three Philosophical Sensibilities

4   Aesthetic Philosophy and the Aesthetic Approach

Interlude III opens the second part of the book, which is dedicated to the three philosophical sensibilities that traverse and pervade the study of the aesthetic dimension of the organization. In fact, in Part II, I will discuss that the aesthetic philosophical sensibility, the hermeneutical philosophical sensibility and the performative philosophical sensibility are the principal aesthetic philosophies that have a profound influence on organizational theory.

I used the concept of "philosophical sensibility" for the first time in my chapter for *The Routledge Companion to Philosophy in Organization Studies* edited by Raza Mir, Hugh Willmott and Michelle Greenwood (Strati, 2016). I proposed this notion in order to comprehend the philosophical currents that have and still do influence the configuration of the organizational aesthetics research for two motives. First of all, because the concept of philosophical sensibility renders the term philosophy nuanced thanks to its aesthetic touch—sense, sensible, sensibility. Second, because with the notion of philosophical sensibility, I also intend to emphasize the "connection in action" that I catch in the hybridization between philosophy and organizational theory in the study of art and aesthetics in the organization.

Interlude III also opens to the principal aesthetic philosophies that have a profound influence on my "aesthetic approach" to the study of organizational life. Thus, in this chapter I will first describe the fundamental aspects of my "aesthetic approach" and will debate the relationship between the "aesthetic approach" and the philosophical and sociological topic of "rationality" in organization studies. Then I will emphasize the phenomenological and post-humanist awareness that characterizes the "aesthetic approach" and discuss the "post-humanist aesthetics", which avoids anthropocentrism and connects, instead, in bodily and material relationships, the human with the robot, organization and all forms of life, as pointed out by the French philosophers Gilles Deleuze and Felix Guattari (1980), the American philosopher Donna Haraway (1991) and the Italian philosophers Rosi Braidotti (2013) and Roberto Esposito (2010; 2014).

4.1 Fundamental Characteristics of the Aesthetic Approach

The "aesthetic approach" (Strati, 1992, 1999) is one of the four research styles which compose the area of the study of art and aesthetics in organizational theory, sociology of organization, and management studies (Strati, 2009: 196–202). I shall further illustrate these four different styles of research in Chapter 6, which represents the final chapter of Part II and thus of the book. Here, I want to recapitulate some major features that distinguish these four approaches to the study of organizational life:

- The "aesthetic approach" focuses on the continuous collective negotiation of the organizational aesthetics in the work practices in organizations.
- The "archeological approach" studies the organizational aesthetics in order to understand the organization's symbolism and culture.
- The "artistic approach" investigates the artistic experience in the art worlds in order to grasp insights for the management of the organizational processes.
- The "empathic-logical approach" studies the aesthetic side of organization to comprehend the pre-cognitive forms of organizational experience.

The characteristics of my "aesthetic approach" to the study of the organization resonate in the photopoem of *Interlude III: Homage to Gaspare Traversi*, which constitutes the material and symbolic bridge connecting Part I to Part II of the book. In this tribute to the painting art of Gaspare Traversi, in fact, a micro-practice, that of a surgical operation that occurs some centuries ago, is exhibited in its vivid performance and is embellished with tragicomic details that reveal its operational and organizational context.

Traversi is an important Caravaggist Neapolitan painter (Longhi, 1927; Forgione, 2014) who shows irony and satire in his representations of acts, moments and rituals of the society that is contemporary to him. He worked in Naples, Rome, and in other important capitals of the European culture, like Parma, in the same epoch of the Neapolitan philosopher Giambattista Vico. I tried to emphasize his satirical aesthetics in my tribute to his work. We shall see another examples of "Homage to" in subsequent Interludes. They all represent a dialogue between the aesthetic materiality of the artwork—which can be a painting, like in this case, or an art installation, as in the next—and my "Photopoesia".

In this case, my photopoem does not have its origins in a photograph I took directly, but in an image I found on the Internet. Thus, *Homage to Gaspare Traversi* began in a way similar to that of Joan Fontcuberta, who experiments with his art photography with the Internet. We saw this in Chapter 3: the Catalan art photographer creates the "googlegrams" by finding photographs on the Internet and thus manipulating them through a software program (Fontcuberta, 2008). However, at the same time, the origins of my photopoem on the Internet echo the ordinary photographic practice of using images of the Internet in everyday work in organizations, in organizational communication, in business and leisure: an intrinsically "aesthetic" research, because it is the search for an image on the Internet that can be judged aesthetically appropriate.

In other words, "my situation" was that of the hybridization of the mundane use of photography in the organization and society and the art photography of which I discussed in the previous chapter. I was searching images that would respond to the term "flesh" when, at some point, I fell on the picture that reproduces *L'operazione chirurgica/The operation*, a painting that Gaspare Traversi made in the years 1753–54, and which is now at the Staatsgaleri of Stuttgart. An oil on canvas, not very large, only 77 × 103 cm, that the reader can see in its photographic reproduction of the digital file in the public domain on the Internet at the following link: https://en.wikipedia.org/wiki/Gaspare_Traversi#/media/File:Traversi_Operation.jpg.

But the idea that we can look "through" photography to see a painting is misleading, because the photographic reproduction of a painting represents an interpretation which translates the original artwork *into other terms*, which are novel and different under various respects. Reproducing a subject means transforming it, and reproduction is generally very important, both in routine work and in the art creation process. When reproduction is taken as having "documentary accuracy", notes Barbara Savedoff (2000: 152), this faith in the documentary precision of reproduction makes us less sensitive and critical of "the distortions inherent in photographic reproduction".

> When paintings are seen in photographic form, when they are reduced to their photographically transmittable properties, their distinctive character is lost; and this experience with photographs of paintings can come to inform the way we look at and think about paintings themselves.
>
> (Savedoff, 2000: 153)

And, in fact, what I did by manipulating the digital file that reproduces the painting of Traversi with the Adobe Photoshop software was informing the way in which I look and think about this work of art. In the first place, I framed only a part of the painting, one in which the surgical practice had been particularly focused. Then, I kept in the image the figures that act as a chorus to the practice of surgery, cutting the photo so as to include at least one of the two people who help the surgeon to restrain the patient who is suffering. Finally,

- I changed shapes, tones, proportions, perspectives and shadows.
- I used the strong nuances of black and white photography to almost give the sound of the patient's cry of pain.

- I strengthened the black color of the lines that trace the dynamics of "attention-tension-action" in the surgical practice, but also, at the same time, the ironic description of the stubborn concentration that Traversi paints on the visage of the surgeon.
- I highlighted the hands for their significance of perceiving, acting and communicating, namely

  - the hand of the surgeon who manipulates the patient's flesh by gently tightening the scalpel with his fingers;
  - the strength of the hands on the patient's arm of the person assisting the surgeon;
  - the gesture that the patient makes with his hand, as if to protect himself and at the same time express his suffering.

In one word, I emphasized in my photopoem the sense of touch and the fact that this perceptive faculty is acting together with the sense of sight, of hearing, of smell. All the three visages are carefully depicted to manifest the "concentration in doing" the operation, and I have highlighted the nose of these three faces to show the intensity of being concentrated in the "doing" of a work practice—all three noses, not just the surgeon's nose. Because the surgical practice is realized by the plurality of gestures, attention and focus, the skills to realize the operation—exposed through the photographic manipulation—of the surgeon in action remain predominant. In this way, *Interlude III* anticipates and reveals the fundamental subjects of the dialogue between the philosophical aesthetic sensibility and the organizational theories:

- the materiality of organizational life,
- the importance of the aesthetic dimension of social practice in organization,
- the relevance of the art for describing and communicating professional skills and work organization,
- the pleasure of irony in reliving vivid memories of organizational processes and dynamics.

Looking at *Homage to Gaspare Traversi*, the reader can also grasp the main features of my "aesthetic approach" to the study of organizational life, which range

1. from the micro-practice that constitutes the principal subject of my aesthetic study to the perceptive and sensorial faculties which ground my approach in the materiality of the bodily knowing as activity;
2. from the sensitive aesthetic judgement—that can be grasped, for instance, on the patient's visage, on the eyes, on the mouths and on the hand protecting the mouth in an evident act of screaming, even if we cannot hear the scream—until reference to the categories of

aesthetics—such as the "tragic" and the "comic"—to aesthetically judge how the practice of the surgical operation is exhibited through the art of painting;
3. from the experiential flux that connects-in-action the surgeon, the assistant and the patient in the painting to the connection of this painting, with its photographic reproduction, its exposition on the Internet, my photopoetic transformation, the Routledge typographic print and the reader's aesthetic interpretation;
4. from the Caravaggist style in which lights and shadows are explored and expressed to the Rococo irreverence that also characterizes the choice of the specific subject of the surgical operation performed by Traversi.

The aesthetics—of the mundane surgical operation—and the art—of the painting—are both constituent elements of the ongoing performative process, and they hybridize it. At the same time, all interactions, those "internal" to the painting, i.e., those between surgeon, assistant and patient, as well as those "external" to the painting, which connect the art of painting with art photography, book production and the reader, are all immersed in the negotiation of aesthetics. They are rooted, in other terms, in the materiality of the execution of a professional practice—the operation—and in the corporeity of "doing the operation".

This means that they are grounded in perception and sensitive judgment, in imagination and in aesthetic judgment, in personal knowledge and in collective performance, in experimentation of the senses and the aesthetic research. Furthermore, the art of painting shows the art of performing a surgical operation and, at the same time, the opposite also happens, in the sense that the art of doing an operation shows the art of painting by Gaspare Traversi.

Now, in place of who or of what, would the reader want to be with his/her imagination to understand empathetically and have an aesthetic experience of this surgical practice? The patient? The surgeon? The assistant? The scalpel? The hand? And which hand?

These are some of the interrogatives that, in any case, the researcher must put to him/herself when s/he adopts my "aesthetic approach" to the study of organizational life.

4.1.1 Rationality: An Old Story

I illustrated in the previous section the fundamental characteristics of the "aesthetic approach". Obviously, the analytical and logical intelligence that is not only necessary, but also crucial, for the art of doing a surgical operation, as well as for the art of painting, is not omitted or neglected in my "aesthetic approach", even though it is the aesthetic that constitutes its principal subject. Who, for example, empathetically imagining being in the patient's place of *Homage to Gaspare Traversi* in *Interlude III*, would fantasize to be benefited by the irrational organization of this work team and even the medical structure in which they operate? As Jon Elster put it beautifully, the idea "that all would benefit if all acted irrationally is neither here nor there" (1989: 29).

We shall see in this section the philosophical foundations concerning the relationship between the "aesthetic approach" and the concept of rationality in organizational theories and in the social sciences, and also that this relationship is grounded on my empirical study of organizational life. Beginning with the considerations highlighted by Alfred Schütz during the "Harvard Rationality Seminar" held at Harvard University during the academic year 1939–1940, the

> term "rationality", or at least the concept it envisages, has, within the framework of social science, the specific role of a "key concept".
> (2018: 88)

The Harvard Rationality Seminar has been "an unusual interdisciplinary seminar on the general topic of Rationality" write Helmut Staubmann and Victor Lidz (2018a: 1) in their introduction to the book that—finally—publishes all the essays of those who participated in this important event, which included Alfred Schütz, Joseph Schumpeter, Talcott Parsons, Donald McGranahan, Wilbert Moore, Rainer Schickele and an "Unknown Author", and which also collects more recent contributions to illustrate the current perspectives on rationality (Staubmann and Lidz, 2018b). This debate did not have the resonance of that of the *Methodenstreit* during the early years of the last century, to which I will return later on in this section, but was significant for the construction of sociological and, more generally, of social theory during the years of World War II and the first two decades after.

> Rationality was in 1939 and remains today one of the fundamental theoretical and empirical issues in all of the social sciences. Since the early attempts to approach human action in modern scientific terms, the question of rationality has stood at the center of conceptual frameworks and methodological premises.
> (Staubmann and Lidz, 2018a: 4)

This "key concept" has been widely debated in organizational theories and, as I wrote in my essay for the Staubmann and Lidz's book (Strati, 2018: 190), "once upon a time", rationality was "the grand concept" that received a deep consideration to configure the styles of management and the organizational theories as well as to discuss in philosophy, sociology, social history, economic and other social sciences. Richard Scott put the term "rational" in the title of his influential handbook *Organizations: Rational, Natural, and Open Systems* (1981), also emphasizing in this way the sociological relevance of rationality in organizational theories. "Rational" is, in fact, one of the three main perspectives of Scott in the study of organization, but "rational" is also one of the three main approaches to the study of the organization identified by Edward Gross and Amitai Etzioni (1985) in their handbook: rational, interactionist and structuralist models.

But, at the same time, a strong critique of rationality pervaded organizational theories, and a fierce controversy contrasted the dominance of the rational and positivistic paradigm in organization studies because of the excessively rational image of organizational life and of the organizational structuring depicted by this paradigm (Zey-Ferrel, 1981). Alfred Schütz emphasized a philosophical and sociological awareness in his contribution to the Harvard Rational Seminar of 13 April 1940: rational action, together with its antithesis defined by Max Weber in terms of "traditional" action, constitutes a sociological "ideal type" that can rarely be observed in everyday life, since "the ideal of rationality is not and cannot be a peculiar feature of everyday thought, nor can it, therefore, be a methodological principle of the interpretation of human acts in daily life" (Schütz, 2018: 90).

This was what happened when I "discovered"—as I like to emphasize with a touch of irony—the organizational relevance of aesthetics in daily working life. I was conducting an empirical research study to understand organizational cultures in the Department of Mathematics, that is, in an organization that, according to my typifications, was to constitute the realm of rationality and "rational quality". As I described in Chapter 1, while I was researching how the symbolism of rationality, in its purity, was able to characterize departmental organizational cultures, my research results gave rise to the aesthetic dimension of organizational life of the prestigious mathematics department of one of the most ancient universities in the world.

The "cultural turn" that took place during the 1980s circumscribed the relevance of rationality in organizational life; rationality and rational action represent nowadays a topic which no longer has the appeal and status of the "grand concept" which has existed for several decades in organizational theories. But just as "art" was the central philosophical problem we discussed in Chapter 3 and that the recent trends in aesthetic philosophy had and wanted to address to comprehend the aesthetics of everyday life, "rationality" was the central theoretical problem for the flourishing of new approaches in organization theory, sociology of organization and management studies.

In this, for my "aesthetic approach", it was the *Methodenstreit* debate between the nineteenth and twentieth centuries that was of fundamental importance, and in particular, the contribution given by the philosopher and historian of culture Wilhelm Dilthey and by the sociologist Max Weber. This debate aimed to redefine the epistemological bases of human inquiry and pervaded science and philosophy, from sociology to economic thought, and involved historicism, neo-idealism, logical-empiricism and neo-Kantianism.

The *Methodenstreit* gave rise to the modern philosophical legitimation of "rationality" and causal-based explanation, favoring the aesthetics of objectivity. But also "empathy" and empathic and artistic understanding was central to the *Methodenstreit* debate as a legitimate form of knowing processes, dynamics and motivations of intentional action in society. Empathy, as David Freedberg notes (2017: 147), is "fundamentally a matter of bodily engagement", and this engagement is "with the movements of others", while "the form of immersion it entails is often a critical preliminary stage in aesthetic judgement".

Every action and every movement, even in an image, activates in the observer, the reader, the spectator, an immediate motor imagery, and accentuates soma-kinetic auto-affections—in short, "embodied simulation" (Gallese, 2005) and the "mimetic empathy" that António Damásio (1999) formulated in terms of the "*as-if*" hypothesis. According to this hypothesis, which is also found in Merleau-Ponty, writes Filippo Fimiani (2013: 333), it is the "entire body" of the observer, the reader or the spectator

> who sees, just *as-if s/he* were himself an actor, *as-if s/he* were currently engaged in the same activities and passions contemplated, *as-if s/he* were confronting the same events and performing the same displacements as the bodies (living or not) represented, *as-if s/he* expressed and supported the movements and the emotions put in images.

Empathic understanding is the crucial distinction of the "aesthetic approach" and the "empathic-logical approach" from the other two approaches, "archaeological" and "artistic". Both Dilthey and Weber pointed out the importance of empathic understanding of social action:

- Dilthey (1914–36) to delineate that the investigating being belongs to and partially coincides with the investigated being, and is not monolithic but rather resembles a woven fabric from a variety of threads;
- Weber (1922) to take due account of the legitimacy of the different forms of comprehension (*Verstehen*) of intentional action, because whenever an explanatory comprehension of causal type fails, empathic and artistic understanding—*Einfühlung* in Theodor Lipps terms (1913)—can legitimately be privileged.

Since then, empathic understanding has been a source of epistemological and methodological controversy and, during the second half of the last century, the operationalization of the concept of empathy as a method, its scientific validity and its epistemological principles were fiercely debated.

Among the various contributions that followed each other for some decades, I want to mention here that of Carl G. Hempel (1942), who proposed to confine the intuitive comprehension of the empathic understanding to the sphere of the formulation of the hypotheses necessary to design research and study, because this is exactly the opposite of what my "aesthetic approach" proposes.

In the study of the aesthetic dimension of organizational life, in fact, drawing from the methodological considerations of Max Weber (Bruun and Whimster, 2012), the concept of empathy denotes an autonomous method for investigating social action in the organization and an independent philosophical and epistemological frame to understand organization.

In particular, the empathic understanding of organization has a heuristic value (Sousa Lopes, Rocha Ipiranga and da 'Silva, 2017) which is based on the following theoretical presuppositions for the "aesthetic approach" (Strati, 1999: 67–74):

1. *willingness of the researcher* to position himself/herself in the place of the organizational actor through the imaginary aesthetic self-immersion in the aesthetic flow of the experiential processes in the organization, and activating the perceptive faculties and the aesthetic judgment of the researcher;
2. *knowledge-gathering methods* based on self-observation, intuition, analogy, and the reliving of experience in the imagination;
3. *definition of the situation of empathy* in terms of imaginary participant observation and of the sharing of experience;
4. *architecture and style of description and communication* of the knowledge gathered by the empathic method;
5. *choice of the feature dominant in the knowledge process*, which can be merely cognitive, or emotionally involving, or aesthetic to favor sensory and evocative understanding.

Configured in this way, the dialogue and the controversy that interconnect rationality with empathy could position—imaginatively—the "aesthetic approach" at the intersection of two of the four sociological paradigms (Strati, 2004: 80–82; 2013: 237–238)—*radical humanist, interpretative, radical structuralist* and *functionalist*—proposed by Gibson Burrell and Gareth Morgan (1979) to identify the main epistemological characteristics of schools, perspectives and models that composed the rich and fascinating panorama of organizational theories. All four approaches that make up the organizational aesthetics research—"aesthetic approach", "archeological approach", "artistic approach" and "empathic-logical approach"—briefly introduced at the beginning of this chapter, could be placed among the "interpretative paradigm" and the "radical humanist paradigm" (Figure 4.1).

Research on organizational aesthetics could extend, in fact, through the two sociological paradigms that underline the organizational interaction and the collective construction of the organization. This is because the radical humanist paradigm privileges intuition and the evocative

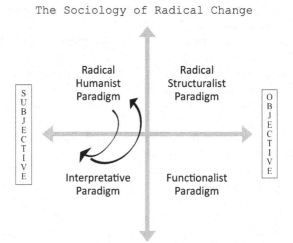

The Sociology of Radical Change

Figure 4.1 Organizational aesthetics research paradoxically projected on Burrell and Morgan's sociological paradigms

process of knowing the organizational life, that is, the empathic understanding rather than the rational explanation. Moreover, both the radical humanist and the interpretative sociological paradigm oppose positivism and the dominion of rationality in the social sciences, and they manifest a profound criticism against the vision of the organization as the social form of modern and contemporary societies consisting of an objective reality which is independent from the continuous interactions between human and non-human elements.

Of course, the fact of projecting the "aesthetic approach" and all the area of the study of the aesthetic dimension of organization on the epistemological map created by Gibson Burrell and Gareth Morgan can appear a paradoxical way to reflect on the paradigmatic foundations of organizational aesthetics research. First of all, this is because the aesthetic discourse on organization was created and configured *after* the publication of the theoretical model of the four sociological paradigms that outline and comprehend organizational theories. It could also be argued that it would certainly be more appropriate to project the aesthetic study of organization onto an epistemological map that also contemplates the variety of approaches that were created during the crisis of rationality and rational action in the sociology of organization, organizational theories and management studies. As John Hassard points out, in fact,

> a significant development for the field, therefore, would be a research programme directed at revisiting paradigm models in order to

determine if they still have explanatory power for interpreting the "post-paradigm times" of contemporary OT [Organization Theory].

(2016: 506)

The post-paradigm times of the most recent organizational theory have given rise, in fact, to new sociological paradigms, which are different from the four sociological paradigms proposed by Burrell and Morgan. John Hassard and Julie Wolfram Cox indicate and discuss three sociological paradigms, the *structural paradigm*, the *anti-structural paradigm* and the *post-structural paradigm*.

> Based on their political and ideological characteristics we argue therefore that our three paradigm fields reflect the following research domains: *normative structural*; *critical structural*; *normative anti-structural*; *critical anti-structural*; *normative post-structural*; and *critical post-structural*. In terms of their meta-theoretical assumptions the first four basically reflect the original Burrell and Morgan paradigms—i.e. normative structural *qua* functionalist; critical structural *qua* radical structuralist; normative anti-structural *qua* interpretive; critical anti-structural *qua* radical humanist.
>
> (2013: 1714)

The distinction "normative/critical" is considered more appropriate by Hassard and Wolfram Cox (2013: 1714) in order "to classify research in terms of underlying political and ideological assumptions, rather than deploy Burrell and Morgan's original bifurcation of the sociologies of regulation and radical change" that was the basis of the construction of their epistemological map in the late 1970s. And, as regards the *post-structural paradigm*:

- In its *normative* domain, we find the post-structural or post-modern theorizations in the organizational theories that are based on the philosophical thought of the French philosophers of the twentieth century, such as Georges Bataille, Jacques Derrida or Michel Foucault. This is a philosophical tradition "that wishes to dissolve the subject, attack historicism (notably historical materialism) and promote a critique of meaning" (2013: 1715), and which underlines the performative action of the reader in his/her interaction with the text. For instance, observe John Hassard and Julie Wolfram Cox (2013: 1715), the Actor Network Theory proposed by Bruno Latour and Michel Callon at the École des Mines in Paris, France, "despite being regularly described as a critical or alternative method for organizational research" because of their stress on the relationship "human and nonhuman"—that is, a foundation of the post-humanistic awareness, as we shall see in the next section with regard to the "aesthetic approach"—has "frequently been denounced as sociologically normative, apolitical and even conservative" and, therefore, constitutes a component of the normative post-structural paradigm.

- In its *critical* domain, instead, we find the writings on feminism and the body by a number of socialist post-structuralist feminists such as Julia Kristeva, Luce Irigaray and Donna Haraway; the writings on the post-colonialism of Gayatri Spivak and Homi Bhabha; the writings on "autonomism"—the self-activity, in neo-Marxist terms, of the working class—during the 1960s and the 1970s by Italian intellectuals, such as Raniero Panzieri, Mario Tronti, Mariarosa Dalla Costa and Antonio. Negri, and published in the Italian New Left journal *Quaderni Rossi*; and the writings on "postmodern capitalism", such as those of Maurizio Lazzarato, that is on "capitalism's extensive deployment of information technologies in order to achieve unprecedented levels of workplace automation, societal surveillance and global mobility" (Hassard and Wolfram Cox, 2013: 1716).

The debate concerning the significance and the value of the philosophical concept of paradigm in the sociology of organization and in organizational theory has also touched on the issues of the multiplicity of paradigms, the paradigmatic incommensurability, the choice between competing paradigm, and the paradigmatic fragmentation (Burrell, 1996; Calás and Smircich, 1999; Cooper and Burrell, 1988; Jackson and Carter, 1991; Kaghan and Phillips, 1998; Willmott, 1993). However, as noted by John Hassard (1993) in the course of this debate, the paradigm is a philosophical concept that has lost some of the rigor imposed by the philosopher of science Thomas Kuhn (1962). In organizational theory, in particular, the concept of paradigm constitutes a "theoretical space" that is created and realized by philosophical, epistemological and methodological traditions that are in conflict with each other and which is subject to decisive aesthetic considerations (Kuhn, 1962; Strati, 1996).

In any case, the importance and use of the concept of paradigm in organizational theories reveals how relevant philosophy is in organizational theories. Moreover, the vast popularity of Burrell and Morgan's book consolidates the image of the relevance of philosophy, while at the same time, their epistemological map represents a "self-explanatory common place"—I would claim—by virtue of its evocative process of knowing the sociology of organization and organizational theory. And, indeed, the paradox of projecting the organizational aesthetics research into the four sociological paradigms identified by Gibson Burrell and Gareth Morgan is in any case capable to

- stimulate evocative knowledge with respect to organizational theories,
- highlight some principal characteristics of the paradigmatic foundations of the study of the aesthetic dimension of organizational life, and
- re-echo the relevance of philosophical roots in order to broaden the scope of research and theorization of organizational theory, and expand its boundaries.

4.2 Phenomenological and Post-Humanistic Awareness

The "aesthetic approach", as we have seen with regard to its relation with the concept of rationality, has no desire to give form to an ontological theory of organization—also because the philosophical roots of this approach are grounded in the Italian philosophy of the "Weak Thought" (Vattimo and Rovatti, 1983)—presented in the Prelude of the book and thoroughly discussed in Chapter 1. Thus, with modesty, the "aesthetic approach" seeks an understanding of organizational life and a theorizing of the discourse on organization that are characterized by a phenomenological and post-humanistic awareness, and that are based on the following three key dimensions:

- sensorial know*ing*
- aesthetic judg*ing*
- poetic perform*ing*

These three key dimensions for the "aesthetic approach" are highlighted in Figure 4.2, where the written texts underline the ongoing interaction between a wallaby and my left hand shown in the photograph

Figure 4.2 Key dimensions of the "aesthetic approach": sensorial knowing, aesthetic judging, poetic performing

I took at "Kangaroo Point" in Brisbane, Australia. The written texts of the three key dimensions of my "aesthetic approach" make explicit that the interaction "wallaby/my left hand" is intrinsically aesthetic, phenomenological and post-humanist. This is because this interaction is based on:

- the external perceptive faculties of smelling, touching and seeing;
- the sensitive aesthetic judgment activated by the senses of smell, touch and sight;
- the internal proprioceptive kinaesthetic faculties that allow both the wallaby and my left hand to maintain the physical balance necessary to establish and perform the interaction between them;
- the "smell the atmosphere" that has been fundamental to create the mutual trust between the wallaby and myself in order to approach carefully and appropriately;
- the poetic performance of this interaction that has a certain mystery and shows intensity;
- the invisible but perceivable presence of my right hand, which is performing the task of taking the photograph of the interaction between the wallaby and my left hand thanks to its acquired photographic skills and to its sensible knowledge;
- the aesthetic communication of the relationship created between the wallaby and my left hand, as the written texts and photography blend together and form a unique image that emphasizes the phenomenological and post-humanist awareness that characterizes the "aesthetic approach";
- the affectivity that is expressed in the gestures that depict the ongoing interaction in the photograph and which also concerns the photographic memory of the interactivity between the wallaby and my body.

In a more personal frame, affectivity is the intimate relationship that connects-in-action my "aesthetic approach" with the three written texts that represent its key dimensions that blend with photography. The "linguistic signifier", writes Rosi Braidotti (2013: 166),

> is merely one of the points in a chain of effects, not its centre or its engame. The source of intellectual inspiration comes from the never-ending flow of connections between the texts and their multiple "outsides". Creativity constantly reconnects to the virtual totality of a block of past experiences, memories and affects.

These "speech acts"—in Wittgenstein's terms (Wittgenstein and Barrett,1966)—constitute assessment and action of the superimposed texts of the three key dimensions of the "aesthetic approach" on the photograph that represent the material memory of the ongoing interaction and the process of mutual knowing that involved both the wallaby and myself. Even the speech acts were materially produced and composed to merge with the photograph. Their materiality is digital and, therefore, "immaterial" or virtual, since it was produced using Adobe Photoshop software. Just as "immaterial" is the materiality of the "virtual body" of the digital photograph that I shot with my Leica M9 and then manipulated with Adobe Lightroom photographic software to realize the black and white image that can be seen in Figure 4.2. All this emphasizes

- the corporeality of the living beings which connect-in-action with a deeper or a less profound intensity, i.e., the tree and the grass of Kangaroo Point, the wallaby, myself;
- the physical materiality of the camera, as well as that of the Routledge printed book;
- the immaterial materiality of the digital environment engineering for photographing and for writing;
- the organizational materiality of the photographic industry, of the computer industry and the software production industry, of the entertainment industry and of the animals' park;
- the institutional materiality of universities and publishing houses;
- the ordinary materiality of photographing and writing.

4.2.1 The Aesthetic Materiality of the Aesthetic Approach

Materiality *is not a single thing*, and every element of materiality is characterized by a variety of different aspects and qualities. The "speech acts" that merge with the photograph resonate the philosophical considerations on the "material-semiotic actor" made by Donna Haraway in the early 1990s:

> I wish to translate the ideological dimensions of "facticity" and "the organic" into a cumbersome entity called a "material-semiotic actor". This unwieldy term is intended to highlight the object of knowledge as an active, meaning-generating axis of the apparatus of bodily production, without *ever* implying immediate presence of such objects or, what is the same thing, their final or unique determination of what can count as objective knowledge at a particular historical juncture. Like King's objects called "poems", which are sites of literary production where language also is an actor independent of intentions and authors, bodies as objects of knowledge are material-semiotic generative nodes.
>
> (1991: 200)

The words that describe the three key dimensions of the aesthetic approach are positioned over the picture so that it is the photograph that underlines and emphasizes their meaning and their value. Said in a different way, they represent speech acts enhanced by the sight and the smell of the wallaby, the act of offering the skin of my left hand, the perspective that frames the animal body together with the human body in a natural environment. The three key dimensions become codified acts that are added to the coded interactions visible in the photograph. These interactions highlight the sense of smell, and while the wallaby is immersed in the smell of the skin of my fingertips, I am concentrated in the smell of the atmosphere of the situation and intent on facilitating the interactions in course (Böhme, 1993; Julmi, 2017; Strati, 2009, reprint 2012: 203–204). Both, however, are also immersed in the natural environment provided by an organization, "Kangaroo Point", and, since this environment constitutes "our surroundings", notes Allen Carlson,

> impinges upon all our senses. As we occupy it or move through it, we see, hear, feel, smell, and perhaps even taste it. In short, the experience of the environmental object of appreciation from which aesthetic appreciation must be fashioned is initially intimate, total, and engulfing.
> (2000: XVII)

But, in Figure 4.2, I am not visible and only my hand is part of the picture. However, looking at the picture, the reader cannot avoid imagining the presence of my whole body. This observation is important under two respects. The first is that it is quite a common general situation to be in a technologically mediated relationship with just parts of a human body, animal bodies, plant bodies and bodies of artifacts. Especially at work in the organization, the technology in use can bring our corporeal presence as the sound of our voice coming out of a phone or simply the image of a face that appears on the computer screen.

In any case, however, we are perceived in a more holistic way. This can only be just a mere cognitive and rational act of deduction, of imagination, or just the habit of taking the whole of our body for granted. But, and this is the second consideration, it can also be an aesthetic and phenomenologist form of knowing and interacting, as evidenced by the French philosopher Maurice Merleau-Ponty. When I look at the lamp placed on my table, notes Merleau-Ponty (1945: 82), I attribute to the lamp not only the perceptible qualities that I can see, since they are visible from my place, but also those qualities that are not for me and that instead the table, the walls and the fireplace can "perceive" and "see", while those qualities remain invisible for my sense of sight.

> Though we see it only from a limited perspective—our perspective— this space is nevertheless where we reside and we relate to it though our bodies. We are rediscovering in every object a certain style of being that makes it a mirror of human modes of behaviour. So the way we relate to the things of the world is no longer as a pure intellect

trying to master an object or space that stands before it. Rather, this relationship is an ambiguous one, between beings who are both embodied and limited and an enigmatic world of which we catch a glimpse (indeed which we haunt incessantly) but only ever from points of view that hide as much as they reveal, a world in which every object displays the human face it acquires in a human gaze.

(Merleau-Ponty, 2002; Eng. trans. 2004: 53–54)

The concept of materiality illustrated and discussed in this section with regards to the "aesthetic approach" to the study of organizational life is an aesthetic concept, in the sense that the interactivity between the wallaby and my left hand is concrete, carnal, corporeal:

- in the breathed atmosphere;
- in the environment of the interaction constituted by the tree and the grass of Kangaroo Point in Brisbane that are visible in the picture, and also of those that could be perceived only imaginatively;
- in the flesh of both the wallaby and of my hand;
- in the bodily interaction between the smelling nose of the wallaby and of my left hand, that is, in the act of offering itself to be smelled and touched by/through its skin. The skin is "a visual surface to be regarded, a source of odours to be smelt, and a sentient surface to be felt", writes David Howes (2018: 226). As such, the skin straddles the visual, the odorous and the touchable.

This is the principal point I wanted to make by creating Figure 4.2. The philosophical foundations of the "aesthetic approach" are rooted in a concept of aesthetic materiality, where the aesthetic quality does not belong exclusively to human beings and comprehends the aesthetic knowing and performing activated by other life forms, such as that of the wallaby, and the aesthetic interaction is characterized by the polysemy, mystery and intensity we saw in Chapter 1.

4.2.2 Post-Humanism and Italian Thought

The philosophical foundation of aesthetic materiality stimulates two other considerations before concluding this section dedicated to the phenomenological and post-humanist awareness of the "aesthetic approach" to the study of organization.

The first consideration concerns the fact that the image in Figure 4.2 highlights the aesthetic process of knowing through the senses of the smell and the view of the wallaby, both focused on the tip of my fingers, as well as through my perceptive faculty of touch—offering the skin of my hand—and of the sight—observing the wallaby's moves to understand them and also to facilitate them. The photographic perspective reveals that the camera was held in my right hand—which is invisible for this motive—situated at the appropriate level to frame the interaction between my left hand and the nose and the eyes of the wallaby, and oriented towards the ongoing process of knowing. What the perspective of the photograph cannot reveal is that I was watching the moves of the wallaby rather than looking through the viewfinder to frame the photograph, and it was my right hand that "looked at" each other's interaction.

In other words, the memory of the aesthetic interaction between my body and the body of the wallaby located in the context of the grass and the tree of Kangaroo Point was realized by framing "in the right way" and pressing the shutter of the Leica "at the right moment" thanks to a mix of luck, my photographic skills, my manual abilities, the absorption of both wallaby and myself in the knowing interaction, the professional camera and the lens, the integrated Leica M9 software and the natural light of the park. It was an aesthetic performance which highlighted the relevance of aesthetic sensorial knowing and its complexity due to the intertwined interactions between the external perceptive faculties and the internal proprioceptive faculties. Richard Shusterman (2008: 53) illustrates the diversity of external and internal sense organs by writing that:

> I can consciously sense the position of my hand by looking at it and noting its orientation, but I can also close my eyes and try to sense its position by proprioceptively feeling its relation to my other body parts, to the force of gravity, to other objects in my field experience.

Now, the emphasis on the external and internal sensory faculties of both the wallaby and myself and on the concrete carnal corporeality of aesthetic materiality raises the issue of the privilege accorded by the "aesthetic approach" to animal and human corporeal compared to the other elements—from the grass of the park to word processing software—which, as we have seen, compose the aesthetic materiality of the image in Figure 4.2. Furthermore, this privilege can translate itself into the symbolic sacralization of the body that Ivan Varga points out as an aspect that characterizes postmodern thought in sociology and in social science:

> Postmodernity largely, albeit not fully, accomplishes the mind (spirit or *pneuma*)—body separation by giving primacy or at least preference to the body. The preoccupation with the body and corporeal processes is a strong indication that the body has become sacred, if not "the sacred" but at least "a sacred", in hypermodernity.
>
> (2005: 231)

However, the body/mind dualism is absent in the "aesthetic approach", which is instead inclined to comprehend the body in terms of a knowing body which is a *floating body*, such as Anu Valtonen et al. (2017) emphasize, that is, a body that is never stationary but interwoven between the forms of "wakefulness" and "dormant" existence. This is the opposite of the watershed that "divides the world of life, cutting it into two areas defied by their mutual opposition", as Roberto Esposito (2014: VII–VIII) observes, and you are on the side of the divide "with the persons", or on the other side "with the things". All this, Esposito continues, takes place above all "in the domain of knowledge", that is, as regards the world of organizations, in the domain of the organizational theories, rather than in the domain of practices in organizations (Gherardi and Strati, 2012; Strati, 1999). This watershed, in fact,

> did not take place in the domain of practices, of course, which has always revolved around the body; nor in the domain of power, which is measured by the distinct capacity to control what the body produces. But in the domain of knowledge the body certainly was excluded, especially in legal and philosophical thought, which, generally speaking, has aimed to eliminate its specificity. Because it falls neither under the category of person nor under that of thing, the body has no long oscillated between one and the other without finding a permanent place.
>
> (Esposito, 2014: IX–X)

Equally absent in the aesthetic approach is the human/others dualism that characterizes anthropocentrism, which places human beings at the center of organizational life and of society. Certain dualisms, writes Donna Haraway (1991: 177),

> have been persistent in Western traditions; they have all been systemic to the logics and practices of domination of women, people of colour, nature, workers, animals—in short, domination of all constituted as others, whose task is to mirror the self. Chief among these troubling dualisms are self/other, mind/body, culture/nature, male/female, civilized/primitive, reality/appearance, whole/part, agent/resource, maker/made, active/passive, right/wrong, truth/illusion, total/partial, God/man.

These are dualisms that the "aesthetic approach" contrasts, as it also opposes other dualisms, such as science/art, work/play, routine/creativity, norm/improvisation, theory/practice, human/technology. The "aesthetic approach", in fact, favors the evocative process of knowing in the study of work and organization, and considers aesthetics as a dialogue for non-causal knowledge and which avoids normative knowledge (Strati, 1999: 102–114). The elusiveness of aesthetics in organizational life highlights the crucial importance of investigating the non-causal and non-normative significance of the aesthetics of organizational forms, organizational practices, and organizational corporeal and material interactions.

The second consideration regards the fact that the image in Figure 4.2 will acquire a novel materiality with the Routledge typographic print.

This consideration draws attention to the point raised by Umberto Eco and discussed in Chapter 3: "*every image is born of a series of successive transcriptions*" (1982: 33) and then to the following question: Who/what is the *auteur* of Figure 4.2?

The reader will observe that I have already dealt with the author's argument precisely in Chapter 2 and Chapter 3 of this book. My aesthetic investigation of the process of creation has revealed that its author was configured by a plurality of heterogeneous protagonists—which were human beings, algorithms, robots, institutions and companies—that were all connected-in-action. The author of "my" photopoems illustrated in the Interludes—I pointed out—is a "collective artist" composed of art photographer, information engineer, photographic industry and public. An art photograph—I also stressed in Chapter 3—could be made by an anonymous photographer. In the case of Figure 4.2, authorship can look like the connection-in-action of the animal, the human, the engineering, the artifactual, the organizational, the environmental.

This authorship enhances the relevance of the post-humanistic awareness that characterizes the "aesthetic approach" and the three key dimensions of this approach to the study of organizational life that Figure 4.2 illustrates. But what post-humanism does it highlight? Francesca Ferrando writes that post-human represents both a key notion and an umbrella term.

> In contemporary academic debate, "posthuman" has become a key term to cope with an urgency for the integral redefinition of the notion of the human, following the onto-epistemological as well as scientific and bio-technological developments of the twentieth and twenty-first centuries. The philosophical landscape, which has since developed, includes several movements and schools of thought. The label "posthuman" is often evoked in a generic and all-inclusive way, to indicate any of these different perspectives, creating methodological and theoretical confusion between experts and non-experts alike. "Posthuman" has become an umbrella term to include (philosophical, cultural, and critical) posthumanism, transhumanism (in its variants as extropianism, liberal and democratic transhumanism, among other currents), new materialisms (a specific feminist development within the posthumanist frame), and the heterogeneous landscapes of antihumanism, posthumanities, and metahumanities.
>
> (2013: 26)

Post-human post-humanism can be the way to understand post-humanism, affirms Cary Wolfe (2010), one of the most influential voices of the post-humanist philosophical discourse. Gavin Rae (2014: 65–66) illustrates Wolfe's point, underlining that among the various modes of understanding, in the relationship between humanism and post-humanism, only the "posthuman posthumanism, wherein an 'internally' disordered, malleable, emergent human self exists in a relation of entwinement with a differential and differentiating 'external' world" does not "end up reaffirming the humanism to be overcome". Thus, continues Rae (2014: 65–66), Wolfe's choice is to privilege

> a posthumanist approach to posthumanism (2008: 7) because it is only through this approach that (1) the self-referential notion of human being underpinning humanism is called into question; (2) the non-human is thought in differentiated, changing and emergent ways; and (3) the binary relationship between "the human" and "the non-human" of humanism is blurred to reveal "the embeddedness and entanglement of the 'human' in all that it is not, in all that used to be thought of as its opposites or its others".
>
> (2003: 193)

On another side, another influential voice, that of Rosi Braidotti (2013), proposes the choice of critical post-humanism that she considers as one of the three major strands in post-human thought, together with the strand related to moral philosophy and the strand of science and technology studies—which has an important reference in the work of Bruno Latour and Michel Callon at the "École of Mines" in Paris, France (Latour, 2005). Her philosophical choice is rooted in the anti-humanist philosophy of subjectivity, and in particular, in "the epistemological and political foundations of the post-structuralist generation", writes Rosi Braidotti (2013: 38), and is a choice that "moves further", because the

> alternative views about the human and the new formations of subjectivity that have emerged from the radical epistemologies of Continental philosophy in the last thirty years do not merely oppose Humanism but create visions of the self. Sexualized, racialized and naturalized differences, far from being the categorical boundary-keepers of the subject of Humanism, have evolved into fully fledged alternative models of the human subject.

In the context of the phenomenological debate in Continental philosophy and that goes, more specifically, from Merleau-Ponty to Deleuze, Enrica Lisciani Petrini (2007: 408) observes that *every idea of conscious subject, of inner thought, of feeling or human perception, and even of* "affection", *is dismantled at the root, is not at all constituted by the individual,* "but *happens to* the individual". Above all, with Gilles Deleuze—continues Lisciani Petrini (2007: 409)—this philosophical debate creates another way of conceptualizing the individual, a way that "stands outside the notion of person" and which situates the individual "*in the 'outside' of the person*".

Returning to the image in Figure 4.2 and the topic of authorship as the connection-in-action between living animals, humans, plants, nature in general and artifacts that obviously include organizations, the way in which Rosi Braidotti defines the "critical posthuman subject" resounds evocatively:

> the critical posthuman subject within an eco-philosophy of multiple belongings, as a relational subject constituted in and by multiplicity, that is to say a subject that works across differences and is also internally differentiated, but still grounded and accountable. Posthuman subjectivity expresses an embodied and embedded and hence partial form of accountability, based on a strong sense of collectivity, relationality and hence community building.
>
> (2013: 49)

Community building is a concept that is relevant to the "aesthetic approach" because the negotiation of aesthetics in the organization aggregates and discriminates, thus creating communities that differ from one another. Community—as well as immunity—opens up novel perspectives, underlines Roberto Esposito (2010; Eng. trans. 2012: 256), if it is understood in its "more originary term—the Latin *munus*, understood as the law of reciprocal giving or donation—from which the concept *communitas* derives", and this approach to the concept of community

> allows a precise meaning to be given to the empty spot around which community takes form, like a "nothing in common", calling into question the subjective logic of the presupposition: rather than being presupposed, the subjects in common are exposed to that which deprives them of their status as such.

Concluding Remarks

The relationality activated by mutual donating that distinguishes the philosophical concept of community (Esposito, 1998) is central to the posthumanist awareness of the "aesthetic approach", as well as is the sense of finitude, the process of hybridization, and the opening to otherness. But there is something more that is crucial for the "aesthetic approach" that comes from the Italian philosophical debate on post-humanism and which also evokes the Italian philosophical tradition from Machiavelli to the contemporary philosophy of "Living Thought". Something "perhaps even more disqualifying", writes Roberto Esposito (2010; Eng. trans. 2012: 277), which

> regards the differential character (anything but undifferentiated, in other words) indicated by the thought of the impersonal that was sparked by the deconstruction of the metaphysics of the person. As we have said, from the beginning of the Italian tradition, the impersonal has referred to a category of life that is not separate from— and, indeed, is always joined differently with—those of history

and politics. It is precisely this rootedness in a historical-political horizon—sometimes antinomic but always active—that drives the critique of the person in Italy, formulated and developed, then as now, in a sphere of meaning marked by difference and by conflict. How else could it be, for that matter, in a tradition originating in the thought of Machiavelli?

This impersonality, this openness to otherness and the fact that in a post-humanist vision, the human is therefore the fruit of a hybridization, "of an anthropo-decentrative event, of an epiphany that inaugurates new perspectives of being there" represent a profound caesura in philosophical thought, observes Roberto Marchesini (2017: 40). This concern is also an important aspect of the post-humanistic and phenomenological awareness which characterizes the "aesthetic approach". In particular, post-humanist awareness involves an aesthetic style of research and theorizing of organizational life that is different because of the following aspects:

- The human subject is de-centered; it is only a component among the various authors of the creation process, as we have seen in various parts of this book.
- The sensible knowing is not only of human beings, but also of other living beings. As I pointed out in Figure 4.2, it is an experiential flux which goes back and forth from the wallaby to my hand.
- The artefact acts aesthetically on the pre-cognitive assumptions of the human beings thanks to its *pathos*.

We will continue to take due account of the phenomenological and post-humanistic awareness of the "aesthetic approach" in the next chapter, which is dedicated to highlighting the fundamental importance of the aesthetics of practice for this approach to the study of organization.

But before moving on to Chapter 5, the reader—if s/he wishes—can interrupt the experiential flow stimulated by my writing and immerse him/herself in the visual language of *Interlude IV: Riviera Mediterranea*.

References

Böhme, G. (1993). Atmosphere as the fundamental concepts of new aesthetics, *Thesis Eleven*, 36 (1): 113–126.

Braidotti, R. (2013). *The Posthuman*. Cambridge: Polity Press.

Bruun, H. H. and Whimster, S. (eds.) (2012). *Max Weber: Collected Methodological Writings*. London: Routledge.

Burrell, G. (1996). Normal science, paradigms, metaphors, discourses and genealogies of analysis, in Clegg, S. R., Hardy C. and Nord, W. R. (eds.), *Handbook of Organization Studies*. London: Sage. pp. 642–658.

Burrell, G. and Morgan, G. (1979). *Sociological Paradigms and Organizational Analysis*. Aldershot: Gower.

Calás, M. and Smircich, L. (1999). Past postmodernism? Reflections and tentative directions, *Academy of Management Review*, 24 (4): 649–671.

Carlson, A. (2000). *Aesthetics and the Environment: The Appreciation of Nature, Art and Architecture*. London: Routledge.

Cooper, R. and Burrell, G. (1988). Modernism, postmodernism and organizational analysis: an introduction, *Organization Studies*, 9 (1): 91–112.

Damásio, A. R. (1999). *The Feeling of What Happens: Body, Emotion and the Making of Consciousness*. New York: Harcourt Brace & Company.

Deleuze, G. and Guattari, F. (1980). *Mille plateaux: capitalism et schizophénie*. Paris: Éditions de Minuit. (English trans.: *A Thousand Plateaus: Capitalism and Schizophrenia*. Ed. Massumi, B. Minneapolis: University of Minnesota Press, 1987).

Dilthey, W. (1914–36). *Gesammelte Schriften*. Stuttgart: Teubner.

Eco, U. (1982). Critique of the image, in Burgin, V. (ed.), *Thinking Photography*. London: Macmillan, pp. 32–38.

Elster, J. (1989). *Nuts and Bolts for the Social Sciences*. Cambridge: Cambridge University Press.

Esposito, R. (1998). *Communitas: Origine e destino della comunità*. Torino: Einaudi. (English trans.: *Communitas: The Origin and Destiny of Community*. Stanford, CA: Stanford University Press, 2010).

Esposito, R. (2010). *Pensiero vivente. Origine e attualità della filosofia italiana*. Torino: Einaudi. (English trans.: *Living Thought. The Origins and Actuality of Italian Philosophy*. Stanford, CA: Stanford University Press, 2012).

Esposito, R. (2014). *Le persone e le cose*. Torino: Einaudi. (English trans.: *Persons and Things: From the Body's Point of View*. Cambridge: Politi Press, 2015).

Ferrando, F. (2013). Posthumanism, transhumanism, antihumanism, metahumanism, and new materialisms: differences and relations, *Existenz*, 8 (2): 26–32.

Fimiani, F. (2013). De l'incorporation et de ses valeurs d'usage, in Gefen, A. and Vouilloux, B. (eds.), *Empathie et esthétique*. Paris: Hermann Éditeurs, pp. 329–349.

Fontcuberta, J. (2008). *Joan Fontcuberta*. Tours: Actes Sud.

Forgione, G. (2014). *Gaspare Traversi (1722–1770)*. Cremona: Edizioni dei Soncino.

Freedberg, D. (2017). From absorption to judgement: empathy in aesthetic response, in Lux, V. and Weigel, S. (eds.), *Empathy. Epistemic Problems and Cultural-Historical Perspectives of a Cross-Disciplinary Concept*. London: Palgrave-Macmillan, pp. 139–180.

Gallese, V. (2005). Embodied simulation: from neurons to phenomenal experience, *Phenomenology and the Cognitive Science*, 4 (4): 23–48.

Gherardi, S. and Strati, A. (2012). *Learning and Knowing in Practice-based Studies*. Cheltenham: Edward Elgar.

Gross, E. and Etzioni, A. (1985). *Organizations in Society*. Englewood Cliffs, NJ: Prentice-Hall.

Haraway, D. J. (1991). *Simians, Cyborgs, & Women: The Reinvention of Nature*. New York: Routledge.

Hassard, J. (1993). *Sociology and Organization Theory. Positivism, Paradigms and Postmodernity*. Cambridge: Cambridge University Press.

Hassard, J. (2016). Paradigms, the philosophy of science and organization studies, in Mir, R., Willmott, H. and Greenwood, M. (eds.), *The Routledge Companion to Philosophy in Organization Studies*. London: Routledge, pp. 499–507.

Hassard, J. and Wolfram Cox, J. (2013). Can sociological paradigms still inform organizational analysis?, *Organization Studies*, 34 (11): 1701–1728.

Hempel, C. G. (1942). The function of general laws in history, *Journal of Philosophy*, 39 (1): 35–48. (reprinted in Martin, M. and McIntyre L. C. (eds.), *Readings in the Philosophy of Social Science*. Cambridge, MA: The MIT Press, 1994, pp. 43–53).

Howes, D. (2018). The skinscape: reflections on the dermalogical turn, *Body & Society*, 24 (1–2): 225–239.

Jackson, N., and Carter, P. (1991). In defence of paradigm incommensurability, *Organization Studies*, 12 (1): 109–127.

Julmi, C. (2017). The concept of atmosphere in management and organization studies, *Organizational Aesthetics*, 6 (1): 4–30. (http://digitalcommons.wpi.edu/oa/vol6/iss1/2).

Kaghan, W. and Phillips, N. (1998). Building the Tower of Babel: communities of practice and paradigmatic pluralism in organization studies, *Organization*, 5 (2): 191–215.

Kuhn, T. (1962). *The Structure of Scientific Revolutions*. Chicago: University of Chicago Press.

Latour, B. (2005). *Reassembling the Social: An Introduction to Actor-Network-Theory*. Oxford: Oxford University Press.

Lipps, T. (1913). *Zum Einfühlung*. Leipzig: Engelmann.

Lisciani Petrini, E. (2007). Fuori della persona. L'"impersonale" in Merleau-Ponty, Bergson e Deleuze, *Filosofia Politica*, 21 (3): 393–409.

Longhi, R. (1927). Di Gaspare Traversi, *Vita Artistica*, 2: 145–167.

Marchesini, R. (2017). Possiamo parlare di una filosofia postumanista?, *Lo Sguardo. Rivista di Filosofia*, 24 (2): 27–50.

Merleau-Ponty, M. (1945). *Phénoménologie de la perception*. Paris: Éditions Gallimard. (English trans.: *Phenomenology of Perception*. Ed. Williams, F. and D. Guerrière. London: Routledge, 2012).

Merleau-Ponty, M. (2002). *Causeries 1948*. Paris: Éditions du Seuil. (English trans.: *The World of Perception*. New York: Routledge, 2004).

Rae, G. (2014). Heidegger's influence on posthumanism: the destruction of metaphysics, technology and the overcoming of anthropocentrism, *History of the Human Sciences*, 27 (1): 51–69.

Savedoff, B. E. (2000). *Transforming Images: How Photography Complicates the Picture*. Ithaca, NY: Cornell University Press.

Schütz, Alfred (2018). The problem of rationality in the social world, in Staubmann, H. and Lidz, V. (eds.), *Rationality in the Social Sciences: The Schumpeter/Parsons Seminar 1939/40 and Current Perspectives*. New York: Springer International Publishing, pp. 85–102.

Scott, R. W. (1981). *Organizations: Rational, Natural, and Open Systems*. Englewood Cliffs, NJ: Prentice-Hall.

Shusterman, R. (2008). *Body Consciousness: A Philosophy of Mindfulness and Somaesthetics*. Cambridge: Cambridge University Press.

Sousa Lopes, L. L., Rocha Ipiranga, A. S., da Silva, J. J. Jr (2017). Compreensão empática e as possíveis contribuições para a pesquisa nos estudos organizacionais: reflexões a partir da experiência do lado estético das organizações, *Cadernos EBAPE.BR*, 15 (4): 831–845.

Staubmann, H. and Lidz, V. (2018a). Editors' introduction: the Harvard Rationality Seminar, in Staubmann, H. and Lidz, V. (eds.), *Rationality in the Social Sciences: The Schumpeter/Parsons Seminar 1939/40 and Current Perspectives*. New York: Springer International Publishing, pp. 1–25.

Staubmann, H. and Lidz, V. (eds.) (2018b). *Rationality in the Social Sciences. The Schumpeter/Parsons Seminar 1939/40 and Current Perspectives*. New York: Springer International Publishing.

Strati, A. (1992). Aesthetic understanding of organizational life, *Academy of Management Review*, 17 (3): 568–581.

Strati, A. (1996). *Sociologia dell'organizzazione: paradigmi teorici e metodi di ricerca*. Roma: NIS-Carocci. (English trans.: *Theory and Method in Organization Studies: Paradigms and Choices*. London: Sage, 2000).

Strati, A. (1999). *Organization and Aesthetics*. London: Sage.

Strati, A. (2004). *L'analisi organizzativa. Paradigmi e metodi*. Roma: Carocci.

Strati, A. (2009). "Do you do beautiful things?": aesthetics and art in qualitative methods of organization studies, in Buchanan, D. and Bryman A. (eds.), *The Sage Handbook of Organizational Research Methods*. London: Sage, pp. 230–245. Reprinted in Gherardi, S. and Strati, A. (2012). *Learning and Knowing in Practice-based Studies*. Cheltenham: Edward Elgar, pp. 194–209.

Strati, A. (2013). Becoming or process: what future for the aesthetic discourse in organizations, in King, I. W. and Vickery, J. (eds.), *Experiencing Organisations: New Aesthetic Perspectives*. Faringdon: Libri Publishing, pp. 223–248.

Strati, A. (2016). Aesthetics and design: an epistemology of the unseen, in Mir, R., Willmott, H. and Greenwood, M. (eds.), *The Routledge Companion to Philosophy in Organization Studies*. London: Routledge, pp. 251–259.

Strati, A. (2018). Ordinary beauty, ordinary ugliness, and the problem of rationality, in Staubmann, H. and Lidz, V. (eds.), *Rationality in the Social Sciences: The Schumpeter/Parsons Seminar 1939/40 and Current Perspectives*. New York: Springer International Publishing, pp. 189–206.

Valtonen, A., Meriläinen, S., Laine P. M. and Salmela-Leppänen, T. (2017). The knowing body as a floating body, *Management Learning*, 48 (5): 520–534.

Varga, I. (2005). The body—the new sacred? The body in hypermodernity, *Current Sociology*, 53 (2): 209–235.

Vattimo, G. and Rovatti, P. A. (eds.) (1983). *Il pensiero debole*. Milano: Feltrinelli. (English trans.: Dialectics, difference, weak thought, in Vattimo, G. and Rovatti, P. A. (eds.), *Weak Thought*. Ed. Carravetta, P. Albany: State University of New York Press, 2012).

Weber, M. (1922). *Wirtschaft und Gesellschaft. Grundriss der verstehenden Soziologie*. Tübingen: Mohr. (English trans.: *Economy and Society: An Outline of Interpretive Sociology. I–II*. Berkeley: University of California Press, 1978).

Willmott, H. (1993). Breaking the paradigm mentality, *Organization Studies*, 14 (5): 681–719.

Wittgenstein, L. and Barrett, C. (1966). *Lectures and Conversations on Aesthetics, Psychology and Religious Belief*. Oxford: Blackwell.

Wolfe, C. (2003). *Animal Rites: American Culture, the Discourse of Species, and Posthumanist Theory*. Chicago, IL: Chicago University Press.

Wolfe, C. (2008). Flesh and finitude: thinking animals in (post)humanist philosophy, *SubStance*, 37 (3): 8–36.

Wolfe, C. (2010). *What is Posthumanism?* Minneapolis: Minnesota University Press.

Zey-Ferrel, M. (1981). Criticisms of the dominant perspective on organizations, *Sociological Quarterly*, 22 (Spring): 181–205.

nterlude IV: Riviera Mediterranea, 1990

mulsions lift Polaroid 20 × 25cm T 809 stretched on watercolor paper 30 × 40 cm (detail)

5 Practice and the Italian Aesthetic Philosophies

Interlude IV introduces the subject of the relevance of practices in organizations for the "aesthetic approach" and the philosophical roots of this concept in the Italian philosophical aesthetics of the last century that gave pre-eminence to the topic of "practice". The photopoem shown in it, *Riviera Mediterranea*, was made in 1990, and was then purchased by the Polaroid International Collections of Cambridge, Massachusetts, and included in the exposition "Polaroid 50: Art & Technology. An exhibition from the Polaroid Collections" held in Cologne, Germany, in the prestigious *Fotokina* in 1996.

The "Polaroid 50" exhibition was organized to celebrate the relationship between art and technology that has characterized the Polaroid's industrial policy since its foundation for half a century through fifty art photographs, and *Riviera Mediterranea* has been exhibited to represent the novelty in art and technology that took place in 1990. For the other years, photographs of famous artists and photographers such as Ansel Adams, Andy Warhol, Lucas Samaras, Minor White, Robert Frank, Paul Caponigro and other well-known art photographers have been exhibited, as the Polaroid website documented for a certain time (Strati, 2000: 68).

Riviera Mediterranea has a rather mundane subject: a large palm frond in the Ligurian Riviera, which can be considered an ordinary "photographic common place" of conventional professional or amateur photography. But what makes this photopoem artistically significant to the point of being chosen to represent, for one of the fifty years of Polaroid, "the technical innovations that hallmark the continuing innovations of Polaroid and show the creativity of artists who selected the instant medium", as Barbara Hitchcock, director of the Polaroid International Collections, wrote in her presentation of the exhibition on the Polaroid website (Strati, 2000: 67)?

I will explore this interrogative in this chapter, where I intend to illustrate and discuss the importance for the "aesthetic approach", in addition to Futurism and the Marxist aesthetics, of the two philosophical schools that arose in Italy during the period of post-war reconstruction: that of Turin, whose main protagonist was Luigi Pareyson (1954)—his existentialist and hermeneutic aesthetics is a reference for the "aesthetic approach"—and that of Milan, where instead Antonio Banfi (1988), with his "open" and phenomenological aesthetics, has been the philosopher of the utmost importance before and after World War II.

5.1 Formativeness and the Aesthetic Approach

The sense of *Interlude IV: Riviera Mediterranea* is twofold. On the one hand, it shows the relevance of the *Teoria della formatività*—the theory of formativeness which constitutes the philosophical aesthetics of Luigi Pareyson—for the "aesthetic approach" in the study of practices in organizations. On the other hand, it emphasizes the argument "for human freedom within the area of automated, programmed and programming apparatuses" underscored by Vilém Flusser (1983; Eng. trans. 2000: 82) and mentioned in Chapter 3, which deals with photography as a metaphor for organizational aesthetics.

The origins of *Riviera Mediterranea* are organizational, which means that at the beginning, it was an industrial photographic organization, the Polaroid company, which constituted both the context of my situation and the principal actor of the creation process. In fact, I was about to offer some of my photographs to be acquired by the Polaroid International Collections when the Polaroid Italia officials asked me: Antonio, would you like to explore the possibilities of the new Polaroid material, the "T809"?

At that time—at the end of the 1980s—besides some experimental art photography, the analogical environment was the standard in professional and amateur photography. The photographic film, the photographic paper, some electronic equipment and the large variety of mechanical technology—cameras, lenses, enlargers, tripods, artificial lights, darkrooms and studios—were the basic elements of photography, which was based on the photograph rather than the digital file, and was a physical matter rather than the "virtual body" of the digital environment discussed in Chapter 2.

These specific characteristics of the aesthetic materiality of the artifacts used to create an art photograph are important for understanding the aesthetic practice of its creation process. "Long before digital technology made instant viewing a standard part of picture making", observes Sylvia Wolf (2010: 31–32), the invention of "the one-step process for producing a finished photograph" was the project of the Polaroid Corporation, and

> Polaroid cameras and film gave rapid results. Moreover, with instant imaging a photographer could share pictures with a subject on the spot, and offer a photograph to take away, which opened the door to a sense of joint authorship not previously possible. By the time cameras in cell phones allowed users to instantly capture, store, and send

pictures within the blink of an eye, the appetite for instant imagery once cultivated by Polaroid photography had grown to be voracious and wide-spread. How this all-pervasive image culture translates into the world of art is a story in and of itself.

And, in fact, due to the widespread use of the manipulated image in the contemporary digital environment of photography, even if *Interlude IV* shows the distinctive characteristics of analogue photography of *Riviera Mediterranea*, these characteristics may not be perceivable by the reader—also because of the distortions inherent in the reproduction process discussed in the first section of the previous Chapter 4.

But the following description of the analogical environment in which the technological and product invention pertaining to the Polaroid T809 takes place and, therefore, to professional large-format instant photography, should lead the reader to understand the specific aesthetic materiality of the creation process of the photopoem in *Interlude IV* and to grasp in this way the meaning and importance of the concept of practices in organizations for the aesthetic approach.

5.1.1 *The* Riviera Mediterranea *and Pareyson*

The new Polaroid material, the "T809", was a negative/positive professional film created to produce instant large-format color photographs— 20 × 25 cm or 8 × 10 inches—which did not have to be the final image, but an intermediate image. This instant photograph, in fact, had to be useful to the photographer to evaluate the colors, the lights and shadows, and the whole image before realizing, with other appropriate films, the final photograph of, for example, a commercial advertisement of an industrial design product.

I made my first pictures and started to master both the new film and the equipment to work on it. This photographic material fascinated me. My photos were becoming more and more beautiful. But where was that "I don't know what" that would identify them with me, with my "Photopoesia"?

"I do not know something", writes Luigi Pareyson (1950; Eng. trans. 2009: 82–83), "unless I express myself",

> and in expressing myself I declare knowledge of something. This is the principle of the aesthetic nature of knowledge. Of course, knowing is always aesthetic, that is expressive; but it is knowing all the same, because expressing is not creating [. . .]. It is my way of seeing things, so, when I know things, I express myself in my way of seeing them; but they are nevertheless things I see in my way of seeing, so, when I express myself, I state things in whatever transfiguration, or rather figuration, I make of them.

My situation—in Pareyson's terms illustrated in Chapter 1—that is, the concrete material situation of the creation process, was that of the "organizational context" of the cultural initiative of Polaroid Italia and of the technological innovation of the photographic products of the Polaroid Corporation. But I could not simply reduce myself to it and just make beautiful pictures, nor was I asked to do it by the Polaroid company, given its focus on innovation, creativity and art (Hitchcock, 2005). "I do not reduce myself to my situation, but I choose it", observes Luigi Pareyson (1943; Eng. trans. 2009: 44), and this choice, "through which I assume my situation, acts so that I do not identify myself with it", because my concrete, material incarnation in my situation constitutes "a *choice*" that "cannot be a reduction of the singular to fact". Where was "my choice", that is, my personal knowing and my art, if I had only realized beautiful images? So I changed everything, as I described elsewhere (Gherardi and Strati, 2017a: 118; Strati, 2000: 67; Strati and Gherardi, 2015: 26–28):

1. I left my large format studio camera—a folding 8 × 10 Fatif DS2—for which this material was thought and I selected, instead, from my photo archives, some medium format slides made previously with the Hasselblad camera and that for some reason were significant for my imagination since they lived in my visual memory and I felt a certain affection towards them;
2. I projected one of these 6 × 6 cm slides on the negative of Polacolor T809 through the enlarger;
3. I also set aside the specific device to develop the T809 and make the 20 × 25 cm prints that I had been sent with the new film T809;
4. I preferred a rolling pin, to be handled by hand, to the well-calibrated rollers of the sophisticated photographic equipment sent to me to accurately distribute the chemical substances positioned between the negative and the print and obtain in such a way almost instantaneously the photo.

In this way, I began *to give form* to my choice and then to assume my situation and interpret it. Interpretation, observes Pareyson (1971; Eng. trans. 2009: 182–183), "is an endless process" which requires "a continuous and incessant deep investigation" that the analogy with art can better highlight, "so that it must appear evident that one of the cardinal concepts of hermeneutics is, indeed, the compatibility, or rather the essentiality, of possession and process, of achievement and inquiry, of mastery and deepening". The interpretation, notes Paolo Diego Bubbio in his Introduction to the English publication of Pareyson's selected writings he edited, is a process where an

> alleged "given datum", that is, an uninterpreted object, does not exist. More precisely, the form is not just the outcome of a previous

and concluded process, since insofar as it is interpretation, the form is always a continuing process. Form is always "on the move". Here Pareyson fully accepts Gadamer's notion of the hermeneutic circle. But he goes further. If what has been (improperly) called the object of interpretation is a form (not a static object, but "a moving being"), then it can be grasped only by another movement, by knowledge in progress. This knowledge—or, better, this *knowing*—is interpretation. This is the reason why Pareyson defines interpretation as "knowledge of forms by persons". Form is the outcome "on the move" of the continuous process of interpretation. [. . .] Being reveals itself through forms, and forms can be grasped from many points of view. Interpretation is a process in which the more the subject expresses herself, the more the form reveals itself.

(2009: 15)

And, in fact, the form—the Polacolor T809—revealed itself more and more as I expressed myself. The work organization to produce instant prints in large format for professional use as an intermediate stage of the creation of the negative, or final slide of 20 × 25 cm from which to print the final image, was deconstructed, interpreted and mastered in the continuous dialogue between my learning a *savoir faire* (expertise) and the revelations of the Polacolor T809 through the changes of its form.

5.1.2 Aesthetics of Practice: Doing While Inventing the Way to Do

Experimenting with my art photography did not only mean interpreting and mastering the organization of work and the know-how foreseen by the Polaroid Corporation, which was embedded into the technological innovation of the T809 film and the sophisticated equipment to process it. It also meant expressing human freedom, as emphasizes Vilém Flusser in his phenomenological philosophy of photography (1983), and that Pareyson sharpens in terms of *practice of the freedom of interpreting*, that is, of the personal interpretation, the infinity of the work and the variety of performances:

Interpretation is not "subjective", but "personal". It does not deplete the worth of a work in the process of performance, but rather it maintains its independence precisely in order to execute it, so that performance always contains both the diversity of the interpreters and the independence of the work, and it always has a dual and yet single direction—towards the work, which the single interpreter must render and bring alive as it desires, and towards the person of the performer, who in every case expresses herself in the new way in which the work is made to live.

(1954; Eng. trans. 2009: 114–115)

My personal interpretation is that the independence of the forms assumed by Polacolor T809 and the variety of performances have "given form" to the creation of the new characteristic of these large-format instant prints: they were already the definitive photograph, rather than being a simple intermediate test of the photograph to be made. "By virtue of its completeness", affirms Pareyson (1954; Eng. trans. 2009: 129), the work of art "provokes, arouses, stimulates innumerable interpretations of itself, and at the same time is not exhausted in any of them, and remains above them all, even though it identifies with each one every time".

The point is thus to understand, even empathically, writes Bernard Vouilloux (2013: 299), how the completed and finished work of art "can account for its own elaboration, how its *form* refers to its *formation*, how the forms it gives us to perceive bear testimony of the relationship that the artist's perception establishes with the forms to be constructed". Because, observes Simmel (1916; Eng. trans. 2005: 155), the "achievements of intellectual history", the achievements of human action, "are shot through with a contrast that can be characterized as that between the *capacity to create* [*Schöpfertum*] and the *capacity to fashion* [*Gestaltertum*]", and social reality "cannot exist independently of its form" (Staubmann, 1997: 603). Human beings, however, need a given material to create and fashion simultaneously, that is, to reshape with their creativity, since humans are historical beings, and,

> precisely because they do not merely repeat but create something new, cannot start anew each time. Rather, they need a given material, a given antecedence on which, or on the basis of which, they accomplish their achievements as a reshaping [of the material]. We would not, however, be historical beings were we absolutely creative; were our work to create the new as such.
>
> (Simmel, 1916; Eng. trans. 2005: 155)

The "definitive instant print" was my photopoetic expression of human freedom in the midst of the organizational and technological innovation of photography. Polaroid Italia has immediately published some of these photopoems in its magazine dedicated to professional photographers to illustrate my way "to overcome the technical aspect in order to crystallize a work of art and elevate it to the dignity of symbolic work that can be appreciated from an aesthetic point of view" (Saporiti, 1990: 20).

Furthermore, while I was "giving form" to the definitive large-format instant photograph, I also invented the "way to give form" to it. That is, I invented a method to do it and an organization of work, that is, a "practice" based on non-professional and non-*ad hoc* technological equipment, and therefore profoundly different from those envisaged and stimulated by the Polaroid Corporation.

Pareyson states that this is "formative activity", that is, "to give form" by doing and at the same time "inventing how to do it"—the method and the organization to do it as it has to be done—represents the foundations of aesthetics in art and in society: "speculative and practical operations consist of a formative activity which, in a specific field, does things at the same time as it invents how they should be done" (Pareyson, 1954, reprint 1988: 23).

What did I do, in fact? I detached the photographic layer—the emulsion—of his original support very gently after having been in luke-warm water for a while. The emulsion, having lost its support, no longer had its original shape and was no longer a photograph, even though it contained all the elements of photography. I then manipulated it with my hands to extend it on a 30 × 40 cm watercolor paper. The emulsion resumed the shape of a photograph, but larger, and evoked the image of the 6 × 6 slide instead of being its reproduction.

Then I studied the forms that I had built with the touch of my fingers, I evaluated the lights, shadows and colors of the emulsion, and I interpreted the "sense" of the photograph that I was making in the light of my photopoetic research. Once the emulsion was dry, I repeated the same "practices" in order to overlay a second wet emulsion ready to be manipulated. I stretched it on the first emulsion, saturating the colors, creating new shapes, giving texture to the photography, and revealing the coexistence of the different layers, as the reader can see in *Interlude IV*.

I repeated the same practice and the same process for the third layer, when I felt that the photopoem was made. Each time, however, if the stages of the work organization remained in the same sequence, the pace changed due to manual performance and low standardization of each stage of the creation process. The new practice and the new work organization constituted my "formative activity", that is, as indicated above,

> a doing that as it is being done, *invents how it is to be done*. This is doing without how it is to be done being predetermined and imposed so that it suffices to apply it to do well: it must be found by doing, and only by doing can one discover it, so that, properly speaking, it is a matter of inventing, without which the operation fails [. . .]. To form, therefore, means to "do" and "know how to do" together: to do while inventing at the same time how in the particular case what is to be done lets itself be done.
>
> (Pareyson, 1954, reprint 1988: 59)

During my "formative activity", I was in direct contact with the film Polacolor T809. My sight and, above all, my touch have made the photographic image, together with the Hasselblad slide, the timer, the enlarger, the rolling pin, the warm water, the spatula, the watercolor paper, the space and the furniture in my studio. Forming, writes Pareyson, "means 'being able to do', that is, doing in a way that, without appeal to pre-established technical rules, one can and must say that what has been done has been done as it should have been done" (1954, reprint 1988: 59). That is, for *Riviera Mediterranea*, with my hands: my fingers had the "last word" compared to the technologically sophisticated photographic equipment.

The sense of touch is *in* the photopoem, it is in its texture. Barbara Hitchcock (2005: 6) wrote that these images, that were "the first Polaroid Emulsion Lifts" that she had ever seen, were "characterized by a dimensionality" that she "had never before witnessed"; that with "a delicate touch, you could feel the bas-relief of the emulsion beneath your fingers".

The photograph is not only to be looked at, but also to be touched—and this, while reaffirming the relevance of the sensorial and perceptive faculties for the "aesthetic approach", also underlines the figurative motif of the "hand" which creates a symbolic link between the formative activity that shaped the bas-relief texture of the photopoem *Riviera Mediterranea*, the knowing interaction between my left hand and the nose and the eyes of the wallaby (Figure 4.2), the surgical operation in the painting done by Gaspare Traversi (*Interlude III*).

This is a symbolic link that evokes the mixture of the work of art and the work of ordinary beauty that is characteristic of my "aesthetic approach" and which is a fundamental aspect of Pareyson's aesthetic philosophy, that is, of his *Teoria della formatività*. Because if "artistic operation is a process of invention and production undertaken, not to achieve speculative or practical works, or others besides, but only for itself: forming to form, only pursuing the form for itself" and "*art is pure formativeness*", Pareyson (1954, reprint 1988: 23) emphasizes that *formativeness does not belong only to the arts, but to the everyday social activities*, since "every operation is aesthetic in the sense that it is *formative*, in the sense that it cannot be itself without forming, and one cannot think or act without forming", as we shall see in the next section.

5.2 Practice as a Trait of Italian Philosophical Aesthetics

The philosophical aesthetics of Luigi Pareyson—his theory of formativeness—became a philosophical reference in organizational theories with the publication of my book *Organization and Aesthetics* twenty years ago. More specifically, Pareyson's aesthetic philosophy has been a reference, in particular, to the "aesthetic approach", that is, essentially to one of the four approaches—"aesthetic", "archeological", "artistic" and "empathiclogical"—which constitute the principal styles of theorizing the aesthetic discourse on organization, as I briefly illustrated in the first section of Chapter 4:

> [W]ith its roots in the eighteenth-century rejection of the thesis that humans are distinguished from animals by their rational capacity, in the phenomenological philosophy of the early Husserl, in the

deconstructionism of Derrida, and in the hermeneutic and existentialist thought of Pareyson, the aesthetic approach seeks after the "sensible" in intentional action within organizations, while at the same
time problematizing the exclusively mental knowledge of the inten-
tionality of such action.

(Strati, 1999: 85)

This was because Pareyson focused his philosophical thought on the aesthetics of concrete and situated experiences. Moreover, these experiences
were not only related to the art world, but also concerned the ordinary,
banal aesthetics of everyday life, of every speculative or practical activity
and of every type of work in society.

Pareyson had, in fact, the same style of aesthetic theorizing that the
American pragmatist philosopher John Dewey (1934/1987) had: the aesthetics of experience is widespread in society, and cannot be considered
coinciding with art and to be bounded to art. In art, which was both the
origins and the main context of Pareyson philosophical considerations,
formativeness has the special character to devote *to shape the form*.

But in the other fields, formativeness is to give form to the *art of* doing
an industrial design product, *of* managing an organization, *of* running
a business, *of* writing a book, *of* performing the maintenance of a car
engine, *of* making a surgical operation, *of* looking after the children in
a kindergarten, *of* cook in a restaurant, *of* inventing an algorithm for a
software program, *of* communicating the beauty of a mathematical theorem. In a word, formativeness is about *giving form to the art of a practice*.

In the Preface that he wrote in 1988 for the fourth edition of *Estetica: Teoria della formatività*, Pareyson specifies that his aesthetic theory
"starts from the aesthetic experience and then returns to it", that his, his
theory of formativeness arose

> from living contact with the aesthetic experience as it results from
> the industriousness of artists, studied both in their ongoing work and
> their valuable thoughts and statements about it, from the activity of
> readers and interpreters and art critics, as well as from the attitudes
> of the producers and contemplators of beauty wherever this is to be
> found, either in the natural sphere or in the practical and intellectual
> one. [. . .] The aesthetics proposed in this book is therefore not a
> metaphysics of art, but an analysis of aesthetic experience: not a defi-
> nition of art considered abstractly in itself, but a study of the person
> who makes art and in the act of doing art. In short, a philosophical
> reflection on the aesthetic experience and intended to problematize
> it as a whole.

(1954, reprint 1988: 8–9)

Pareyson's philosophical interest in investigating the "practical sphere",
and, moreover, the theoretical distance taken in respect of philosophy

as metaphysics, constituted another pillar of the relevance of aesthetic philosophies for the "aesthetic approach" and the configuration of the aesthetic discourse on organization. The practice—and even the micro-practice—in the organizational life was in fact a crucial topic for the "aesthetic approach", and this approach contributed to the development of the research area of "Practice-based Studies" (Gherardi, 2000, reprint 2012: 9–10) through the emphasis on sensible knowledge and the materiality of organizing (Gherardi, 2009, reprint 2012: 161–163; Gherardi, 2012: 49–76; Gherardi, Nicolini and Strati, 2007; Gherardi and Strati, 2012; Gherardi and Strati, 2017a; Strati, 2003, 2007).

In this way, that is, through organizational aesthetics and its focus on practice, Pareyson's aesthetics as a theory of formativeness became a philosophical reference not only to the "aesthetic approach" but also for the intellectual current of "Practice-based Studies" in organizational theories. The contribution

> of Pareyson's aesthetic philosophy to the study of practices comprises three main topics: (1) the concept of formativeness makes it possible to analyze and interpret how the object of a practice acquires form, (2) the idea of the inseparability of knowing and expressing supports an understanding of practice as collective tastemaking, and (3) the inseparability of knowing and sensing explains practice as grounded in sensible knowledge and therefore in the materiality of bodies that work.
>
> (Gherardi and Strati, 2017b: 749)

5.2.1 Practice and Futurist, Marxist and Phenomenological Italian Aesthetics

Pareyson grounded his theory of formativeness in the aesthetics of practice, of doing, of producing, rather than in the aesthetics of contemplation. In the aesthetic philosophies, the attention and the focus on the "*producer* rather than that of the user or the art work", observes Paolo D'Angelo (1997: 174–175), is of particular interest because "an attitude of this kind is relatively rare in the history of aesthetics". Yet, it represents a specific characteristic of the Italian aesthetics and, more in general, of the Italian philosophy since the Renaissance (Barbera, 2018; D'Agostini, 1997; Esposito, 2010). In his conversation with Gianluca Barbera, Roberto Esposito points out the following to the question of whether there is a common thread that holds Italian philosophy together from the Renaissance up to today:

> It is an attitude to contaminate with history and politics absent in other traditions. Unlike the logical and analytical vocation of the Anglo-Saxon philosophy, the metaphysical one of German classical philosophy and the French one, addressed to the interrogation

of subjectivity and inner consciousness, Italian thought is a hybrid, worldly thought, descended into the reality of politics (Machiavelli) and of history (Vico). Even today at the center of Italian philosophy there is a reflection on the relationship between politics and biological life absent or less developed in other traditions. Starting from Giordano Bruno, the theme of life has been and is at the center of Italian philosophy.

(Barbera, 2018: 102–103)

And, at the time when Pareyson wrote his philosophical aesthetics, other Italian philosophical aesthetics, such as the futurist, phenomenological and Marxist aesthetics, emphasized the aesthetics of the practice, rather than focusing pre-eminently on the aesthetics of the artwork. It was a special moment for the Italian philosophical aesthetics because, as Umberto Eco (1968: 10) underlines, one can discern in that time a flourishing of inquiries aimed at rethinking recent European and American aesthetic experiences, "from Bergson to Dewey, from the experiences of the *Allgemeine Kunstwissenschaft* and the theorists of *Einfühlung* to the developments of phenomenology and sociological research", examining all the aesthetic phenomena of changing tastes and styles in contemporary society.

As "part of this phenomenon", continues Eco, "Luigi Pareyson's 'aesthetics of formativeness' occupies a position of considerable prominence: both for the extent of its commitment and the personal way" (1968: 10), a particularly important example of Italian philosophical school on aesthetics that developed in theoretical domains very distant from the idealism of both Benedetto Croce and Giovanni Gentile.

In any case, Croce's philosophical idealism was very influential in Italy and abroad since the publication of his *Aesthetics* (Croce, 1902), in which he theorized the crucial importance of the relationship between intuition and expression. A musical intuition can be appreciated once expressed, he affirmed, and in its final and definitive form. The process of creation, the practice of inventing and giving form to it, and the artistic techniques were openly devalued in the philosophical idealism of Benedetto Croce.

Aesthetics, wrote Luigi Pareyson (1954, reprint 1988: 7), "is the field in which Croce's dominance remained unchallenged for longest" and this dominance persisted also in the years of post-war reconstruction, for "in the immediate post-war period, Croce's aesthetics was the only theory to which reference was made in Italy". Croce's dominance, however, must not give the impression that the panorama of philosophical aesthetics in Italy was not composite in the first half of the twentieth century. The authority of Benedetto Croce was enormous, but his work did not go uncontested; and the process of creation, the artistic genre and the artistic technique, the performance and the aesthetic practice of the art producers, as well as the applied arts and the mundane aesthetics of everyday life, constituted the main topics of the Italian aesthetic philosophies. There were, that is, in the first half of the last century

> thinkers of a different orientation not reducible to, and sometimes very different from, the dominant one, and to whom it is necessary to pay attention, and not only because they wanted [. . .] almost programmatically to exhibit independent positions but also because they gave expression to authentic exigencies of inquiry and, in the best cases, prepared the developments that would come about in the second half-century.
>
> (D'Angelo, 1997: 118)

Among them was the futuristic aesthetic which has been important in spreading at the international level other Italian aesthetics who did not draw on the idealism of Croce and Gentile, and that, beginning with literature, gradually concerned itself also with painting, sculpture, architecture, theater, music and performance art. This was a particular aesthetics, the aesthetics of an artistic avant-garde, so that its arguments about art consisted of instructions and exhortations about "art that was to be done" rather than about the fully accomplished work of art, which was the principal reference of Crocean idealism. A sequence of "manifestos" of Italian futurism—from Marinetti's manifesto published in Paris in 1909 to those published by Umberto Boccioni, Carlo Carrà and Gino Severini for futurist painters in 1910 and by Balilla Pratella for futurist musicians in 1911—urged:

- the production of ostentatiously "ugly" art;
- the exaltation of "mechanical beauty";
- appreciation of the so-called "minor" arts such as variety theater, or arts treated with contempt, like advertising;
- art realized with poor, unusual, new and ephemeral materials.

Mention has also been made of the importance of Marxist aesthetics. Again, this is an aesthetics with an entirely original structure, and which, therefore, between the 1940s and 1960s, was heterodox with respect to the Marxist aesthetics most widespread both in the socialist countries and the Soviet Union, and in Europe to the west of the infamous "Iron Curtain" and the "Berlin Wall". Its main proponent was the philosopher Galvano della Volpe, whom Omar Calabrese (1985: 85) describes as follows:

> the first Marxist scholar to leave the ghetto of what was by now an excessively consolidated sociological aesthetics that judged a work of art only in regard to its 'social' content. Della Volpe instead proposed, again in materialist terms, a methodical "sociological"

aesthetics: that is, an aesthetics attentive not only to the content of the work but also its formal aspects. Hence a work of art was to be judged also on the basis of its technical aspects and in particular the semantic one, given that the "technique" of a work of art is always evaluated in language.

Della Volpe's critique of historicist Marxism in general, and in particular of influential Marxist theorists like György Lukàcs, was also a critique of the aesthetics of Crocean idealism: the different arts cannot be reduced to art; it is not possible to ignore differences in expressive techniques when the diverse experiences of art exhibit substantive differences such that one language cannot be translated into another; one concrete artistic experience cannot be converted into another; nor, wrote della Volpe (1960: 208), can one genre be translated into another "without the decadence of the thoughts translated into the generic and banal or artistically indifferent".

But the other school of the Italian aesthetic thought that, in addition to the Pareyson school in Turin, was relevant for its attention to the aesthetics of practice was the one in Milan of Antonio Banfi. Of particular importance for his aesthetics were the neo-Kantianism of the Marburg philosophers, Rickert's philosophy of values, the sociologist Georg Simmel's life-philosophy and Edmund Husserl's phenomenology. Antonio Banfi published his first writings on aesthetics between the 1920s and 1940s. Later, after the war, he collected in his book *Vita dell'arte* (Banfi, 1988) the most important essays on his "open aesthetics", through which he proposed a philosophy aimed at understanding the complexity of aesthetics from its variety and its empirically verified richness.

Therefore, Banfi's aesthetics opposed Croce's denial of the importance of the diversity of arts and artistic genres, and he insisted on the absurdity of wanting to find a single formula for the aesthetic experience. Banfi, therefore, paid close attention to the practices of doing art, and to the sociological interpretation of the social conditions in which the artistic life is effectively pursued.

Among Banfi's students, Luciano Anceschi in particular is of closest interest to us here, because his aesthetics was inspired by the "primacy of doing". In *Autonomia ed eteronomia dell'arte* (Anceschi, 1936), in fact, he followed Banfi's teachings to investigate the "aesthetic principle"— that sort of law whereby some experiences and not others are defined as art—directly in the complex and concrete manifestation of the artistic experience. He propounded an aesthetics intended to redeem theoretically "those institutions (poetics, genres, styles) within which only works of art find their mode of being" (Restaino, 1991: 219).

Banfi's aesthetics constituted a very important frame of reference for the Italian philosophers who did not endorse Croce's aesthetic idealism. As Pareyson has created a school of aesthetic thought that had as pupils Umberto Eco and Gianni Vattimo, Banfi gave rise to the Milanese school of aesthetic thought, also through the work of some of his students—in particular Enzo Paci, Luciano Anceschi, Gillo Dorfles, Dino Formaggio and Renato Barilli—who then contributed greatly to constructing the Italian philosophical aesthetics that originated from, and developed in, cultural domains that had remained extraneous to Croce's idealism.

The Italian philosophical aesthetics has developed a particular focus on "practice" also because the "Italian thought" is a very different philosophical tradition than the philosophical traditions linked to Descartes or Kant. This is due to the fact that, while the latter have focused on the topics of the "constitution of the subject or the theory of knowledge", observes Roberto Esposito (2010, Eng. Trans. 2012: 10–11), the Italian thought "came into the world turned upside down and inside out, as it were, into the world of historical and political life", and this movement "toward the outside has long been identified by critics as the most consistent trait of the Italian philosophical tradition".

> The point of tangency between them, it could be said, lies in the unique propensity of Italian philosophy for the nonphilosophical. Both its civil commitment and its contamination from other styles of expression result in a rupture with the specialized, self-referential lexicon that characterizes the philosophical discourses of other traditions. While the privileged object of these traditions is philosophy itself—its internal forms and structurations—the content of Italian thought is what presses up against its exterior, somehow urging it to step outside itself to look onto the external space.
>
> (Esposito, 2010; Eng. Trans. 2012: 11)

Concluding Remarks

When practice is viewed from within, writes Silvia Gherardi (2009, reprint 2012: 160), "what is of interest to the researcher is the intellectual, passionate, ethical and aesthetic attachment that ties subjects to objects, technologies, the places of practices and other practitioners". The concept of practice has been recently rediscovered and re-used within organizational theories during the 2000s and, in the "practice turn", the

> aesthetic understanding of practices, in fact, constitutes the principal difference from their interpretation as a set of activities, because it adds to the dimension of doing the more subtle one of the distinction inherent in every doing and of the style of doing that makes the difference.
>
> (Gherardi and Strati, 2012: X)

The "aesthetic approach" studies the practices in organizational life because of its interest in understanding the "texture of organizing of an organization" (Strati, 1996, Eng. trans. 2000: 75–82), which extends through the connections-in-action of the practices both internally and externally to the organization. To assume practices "as the units of analysis of organizations", states Silvia Gherardi (2012: 2), is due to the fact that

> practices are the loci—spatial and temporal—in which working, organizing, innovating or reproducing occurs. At a disciplinary level, this makes it possible to bring the study of work closer to the study of organizing, and to view both of them not only in their interrelations but as processes which take place in time and therefore in a "becoming". The categories of performance, practical accomplishment and becoming will be those that illustrate the temporality and processuality inscribed in practices.

Now, to conclude Chapter 5 and move on to the three philosophical sensibilities—aesthetic, hermeneutic and performative—that characterize the organizational aesthetic research (Strati, 2016), and for which Pareyson's aesthetics of practice constitutes "an important philosophical referent" (Gherardi and Strati, 2017b: 748), the reader can perform, according to his/her desire, the practice proposed with this book: the rhythm of the words will be interrupted and distracted by the visual language of the photopoem in *Interlude V*.

References

Anceschi, L. (1936). *Autonomia ed eteronomia dell'arte. Saggio di fenomenologia delle poetiche.* Milano: Garzanti.

Banfi, A. (1988). *Vita dell'arte. Scritti di estetica e di filosofia dell'arte—Opere.* Vol. V. Ed. Mattioli, E. and G. Scaramuzza. Reggio Emilia: Istituto "A. Banfi" (1st ed. 1947).

Barbera, G. (2018). *Idee viventi. Il pensiero filosofico in Italia oggi.* Milano: Mimesis.

Bubbio, P. D. (2009). Introduction. Luigi Pareyson: the third way to Hermeneutics, in Pareyson, L. (ed.), *Existence, Interpretation, Freedom: Selected Writings.* Ed. Bubbio, P. D. Aurora, CO: The Davies Group, pp. 1–32.

Calabrese, O. (1985). *Il linguaggio dell'arte.* Milano: Bompiani.

Croce, B. (1902). *Estetica come scienza dell'espressione e linguistica generale.* Milano: Adelphi. (English trans.: *Aesthetic as Science of Expression and General Linguistic.* London: Macmillan & Co., 1909).

D'Agostini, F. (1997). *Analitici e continentali. Guida alla filosofia degli ultimi trent'anni.* Milano: Cortina.

D'Angelo, P. (1997). *L'estetica italiana del Novecento.* Roma—Bari: Laterza.

della Volpe, G. (1960). *Critica del gusto.* Milano: Feltrinelli.

Dewey, J. (1934/1987). *Art as Experience—The Later Works, 1925–1953.* Vol. 10: 1934. Ed. Boydston, J. A. Carbondale: Southern Illinois University Press.

Eco, U. (1968). *La definizione dell'arte.* Milano: Mursia.

Esposito, R. (2010). *Pensiero vivente. Origine e attualità della filosofia italiana.* Torino: Einaudi. (English trans.: *Living Thought. The Origins and Actuality of Italian Philosophy.* Stanford, CA: Stanford University Press, 2012).

Flusser, V. (1983). *Für eine Philosophie der Fotografie.* Berlin: European Photography Andreas Müller-Pohle. (English trans.: *Towards a Philosophy of Photography.* London: Reaktion Books, 2000).

Gherardi, S. (2000). Practice-based theorizing on learning and knowing in organizations: an introduction, *Organization,* 7 (2): 211–223. Reprinted in Gherardi, S. and Strati, A. (2012). *Learning and Knowing in Practice-based Studies.* Cheltenham: Edward Elgar, pp. 1–15.

Gherardi, S. (2009). Practice? It's a matter of taste!, *Management Learning,* 40 (5): 535–550. Reprinted in Gherardi, S. and Strati, A. (2012). *Learning and Knowing in Practice-based Studies.* Cheltenham: Edward Elgar, pp. 157–172.

Gherardi, S. (2012). *How to Conduct a Practice-based Study: Problems and Methods.* Cheltenham: Edward Elgar.

Gherardi, S., Nicolini, D. and Strati, A. (2007). The passion for knowing, *Organization,* 14 (3): 309–323. Reprinted in Gherardi, S. and Strati, A. (2012). *Learning and Knowing in Practice-based Studies.* Cheltenham: Edward Elgar, pp. 142–156.

Gherardi, S. and Strati, A. (2012). *Learning and Knowing in Practice-based Studies.* Cheltenham: Edward Elgar.

Gherardi, S. and Strati, A. (2017a). Talking about competence: that "something" which exceeds the speaking subject, in Sandberg, J., Rouleau, L., Langley, A., and Tsoukas, H. (eds.), *Skillful Performance: Enacting Capabilities, Knowledge, Competence, and Expertise in Organizations.* Oxford: Oxford University Press, pp. 103–124.

Gherardi, S. and Strati, A. (2017b). Luigi Pareyson's *Estetica: Teoria della formatività* and its implication for organization studies, *Academy of Management Review,* 42 (4): 745–755.

Hitchcock, B. (2005). When land met Adams, in Crist, S. (ed.), *The Polaroid Book. Selections from the Polaroid Collections of Photography.* Köln: Taschen, pp. 1–6.

Pareyson, L. (1943). *Studi sull'esistenzialismo.* Firenze: Sansoni. (Partial English trans.: Pareyson, L., *Existence, Interpretation, Freedom: Selected Writings.* Ed. Bubbio, P. D. Aurora, CO: The Davies Group, 2009).

Pareyson, L. (1950). Arte e conoscenza: intuizione e interpretazione. *Filosofia,* 2 (2). (Partial English trans.: *Existence, Interpretation, Freedom. Selected Writings.* Ed. Bubbio, P. D. Aurora, CO: The Davies Group, 2009).

Pareyson, L. (1954). *Estetica. Teoria della formatività.* Torino: Edizioni di "Filosofia". Reprinted 1988, Milano: Bompiani. (Partial English trans.: Pareyson, L., *Existence, Interpretation, Freedom: Selected Writings.* Ed. Bubbio, P. D. Aurora, CO: The Davies Group, 2009).

Pareyson, L. (1971). *Verità e interpretazione.* Milano: Mursia. (Partial English trans.: *Existence, Interpretation, Freedom. Selected Writings.* Ed. Bubbio, P. D. Aurora, CO: The Davies Group, 2009).

Restaino, F. (1991). *Storia dell'estetica moderna.* Torino: UTET.

Saporiti, A. A. (1990). Photopoesie di Antonio Strati, *Landscape. Panorama della fotografia professionale,* 9: 20–23.

Simmel, G. (1916). *Rembrandt, Ein kunstphilosophischer Versuch.* Leipzig: Kurt Wolff Verlag. (English trans.: *Rembrandt. An Essay in the Philosophy of Art.* Ed. Scott, A. and H. Staubmann. New York: Routledge, 2005).

Staubmann, H. M. (1997). The ornamental form of the iron cage: an aesthetic representation of modern society?, *International Journal of Politics, Culture and Society*, 10 (4): 591–607.

Strati, A. (1996). *Sociologia dell'organizzazione: paradigmi teorici e metodi di ricerca.* Roma: NIS-Carocci. (English trans.: *Theory and Method in Organization Studies: Paradigms and Choices.* London: Sage, 2000).

Strati, A. (1999). *Organization and Aesthetics.* London: Sage.

Strati, A. (2000). Putting people in the picture: art and aesthetics in photography and understanding of organizational life, *Organization Studies*, 21 (0): 53–69.

Strati, A. (2003). Knowing in practice: aesthetic understanding and tacit knowledge, in Nicolini, D., Gherardi, S. and Yanow, D. (eds.), *Knowing in Organizations: A Practice-based Approach.* Armonck: M.E. Sharpe, pp. 53–75. Reprinted in Gherardi, S. and Strati, A. (2012). *Learning and Knowing in Practice-based Studies.* Cheltenham: Edward Elgar, pp. 16–38.

Strati, A. (2007). Sensible knowledge and practice-based learning, *Management Learning*, 38 (1): 61–77. Reprinted in Gherardi, S. and Strati, A. (2012). *Learning and Knowing in Practice-based Studies.* Cheltenham: Edward Elgar, pp. 77–93.

Strati, A. (2016). Aesthetics and design: an epistemology of the unseen, in Mir, R., Willmott, H. and Greenwood, M. (eds.), *The Routledge Companion to Philosophy in Organization Studies.* London: Routledge, pp. 251–259.

Strati, A. and Gherardi, S. (2015). La philosophie de Luigi Pareyson et la recherche esthétique des pratiques organisationnelles: un dialogue, *Le Libellio d'AEGIS*, 11 (3): 21–33, http://lelibellio.com/

Vouilloux, B. (2013). Einfühlung et mimèsis, in Gefen, A. and Vouilloux, B. (eds.), *Empathie et esthétique.* Paris: Hermann Éditeurs, pp. 295–310.

Wolf, S. (2010). *The Digital Eye. Photographic Art in the Electronic Age.* New York: Prestel.

nterlude V: La dame, la licorne et le miroir, 2014

'ile Leica C, software Adobe Photoshop

6 Aesthetic, Hermeneutic and Performative Sensibility

La dame, la licorne et le miroir is the photopoem shown in *Interlude V*, which introduces the "aesthetic", "hermeneutic" and "performative" philosophical sensibilities that characterize the aesthetic discourse on the organization and, therefore, the principal relationship that the organizational theories have established with aesthetic philosophies.

Philosophical sensibility is a concept aimed at delineating the hybridization of organizational theory and philosophy on the aesthetics of the organization. It is a "soft" concept that does not constrain organizational theory in precisely circumscribed fields because of the influence of this or that philosophical thought, but instead evokes how the dialogic discourse of the aesthetic study of organization is composite, equivocal and even paradoxical.

The three philosophical sensibilities outline nuances that shape the differences within the aesthetic discourse of the organization that concern the preferred subjects and study areas, and the research styles, but which do not constitute mutually exclusive research paths. Each philosophical sensibility—the aesthetic, the hermeneutic and the performative—shows the specific fundamental connections-in-action which relate the aesthetic study of organization to aesthetic theory and research in philosophy, art history, sociology and social sciences in general.

In this chapter, I will outline the main aspects of the three philosophical sensibilities through Continental aesthetics, American pragmatism and the sociology of the senses of Georg Simmel. Without claiming—*ça va sans dire*—to exhaust the aesthetic philosophical thought that can be considered relevant for organizational theories, either in this last chapter of the book or in the whole book.

The photopoem represented in *Interlude V* depicts a human being—la dame/the lady, a mythological animal, la licorne/the unicorn, and a mundane artifact, le miroir/the mirror—which are all incorporated into the fabric of a work of art. The sight of the lady is directed towards the eyes of the unicorn, which is looking at the lady and even its own image reflected in the mirror.

The interactivity between the human, the animal and the artifact is shown as a poetic performance, and as sensible knowing and aesthetic judging in the texture of the artwork dedicated to the sense of sight. The "proper" subject of the aesthetics is not the man of reason "as the quintessential European citizen", we can state in resonance with the affirmation of Rosi Braidotti (2013: 169) on the "nomadic vision of the post-human knowing subject" in which a "collectively distributed consciousness emerges from this, a transversal form of non-synthetic understanding of the relational bond that connects us".

The photopoem *La dame, la licorne et le miroir* emphasizes the delicate atmosphere of the interactions between the lady's eyes, the only visible eye of the unicorn and the reflection of the unicorn's eye in the mirror. It does it by framing only a detail of this great 310 × 330 cm tapestry, in wool and silk, exhibited at the Musée de Cluny, Musée National du Moyen Âge, in Paris.

There, in fact, it is possible to aesthetically appreciate six large tapestries—and make photographic reproductions—in a delicately lit hall dedicated to *La dame à la licorne*, which was once oval, while now it is squared. Five of these tapestries each depict one sense: sight—that is partially reproduced in the widely manipulated digital file created with my Leica C and then elaborated with the Adobe Photoshop software to make the black and white photopoem in *Interlude V*, touch, smell, hearing and taste.

In addition, a sixth large tapestry, still in the same hall of the museum, which completes this series of large tapestries, is instead dedicated to language. It is, in fact, the only one in which there are words, only three, which are shown in the inscription in large letters on the tent depicted in the tapestry: A MON SEUL DESIR. To my only desire, that is, to say the "first *cogito*", observes the French philosopher Michel Serres (2003: 67). My desire identifies itself with the "written word" and then "I", carnal, with all my flesh, I do not exist just in five senses but in language.

These six tapestries are thought to have been woven two centuries before the creation of the aesthetic philosophy and of its focus on sensible and perceptive faculties, and on sensitive and aesthetic judgment, that is, between 1484 and 1500. Now, how did all this happen? How has it happened that art—even applied art, like tapestry, is often considered to be—prefigured aesthetics before philosophy, and in such a beautiful and problematic way?

I will address these issues in the next section, dealing with the aesthetic philosophical sensibility. Thus, I will illustrate and discuss both the hermeneutic and performative philosophical sensibilities in section 6.2, and then I will examine the relationships between these three philosophical sensibilities and the organizational theories in section 6.3.

6.1 Aesthetic Sensibility

The aesthetic sensibility has its roots in the origins of philosophical aesthetics, that is, in the European philosophies of the eighteenth century which focused on "wit" with Joseph Addison (1712) in England; on metaphorical thinking and the "logica poetica" with Giambattista Vico (1725) in Italy; on the "Aesthetica" as sensible knowledge in Germany with Alexander Gottlieb Baumgarten (1750–58), who coined this name for this new branch of philosophy; and, always in Germany, on the "aesthetic judgement" with Immanuel Kant (1790).

Furthermore, the aesthetic sensibility is also grounded in the "post-humanist aesthetics" discussed in Chapter 4, which avoids anthropocentrism (Braidotti, 2013; Deleuze and Guattari, 1980; Esposito, 2010; Haraway, 1991), and the theory of aesthetics as "formativeness" (Pareyson, 1954) and its emphasis on practice, widely illustrated in Chapter 5.

In the following sections, I will first illustrate the philosophical and sociological debate regarding the perceptive and sensory faculties with Georg Simmel (1908) and the philosophical topic of "flesh" (*chair*) with Maurice Merleau-Ponty (1945, 1948, 1964, 2002); then, I shall take into consideration the aesthetic and sensitive judgment, the taste, and the poetic understanding with Giambattista Vico (1725).

6.1.1 Senses and Aesthetic Sociology

The roots of aesthetic sensibility, in addition to the post-humanism and formativeness discussed in the previous chapters, are also grounded in the "sociology of the senses" of the early twentieth century by the German sociologist Georg Simmel and the topic of the "flesh" (*chair*) and the world of perception raised around the mid-twentieth century by the French philosopher Maurice Merleau-Ponty, as we shall see in this section.

Interlude V introduces the issue of perception and sensory faculties by representing the snout of the kneeling unicorn "reflected in the looking-glass held out by the Lady, thus clearly indicating that Sight is the sense illustrated here", states Alain Erlande-Brandenburg (1989: 16), former director of the Museum of Cluny.

> It is recognized today that five of the six panels illustrate the five senses, and these are easily explicable. Sight: the unicorn is watching itself in a looking-glass held-out to him by the Lady. Hearing: she is playing at portable organ worked by her servant. Smell: a monkey perched on a stool is sniffing at a carnation while the Lady weaves a wreath of flowers. Taste: a monkey raises a sweetmeat to its mouth, while the young woman chooses another from a comfitdish. Touch: here, she is shown holding the unicorn's horn very gently in her hand.
>
> There remained the last panel [*A mon seul désir*], for which no satisfactory explanation had been found.
>
> (1989: 12–13)

There are no "men", in any case, in these tapestries, remarks Michel Serres (2003: 64), while, on the contrary, the woman is always present. Although "in the visual documents of medieval times, the allegorical characters that represent the five senses are men", writes Anne-Marie De Gendt (2016: 72), and it is by the end of the fifteenth century that one notices that

> there is a change in the sex of these characters: in the majority of visual documents, the five senses will now be represented by women. The tipping point seems to be around 1480, when the famous series of tapestries kept at the Museum of Cluny, called *La Dame à la Licorne*, which is the first testimony of the change of sex in the visual field that has been preserved, is woven.

The number of visual representations of the five senses, however, is rather small until the end of the fifteenth century, observes Anne-Marie De Gendt (2016: 71), and the "mode of representation differs too", because in the Middle Ages "the senses are represented either by an allegorical character accompanied by a relevant attribute or by an animal with symbolic value, unless it is by the image of the sensory organ itself, a kind of physiological hieroglyph".

In the case of the six tapestries of *La dame à la licorne*, the senses are represented by the interactions between the lady and the mythological animal, the unicorn, in the natural environment of a variety of animals and plants, and they are distinguished by specific artifacts' details. Each tapestry is like an oval island, without a sky, as remarked by Michel Serres: "No male at the Cluny museum, no male and no sky" (2003: 64). There we can find flowers and plants of all kinds, pine and oaks, and a variety of animals from lions to monkeys, dogs, rabbits and birds.

Like the lady, the unicorn is always present. Even the artifact that reveals the sensorial faculty of the tapestry is present, but only for four of the five senses: the mirror for sight, the portable organ for hearing, the crown of flowers for smell, the comfit-dish for taste. Instead, for the sense of touch, it is the relationship between the lady's hand and the unicorn's horn that performs the task of revealing the perceptual and sensorial faculty.

It is "the outside world", notes Michel Serres (2003: 61), since the "scholastic thought knew, in the Middle Ages, to divide our *sensorium* in external and internal", and the five senses of "hearing, sight, touch, smell and taste were reputed external". The external senses are now "anti-examples of the moral discourse, sources of happiness, terrestrial and spiritual", observes Olga Anna Duhl (2016: 27), used "as cognitive base for the development of aesthetic models that have a growing autonomy".

If, at the turn of the sixteenth century, the representations of the five senses remain dependent on the hierarchical model fixed by Aristotle and nuanced by the contributions of Arab and scholastic thought, they reveal themselves in a new light thanks to [. . .] the advent and spread of Italian Epicureanism and Neo-Platonism.

(Duhl, 2016: 19)

The external senses are open, delivered to the world. Naïve, they "engage in leaves and branches, rabbits, herons, foxes, the young unicorn without horn"; they are "immersed in the variable and the mixture", they are chaotic, "multiple also, widespread, seeded or scattered", and they "never reach uniqueness, preservation or identity" situated as they are in "these enameled tapestries of all things in the world", writes Serres (2003: 65).

There is a need for a sixth sense, "by which the subject turns on him/ herself and the body on the body" (Serres, 2003: 61–62), and, therefore, a sixth tapestry was necessary for the island of the internal sense, where the "inner sense finally speaks and for the first time the tent imprints itself with burning tongues and crowns itself with writing" (Serres, 2003: 65), where the language "happens": *A mon seul désir*, in which my desire is identified with writing and my carnal "I" exists only in the language, "solitary belonging, given to oneself" (Serres, 2003: 66). During this period of transition from Middles Ages to Renaissance,

an aesthetic of the five senses is emerging that is more and more detached from strictly rational and moral considerations, thanks in particular to the contributions of the Italian humanists, and above all those of Lorenzo Valla (1406–1456). In the famous dialogue *De Voluptate* published under this title in 1431 (first version), the author of the *Elegantiae linguae latinae* makes a veritable apology of the senses by elaborating a theory of pleasure which does not take long to provoke controversies.

(Duhl, 2016: 21–22)

We know now, writes Erlande-Brandenburg (1989: 13), that all six of these tapestries "must have been woven in one of the Northern cities specializing in this technique", perhaps in Brussels, and that they remain "one of the great masterpieces of tapestry" able to express "the poetry of the Middle Ages". Before 1882, when the six tapestries were finally deposited in the museum, they "were disposed in a décor of mid-18th century paneling" in the château of Boussac, and "*Smell, Hearing* and *Touch* were in the *Salon*", while "*Taste, Sight* and *A mon seul désir* in the dining-room" (Erlande-Brandenburg, 1989: 65).

Thus, it was in the dining room of this castle in the Limousin region of France that, before 1882, one could aesthetically appreciate the tapestry of sight, *La vue*, which is at the origins of the photopoem in *Interlude V*.

In the tapestry entitled *La vue*, there is an intense focus in the mirror whirling the vortex of our destiny—the awakening mirror that must be seen without fear, the mirror that finally makes visible the invisible. (In this case, the unicorn is reflected, tiny, the depths of the mirror is nothing but the chasm that steals, ever further, the elusive horn). This mirror called "fidelity" (*de fidélité*), because nothing escapes it, is brother of the Fountain of Life often present near the Virgin welcoming the fertilizing unicorn in her bosom.

(Caroutch, 2002: 97–98)

The mythological animal, the unicorn, is a "male at the Cluny museum"—to make a counterpoint to the words of Serres above—and is a presence that is fundamental for all six panels. The unicorn, in fact, warns Francesca Y. Caroutch (2002: 16–17), at the end of the fifteenth century "was still male, as it remained in Italy and many other countries", and abounded especially in Italy, if one considers the fact that in Siena there is still a district which bears his name, the *contrada del Leocorno*, as can be noticed during the horse race of the *Palio*.

The French language, however, conceals all this because *la licorne* is a feminine name. But the eyes that look at each other in the photopoem *La dame, la licorne et le miroir* are of those of the lady and those of the male mythological animal. Four eyes—two of the lady and two of the unicorn, of which one is a reflection in the mirror—and three subjects of this interaction are depicted along the invisible lines of a triangle: a person, a mythological animal, a reflected image from a small "fidelity" mirror.

A vision that emphasizes the "affective opening-out" towards the philosophical dimension of chaosmosis—in the terms of Felix Guattari (1992)—where "affect and memory become essential elements", to draw attention to the words of Rosi Braidotti (2013: 166–167), elements that are "internally fractured and multiplied over several time-sequences", but also freed from "the logo-centric gravitational force". These few dashed elements bring into focus a relationship that is not merely social, therefore, but post-social, because even the artifacts are in action, and post-humanist. It is an asymmetrical relationship, as I described elsewhere (Strati, 2010a: 100–103), because the unicorn receives the gaze of the eyes of the lady and of his eye reflected in the mirror, but the lady and the mirrored eye receive only that of the unicorn.

One looks into each other's eyes with the Other, writes Georg Simmel in his *Excursus on the Sociology of Sense Impression* (1908; Eng. trans. 2009: 570–584). One cannot "catch the eye" and not give simultaneously, because the sensory organ of sight has just this sociologically important characteristic: the gaze is addressed to the Other; but, at the same time, it is receptive, perceives the Other. He expresses to the Other and receives from him. The act is unique, because the

> closeness of this relationship is borne by the remarkable fact that the perceptive glance directed at the other is itself full of expression, and in fact precisely by the way one looks at the other. In the look that takes in the other one reveals oneself; with the same act, in which the subject seeks to know its object, it surrenders itself to the object. One cannot take with the eye without at the same time giving. The eye unveils to the other the soul that seeks to unveil the other. While this occurs obviously only in immediate eye-to-eye contact, it is here that the most complete mutuality in the whole realm of human relations is produced.
>
> (Simmel, 1908; Eng. trans. 2009: 571)

This is a sociologically relevant process, even if often considered an unimportant relationship in social theory. On the contrary, it is these micro-social interactions that sociology should address with the utmost interest and attention—Simmel stresses this from the very first pages of his *Soziologie* (1908; Eng. trans. 2009: 34)—because they "construct society out of the immediate", out of the "individual material" and are, therefore, "society-constructing forms" which are "parts of social interaction in general", constantly in "physical and mental contact", and alongside "more complicated activities and structures".

The beauty of Simmel's aesthetic sociology is that it analyzes in detail the diversities of the five senses in terms of performance and production of knowledge, that is, of activity, and of the sociological relevance of the micro-interactions they generate.

The sensory organ of hearing, for example, unlike sight, takes without giving. Furthermore, since one cannot detach from hearing, as one can do by closing the eye, the sense of hearing is condemned to take, that is, to hear all that resounds around. The ear cannot close to listening because "hearing is supra-individualistic in its nature: all those who are in a room must hear what transpires in it, and the fact that one picks it up does not take it away from another" (Simmel 1908; Eng. trans. 2009: 575). This fundamental character, being "supra-individualistic", does not in any way negate the intimacy of feeling or feeling with the Other. Try to compare—continues Simmel (1908; Eng. trans. 2009: 576)—two audiences, each marked by a specific sensorial organ, such as a museum audience with a concert audience:

> for the determination of the hearing impression to communicate itself uniformly and in the same way to a crowd of people—a determination by no means simply external-quantitative but bound up deeply with its innermost nature—sociologically brings together a concert

audience in an incomparably closer union and collective feeling than occurs with the visitors to a museum.

In effect, the sociological relevance of the sense of hearing, once compared with the other sense organs, consists in the fact that this sense:

1. is "supra-individualistic", given that

   • we cannot easily prevent ourselves from perceiving with our ears (Strati, 1999: 1–3; 2007, reprint 2012: 86–88),
   • when we listen to a sound or a noise, we do not appropriate this sound or that noise and, therefore, we do not remove them from others and we do not prevent others from perceiving them;

2. is able to create a "communal social relationship" whereby those involved—human beings, animals, artifacts dedicated to detecting or recording and expressing a sound or a noise—share the aesthetic materiality of the specific situation, and eventually also share the same state of mind, as can be the case with music and social ritual to attend a concert, or even the case of a simulation in the digital environment of artificial intelligence, such as those experienced in medicine.

Simmel (1908; Eng. trans. 2009: 575) depicts his comprehension of the sociological relevance of the perceptive faculty of hearing—as he does with other external senses—by understanding the aesthetic materiality of the ear, which is "the quintessentially egoistic organ", since it takes without giving and is profoundly different from the sensory organ of sight for "the absence of that reciprocity that sight produces between eye and eye", as outlined above.

6.1.2 *The* Mielleux *and Concrete Intersubjectivity*

An analogous attention to the micro-interactive processes of our sensory organs shows Maurice Merleau-Ponty regarding the sense of touch when, in the series of speeches given at the French radio in 1948, he described the interactivity that can be observed between an artefact—honey—and human beings or, rather, the hand and fingers. What is brought into focus is the aesthetic materiality of the performance that connects them in an action characterized by the "quality of being honeyed" (*mielleux*).

> Honey is a slow-moving liquid; while it undoubtedly has a certain consistency and allows itself to be grasped, it soon creeps slyly from the fingers and returns to where it started from. It comes apart as soon as it has been given a particular shape and, what is more, it reverses the roles by grasping the hands of whoever would take hold

of it. The living, exploring, hand which thought it could master this thing instead discovers that it is embroiled in a sticky external object.
(2002; Eng. trans. 2004: 46–47)

It is Jean-Paul Sartre (1943; Eng. trans. 1956: 609), the French existentialist philosopher, "who must take the credit for this elegant analysis", and the point is—underlines Merleau-Ponty (2002; Eng. trans. 2004: 47–49)—that artefacts are not "simply neutral *objects* which stand before us for our contemplation": our relationship with them "is not a distant one", but they "dwell within us as emblems of forms of life we either love or hate" and humanity "is invested in the things of the world and these are invested in it". So, the relationship between human beings and artefacts "is no longer one of distance and mastery", states Merleau-Ponty (2002; Eng. trans. 2004: 50–51), and "is less clear-cut".

> When I perceive a cube, it is not because my reason sets the perspectival appearances straight and thinks the geometrical definition of a cube with respect to them. I do not even notice the distortions of perspective, much less correct them; I am at the cube itself in its manifestness through what I see. The objects behind my back are likewise not represented to me by some operation of memory or judgment; they are present, they *count* for me, just as the ground which I do not see continues nonetheless to be present beneath the figure which partially hides it. Even the perception of movement, which at first seems to depend directly on the point of reference chosen by the intellect is in turn only one element in the global organization of the field.
> (Merleau-Ponty, 1948; Eng. trans. 1964: 51)

The proximity between human being and artefact is "vertiginous", underlines Merleau-Ponty (2002; Eng. trans. 2004: 51), and this prevents us from understanding the artifacts as "pure objects lacking in all human attributes" and also "from apprehending ourselves as a pure intellect separate from things", that is, from pure matter.

> Other human beings are never pure spirit for me: I only know them through their glances, their gestures, their speech—in other words, though their bodies. Of course *another human being* is certainly more than simply a body to me: rather, this other is a body animated by all manner of intentions, the origin of numerous actions and words. These I remember and they go to make up my sketch of their moral character. Yet I cannot detach someone from their silhouette, the tone of their voice and its accent. If I see them for even a moment, I can reconnect with them instantaneously and far more thoroughly than if I were to go through a list of everything I know about them from experience or hearsay.
> (Merleau-Ponty, 2002; Eng. trans. 2004: 62)

This is a crucial point with regard to sensible knowledge, as I have emphasized elsewhere (Strati, 2007, reprint 2012: 78), since it does not limit knowing that is sensitive to direct, physical and objectively observable relationships; but it accounts, instead, for the intimate, personal and carnal relationship of the subject with the experience of the world. Addressing, in fact, the "complexities of current organ-isations and their contexts", we know, observes Wendelin M. Küpers and the Senses (2013: 55), that the "corpus of corporation is much more than what can be captured" by "we-senses" and bodily comprehension, but "we are part of those inherent dimensions of embodiment, which refer to more than our mere sensual appearances".

The perceptive-sensorial faculties are not mere terminal sensors that constitute the "instruments of a sovereign consciousness", notes Rossella Prezzo (2004: 8), but "places of the flesh where the flesh of the world becomes visible". Merleau-Ponty, in fact, in his last writings and, in particular, in *Le visible et l'invisible* (1964), observes Todd May (2005: 521), "offers a conception of the body that is neither at odds nor even entangled with the world, but is of the very world itself" and with his "concept of the flesh introduces a point of contact that is also a point of undifferentiation".

> To grasp this remarkable character, it is perhaps worth recalling Gilles Deleuze's concept of the fold. The world is not composed of different parts; there is no transcendent, whether of God or of subjectivity. The world is one. As Deleuze sometimes says, being is univocal. This oneness is not, however, inert or inanimate. Among other things, it can fold over on itself, creating spaces that are at once insides and outsides, at once different from and continuous with one another.
>
> The flesh is a fold of Being in this sense. It is of the world, and yet encounters it as if from a perceptual or cognitive distance. It is a visibility that sees, a tangible that touches, an audible that hears.
>
> (May, 2005: 522)

Whoever posits the Other is a perceiving subject, and the Other is concrete, corporeal, a person's body that is perceived, and, at the same time, seen as perceiving body. It is "never a matter of anything but co-perception", writes Merleau-Ponty (1960; Eng. trans. 1964: 170–171), because "I touch my left hand while it is touching my right"—as we observed above with regards to the *mielleux*—and this is "my incarnation" which summons up within "my most strictly private life" the concrete intercorporeality, the carnal intersubjectivity, in a word, "all other corporeality". In these terms, Maurice Merleau-Ponty addresses the aesthetic materiality of the relationships between living beings and artefacts from his *Phénoménologie de la perception* (1945) up to his last writings, that is, considering that

> all subjectivity is intersubjective, all intersubjectivity is concrete intersubjectivity, concrete intersubjectivity constitutes the social, and

the social is the site of struggle and power. And the body-subject is at the heart of this intertwining, not as transcendental origin but as principle of action. The body is active in the quietest whisper, the most subtle enunciation and the most aggressive and destructive of activities.

(Crossley, 1995: 61)

6.1.3 *Senses, Aesthetic Judgment,* Logica Poetica

There is no name in traditional philosophy, observes Maurice Merleau-Ponty (1964: 181), to designate the generality of the sensible *per se* that we call "flesh" (*chair*). However, flesh is a concept that has a long history, specifies Suzannah Biernoff (2005: 47), as we can see in the writings of the twelfth century, in which the flesh is "both visible and invisible"; it is "an attribute of bodies and thoughts, gazes and shadows" which "transgresses the boundaries separating inside from outside"; or in the Middle Ages, when "the vicissitudes of the flesh often gave rise to theological anxiety and hostility, and also to fantasies of transcendence".

But even before the Middle Ages, "flesh", "carnal" and "incarnation" were concepts in use in the millennial Christian religion, to the point that in the Catholic Church, during the celebration of Mass, there is the rite of symbolically offering the flesh of Christ to the community of believers. Therefore, the concept of concrete and carnal corporeality has not only been learned, but also ritually celebrated in the Christian community throughout the world for over 2,000 years.

Furthermore, the carnal intersubjectivity portrayed by Maurice Merleau-Ponty, in order to emphasize the aesthetic materiality of interactivity in society, evokes the concrete and carnal situation called into question by Luigi Pareyson. I have emphasized this issue from the beginning of this book, in Chapter 1, when I intended to clarify my specific point of view regarding the relevance of philosophical aesthetics for organizational theory: "*my* situation" is my "incarnation", because "I have *this* body, *these* relatives, *these* friends, *this* homeland, *this* job, *these* relations with others and other things: that is I have a very definite position in the universe, a specific place in the world" (Pareyson, 1943; Eng. trans. 2009: 42).

However, neither the phenomenological philosophy of Merleau-Ponty nor the personalistic hermeneutics of Pareyson nor my vision of aesthetic philosophy are directly linked to the Christian religion. On the contrary, they are immersed in the very different *weltanschauung* constituted by the redefinition of the person that has occurred in Western society with the creation of aesthetics as a branch of philosophy during the eighteenth century (Legros, 2005); that is, in a form of knowing and performing that situates the concept of person outside of the domain of theological cosmic orders and also, at the same time, outside of the Cartesian *cogito*.

During the Enlightenment, in fact, the perceptive and sensory faculties that allow the understanding of sensible experience became—with
the aesthetic philosophies of Addison, Vico, Baumgarten and Kant—an
essential part of the social construct that defines the distinctive characteristics of the human person. So, in particular:

- for Merleau-Ponty, who "became disillusioned with the church as
  a young man, frustrated by its lack of political engagement" and
  whose "rejection of Christianity as an institution took place against
  the backdrop of the Second World War" (Biernoff, 2005: 46), the
  philosophical phenomenology of the "flesh" is an ontology of
  the sensible, against the Cartesian separation between the mind and
  the body, and also in polemics with the objectivist ontology that
  defines "perception" in terms of access to reality (Barbaras, 2009:
  104) rather than in terms of "world of perception", of "flesh", of
  "carnal intersubjectivity";
- for Luigi Pareyson, who was instead a Catholic intellectual (Gherardi
  and Strati, 2017), the concreteness of the existence of the human
  being—his/her incarnation in his/her personal situation—is linked in
  a constitutive way to the "practice of freedom" of his/her interpretation, which "is always part of a dialogue", "implies the consideration of interpretation as personal testimony", "requires that the
  subject chooses, *wagers*, brings herself into play", and "grounds a
  hermeneutic theory that is *personalistic* and *ontological*" (Bubbio,
  2009: 18–19).

Regarding my situation and, therefore, my understanding of the relevance of aesthetic philosophies in organizational theories in terms of
"weak thought", that is, not in search of "strong ontologies", I am an
atheist who grew up in a country, Italy, where Catholic culture is widespread and very pervasive. For me, the flesh, the incarnation and the
freedom of interpretation are like the air we breathe, the invisible that is
perceptible in its variety, the atmosphere polluted by our breath and our
smell (Strati, 2009, reprint 2012: 203–204), which is able to arouse the
sensitive judgment (*judicium sensitivum*) of which Alexander Gottlieb
Baumgarten (1735) deals with his aesthetic theory (1750–58), where he
configures this lower-order gnoseology (*gnoseologia inferior*) as a legitimate part of philosophical thought. Georg Simmel gives a vivid picture
of the *judicium sensitivum* when describing the sociological relevance or
sensory organ of smell:

> The personal contact between cultivated people and workers, so
> often enthusiastically advocated for the social development of the
> present, which is also recognized by the cultivated as the ethical ideal
> of closing the gap between two worlds "of which one does not know

how the other lives", simply fails before the insurmountable nature
of the olfactory sense impressions. [. . .] The social question is not
only an ethical one, but also a nasal question.

(1908; Eng. trans. 2009: 577)

This highlights the profound change in the understanding of the senses that
the photopoem *La dame, la licorne et le miroir* has anticipated under several
respects, as discussed above: with the philosophical aesthetics of the eighteenth century, the sensory organs are "analyzed in themselves or for themselves" rather than in the "analogical perspective" of the academic tradition
of the discourse on the five senses in the Middle Ages (Fritz, 2016: 10).

This profound change has affected the forms of perception of sensory
experience, as well as the modes of understanding the sensible knowing,
emphasizes the French philosopher Jacques Rancière (2011), beginning
from the fact that art was no longer art of any kind, as it had been up
to two and a half centuries before, but it became art in itself, for its own
sake. This concerns not only art, but the ways in which our world allows
itself to be perceived even today (Rancière, 2004).

The crucial importance of this change in the understanding of sensible
knowing, which is due to the creation of philosophical aesthetics during the
Enlightenment, is underlined by the German philosopher Ernst Alfred Cassirer, who theorized the philosophy of culture and symbolic forms (1923–29).

For this new configuration of the sensible knowledge, both the philosopher and the human being in general "should not transcend the finite,
but explore it in all directions", writes Cassirer (1932; Eng. trans. 1951:
354). Cassirer explicitly refers to the aesthetics of Baumgarten and notes
that with "the 'humanization' of sensibility" introduced and diffused by
aesthetic philosophies—in addition to the humanization introduced in
the philosophy of ethics, law, politics and religion—the philosophy of the
eighteenth century

> maintains not only the place of the imagination in human knowl-
> edge, but of the senses and the passions as well. The Cartesian doc-
> trine, according to which the passions are supposed to be nothing
> but "perturbations of the soul" (*perturbationes animi*), is gradually
> supplanted; the passions now become the vital impulses, the real
> motivating forces which stimulate the mind as a whole and keep it in
> operation. [. . .] Thus only through the pleasure which beauty affords
> do we experience the inner vitality and the pure spontaneity which
> also dwells in the sensuous, in other words, the "life of sensory cog-
> nition" (*vita cognitionis sensitivae*).
>
> (1932; Eng. trans. 1951: 355–356)

The historian of aesthetics, observes Cassirer (1932; Eng. trans. 1951:
277–278), "must not neglect or underestimate any of these unfinished,

fluctuating, and ephemeral elements" that generated "a new philosophical discipline" and "a new form of artistic creation as well". Joseph Addison (1712) develops an aesthetic theory of taste in which "the aesthetic pleasures of taste are pleasures of imagination", and, interestingly, "Addison's aesthetic theory does not begin with art", notes Emily Brady (2013: 15–16). Taste and feeling are also of fundamental importance for the philosophical aesthetics of Immanuel Kant (1790; Eng. trans. 1952: 35), which assigns "the *aesthetic* judgement the task of deciding" the conformity of a product, in its own form, "to our cognitive faculties as a question of taste (a matter which the aesthetic judgement decides, not by any harmony with concepts, but by feeling)". Giambattista Vico, who Cassirer (1923–29)—in addition to Benedetto Croce—considered the founder of the aesthetic philosophy for the radical anti-Cartesianism of his poetic logic (*logica poetica*), writes that the individuals, when they do not rely on logical understanding to take in the things, they are then able, relying on sensory understanding, to become those things themselves, that is to say, *to transform themselves into them*:

> human nature, so far as it is like that of animals, carries with it this property, that the senses are its sole way of knowing things.
>
> Hence poetic wisdom, the first wisdom of the gentile world, must have begun with a metaphysics not rational and abstract like that of learned men now, but felt and imagined as that of these first men must have been, who, without power of ratiocination, were all robust sense and vigorous imagination. This metaphysics was their poetry, a faculty born with them (for they were furnished by nature with these senses and imaginations) [. . .].
>
> So that, as rational metaphysics teaches that man becomes all things by understanding them (*homo intelligendo fit omnia*), this imaginative metaphysics shows that man becomes all things by *not* understanding them (*homo non intelligendo fit omnia*); and perhaps the latter proposition is truer than the former, for when man understands he extends his mind and takes in the things, but when he does not understand he makes the things out of himself and becomes them by transforming himself into them.
>
> (1725; Eng. trans. 1968: 116 and 130)

6.2 Hermeneutic and Performative Sensibilities

In the previous section dedicated to the aesthetic philosophical sensibility in the study of organization, we have seen the profound change that aesthetic philosophies have brought to the understanding of perception, taste and imagination, and I have also emphasized that the topic of sensible knowledge is of sociological relevance in the comprehension of social, post-social and post-humanist relationships. In this section,

I will illustrate and discuss the other two philosophical sensibilities—the "hermeneutic" and the "performative"—that I consider capable of characterizing, together with the aesthetic philosophical sensibility, the organizational aesthetic research and the aesthetic discourse on organization (Strati, 2016).

I shall begin with the hermeneutic philosophical sensibility and I will underline the relationship between aesthetic theory, interpretation, meaning creation and active involvement of the reader or user of interpretation. The reader will note that I have already discussed these subjects in various parts of the book, and in particular in Chapter 5 with reference to Luigi Pareyson's personalistic hermeneutics. Here, I will discuss these topics with reference principally to the aesthetic hermeneutics of Hans-Georg Gadamer and to the post-structuralist semiotics of Roland Barthes.

With regard, instead, to the performative sensibility, this is a philosophical sensibility that generally remains "invisible" and "unnoticed" while, on the contrary, it represents an organizational comprehension widely diffused in the study of the aesthetic dimension of organization. I will illustrate this issue in this section by underlining some of the main aspects of the American philosophy of pragmatism, since they are relevant for delineating the *humus* of performative philosophical sensibility. I will refer then to John Dewey's reflections on art as experience and his polemics against the philosophical separation of art and aesthetics from the ordinary worldly experience in society, and also to the philosophy of somaesthetics proposed by Richard Shusterman that, as we have seen in Chapter 3, is of particular importance to understand the "performative".

6.2.1 Aesthetic Hermeneutics

À *mon seul désir*, the sixth tapestry of the hall dedicated to *La dame à la licorne* at the Cluny Museum in Paris, which follows the tapestries related to the five senses, inspired the statement of the French philosopher Michel Serres that the advent of language constitutes at the same time the advent of the primacy of language: "I"—carnal—exist only in the language, here is the world, a world that is filled with "categories" and "definitions" in which even the unspeakable, the unconscious or the unknown reintegrate the language, which, alone, gives the data (2003: 143).

Language seems to have become "the epicenter where all trajectories of thought converge", writes Roberto Esposito (2010; Eng. trans. 2012: 6), no matter what perspective one can have regarding the "philosophical quadrant of our time, from logic to phenomenology and pragmatics to structuralism". And while

> analytic philosophy was created explicitly for the critical analysis of philosophical language—of its improper deviations from ordinary language, or at least from given procedural rules that were definable

from time to time—hermeneutics views the interpreting subject as always immersed in a pregiven linguistic situation which determines all its types of practices. Similarly, deconstruction, as it was intended by Derrida in particular, also starts from the assumption of the linguistic nature of all experience and seeks in writing the original key to dismantle the founding categories of Western knowledge by calling into question their hegemonic potential. At issue in each of these strands of thought is the problem of meaning [. . .].

(Esposito, 2010; Eng. trans. 2012: 5)

The "problem of meaning" was also at stake in the recent novel that the French writer Laurent Binet situates in the ambient of "French Theory". This was the problem, in fact, that led the French professor of semiology Simon Herzog to turn to Umberto Eco, saying "We have good reason to believe that Barthes and the three other people were killed because of a document relating to the seventh function of language", and to remind him, at the same time, that in Jacobson's theory, "there are only six functions of language" (Binet, 2015; Eng. trans. 2017: 185)—that is, the obvious "referential" function to talk about something, the "phatic" function to establish communication in itself, the "emotive" or "expressive" function, the "conative" function to command, the "metalinguistic" function to say about other languages, as in scientific discourse, and the "poetic" or "aesthetic" function to see the language in its sensitive-aesthetic dimension.

Binet underlines the embarrassment of the French semiologist before Eco and specifies that Herzog did not want to insult him by pointing out "the functions that the Discourse or the Language generally have to perform according to Jacobson's formalism and structuralism" (Calabrese, 1985: 64). Umberto Eco knows Jacobson's theory "perfectly well" and, according to him, this formalist and structuralist thinking on language "is not entirely correct" (Binet, 2015; Eng. trans. 2017: 185). But the situation is that the police detective Jacques Bayard went to ask the French professor to assist him because he was carrying out his investigation in a bizarre world for him, that of French Theory, where he meets and interrogates *maîtres à penser* as Michel Foucault, Gilles Deleuze, Hélène Cixous, Jacques Derrida, Louis Althusser or Julia Kristeva.

An authentic hermeneutic task was what Bayard asked the semiologist professor, because what hermeneutics realizes, writes Hans-Georg Gadamer (2006: 29), is "this bringing of something out of one world and into another, out of the world of the gods and into that of humans, or out of the world of a foreign language into the world of one's own language". Gadamer (2006: 48) observes that all

human knowledge of the world is linguistically mediated. Our first orientation to the world fulfills itself in the learning of language. But not only this. The linguisticality [*Sprachlichkeit*] of our being-in-the-world articulates in the end the whole realm of our experience [. . .] the communicatively experienced world itself is constantly being handed over to us—*traditur*—as an open totality. It is experience and nothing but experience. It is always co-present when the world is experienced, when unfamiliarity is cancelled, when something becomes clear, when insight happens, when one successfully appropriates a piece of knowledge.

Language, in fact, is not just a mere medium, one among others; it is "experience and nothing but experience", it is "always co-present" and is central to hermeneutical philosophy, to the point that the primary task of hermeneutics *qua* philosophy consists in showing that language is aimed at integrating all the scientific knowledge "we have in the sciences into the 'personal knowing' of the individual 'experience', as Michael Polanyi has shown in his book, *Personal Knowledge*" (Gadamer, 2006: 48).

We saw in Chapter 1 the topic of personal knowledge and the distinction between the tacit and explicit dimensions of knowledge highlighted by the Hungarian philosopher Michael Polanyi. "Though I cannot say clearly how I ride a bicycle", writes Polanyi (1958: 88) to illustrate this distinction, "yet this will not prevent me from saying that I know how to ride a bicycle", as although

the expert diagnostician, taxonomist and cotton-classer can indicate their clues and formulate their maxims, they know many more things than they can tell, knowing them only in practice, as instrumental particulars, and not explicitly, as objects. The knowledge of such particulars is an ineffable process of thought. This applies equally to connoisseurship as the art of knowing and to skills as the art of doing, wherefore both can be taught only by aid of practical example and never solely by precept.

Now, hermeneutics as a philosophical theory seeks the integration of the explicit dimension of knowledge—"all knowledge we have in the sciences"—in the tacit dimension of knowledge, that is, in Gadamer's terms we have just seen above, the personal knowing of the individual experience. This is a very interesting point of view because, contrary to cognitivist theories and rationalist and positivistic philosophies, hermeneutics does not violate the "tacit" dimension of personal knowing willing to make it "explicit".

However, the reader will notice that, in Chapter 1, I discussed the topic of personal knowledge treated by Polanyi in a slightly different way than Gadamer's argument. In fact, with the aesthetic hermeneutics of Hans-Georg Gadamer in particular, and also with hermeneutics more generally—but *not* with the personal hermeneutics of Luigi Pareyson illustrated in Chapter 5—all personal knowledge happens in the language, as underlined by Michel Serres with regard to the sixth tapestry of the hall of *La dame à la licorne,* as we saw earlier in this chapter.

Instead, my understanding of Michael Polanyi's personal knowledge is at odds with that of Gadamer, because, rather than the process of integrating the explicit into the tacit, I consider that this distinction between the explicit and the tacit dimension of knowing is persistent and inevitable. While language dominates the ambits of explicit knowledge, it is the aesthetics which dominates the ambits of the tacit dimension of knowing (Strati, 2003) and provides them with a very different language, and distant from "all knowledge we have in the sciences", because it is based on *logica poetica* (Vico, 1725), that is, on the poetic and metaphorical thought which constitutes "an original procedure that involves the cognitive sphere and not just a linguistic ornament" (Ghiazza, 2005: 203).

6.2.2 Body Speaks, Objects Speak, Destinies Speak

Language, according to Gadamer's aesthetic hermeneutics, is also of fundamental importance to create a sense of commonality, and this aspect has had a significant relevance for the interactions between the police detective and the prominent protagonists of the French Theory. You can already discern this from the first report of Superintendent Bayard, in which he ascertains that

> a man, sixty-four years old, knocked over by a laundry van, Rue des Écoles, Monday afternoon, while on a pedestrian crossing. [. . .] The victim was unconscious when the ambulance arrived, and had no papers on his person, but he was identified by one of his colleagues, a certain Michel Foucault, a lecturer at the Collège de France and a writer. The man, it turns out, was Roland Barthes, also a lecturer at the Collège de France and a writer.
>
> (Binet, 2015; Eng. trans. 2017: 10)

Moreover, the hermeneutical "problem of meaning" was evident once it became known that Barthes was crossing Rue des Écoles just after having lunch with François Mitterrand, who at that time was the socialist candidate for the presidential elections in France. Thus, the accident took on a significance that led Superintendent Bayard to investigate also the mystery of Barthes' discovery of the "seventh" function of language that the semiologist Simon Herzog alluded to Eco. In fact,

> Barthes's stroke of genius is to not content himself with communication systems but to extend his field of inquiry to systems of meaning. [. . .] And yet, language doesn't say everything. The body speaks,

objects speak, history speaks, individual or collective destinies speak, life and death speak to us constantly in a thousand different ways.

(Binet, 2015; Eng. trans. 2017: 8–9)

According to the post-structuralist semiology of Roland Barthes, even the Eiffel Tower of Paris "speaks", as I briefly mentioned recently (Strati, 2016: 255). The Eiffel Tower makes Paris a kind of nature, constitutes the shaman of people in a landscape, brings together memory and sensation, and produces the *simulacrum* of Paris—in Jean Baudrillard's terms (1978)—in our imagination.

Barthes begins his semiological annotations on the meaning of the Eiffel Tower by referring to the habit of Guy de Maupassant, who was one of the intellectuals and artists who signed the "*Protestation des artistes*" against the construction of the Eiffel Tower, published in *Le Temps* on 14 February 1887. The tower was inaugurated two years later, on 15 May 1889, and during the new Universal Exhibition of 1900 in Paris welcomed more than one million visitors. Guy de Maupassant, writes Barthes (1964; Eng. trans. 1985: 236), "often lunched at the restaurant in the Tower",

> though he didn't care much for the food: *It's the only place in Paris,* he used to say, *where I don't have to see it.* And it's true that you must take endless precautions, in Paris, not to see the Eiffel Tower; whatever the season, through mist and cloud, on overcast days or in sunshine, in rain—wherever you are, whatever the landscape of roofs, domes, or branches separating you from it, *the Tower is there*; incorporated into daily life until you can no longer grant it any specific attribute, determined merely to persist, like a rock or the river, it is as literal as a phenomenon of nature whose meaning can be questioned to infinity but whose existence is incontestable. There is virtually no Parisian glance it fails to *touch* at some time of day.

The first meaning of the Eiffel Tower, therefore, is that wherever you are in Paris, you cannot avoid the Tower that is there, rising towards the sky. No monument, no natural place is so thin and so high, so the width is a dimension erased in the verticality of the lines of the Tower, which symbolizes the ascension in a height that is valid for itself, as a pure height exercise, compared to which the horizontal lines constituted, in particular, by the platforms, are in a delicate relationship and of essential linearity. Ascension is a symbol of lightness, and the perforated iron lace of the Tower extinguishes its substance—made of more than 18,000 metal elements with a total weight of more than 10,000 tons—making it empty; but like air, a stem is drawn by two simple lines that, starting from the earth, one distant from the other, go to rejoin in the sky, a heaven that is not divine, but the secular and mundane Parisian sky.

It is an essential movement that *symbolizes* the infinite and that outlines the impossible and the limit of earthly experience and, at the same time, the freedom of the imaginary of human beings, through the pure spectacle of the Tower, which becomes a *metamorphosis* of oneself itself, because it sways with a continuous movement between an object looked upon—from the city or in flight from an airplane—to an object from which one looks.

The Tower is an artefact which sees and is a sight which is seen, because it is a paradox and a continuous metamorphosis rather than an interaction of glances between *La dame, la licorne and le miroir* depicted in the photopoem of *Interlude V*. The Tower, indeed, is a verb, specifies Barthes (1964; Eng. trans. 1985: 238); it "is a complete verb, both active and passive, in which no function, no voice (as we say in grammar, with a piquant ambiguity) is defective", and which transgresses the "habitual divorce of seeing and being seen":

> [T]his radiant position in the order of perception gives it a prodigious propensity to meaning: the Tower attracts meaning, the way a lightning rod attracts thunderbolts; for all lovers of signification, it plays a glamorous part, that of a pure signifier, i.e., of a form in which men unceasingly put *meaning* (which they extract at will from their knowledge, their dreams, their history), without this meaning thereby ever being finite and fixed: who can say what the Tower will be for humanity tomorrow?

6.2.3 Performance and Philosophical Pragmatism

Meaning, symbolizing, signifying: they are situated in a continuous movement in Barthes' semiotics; they are an endless search of the *sense* that the "reader" can create when s/he is not only *seeing* the Tower, and then being at a distance, but also *touching* it, that is, in other words, *performing* and thus making a visit to the Tower.

The concept of "sense" denotes a wide range of aspects, observes the American pragmatist philosopher John Dewey (1934/1987: 27–28), as "the sensory, the sensational, the sensitive, the sensible, and the sentimental, along with the sensuous", to the "sense itself—that is, the meaning of things present in immediate experience". But, continues Dewey,

> sense, as meaning so directly embodied in experience as to be its own illuminated meaning, is the only signification that expresses the function of sense organs when they are carried to full realization. The senses are the organs through which the live creature participates directly in the ongoing of the world about him. In this participation the varied wonder and splendor of this world are made actual for him in the qualities he experiences. This material cannot be opposed

to action, for motor apparatus and "will" itself are the means by which this participation is carried on and directed.

(1934/1987: 28)

To visit the Tower—for admiring the panorama and deconstructing the city to delineate Paris in fragments that are then interpreted and possibly recomposed—means to perform a paradoxical experience, observes Barthes. The visitor does not penetrate into it, but s/he verges on emptiness, that is, grazes the tower without ever ending enclosed in it.

> Here, too, the Tower is a paradoxical object: one cannot be shut up within it since what defines the Tower is its longilineal form and its open structure: How can you be enclosed within emptiness, how can you visit a line? Yet incontestably the Tower is visited: we linger within it, before using it as an observatory. What is happening? What becomes of the great exploratory function of the *inside* when it is applied to this empty and depthless monument which might be said to consist entirely of an exterior substance?
>
> (Barthes, 1964; Eng. trans. 1985: 248)

The Tower develops symbols that belong to the order of total sensations, powerful and indistinct, which are generated not only by external sensory organs—such as sight, smell or hearing—but also by internal sensory organs and thus from the profound life of the body, that is, from those sensations that are called kinesthetic. The act of visiting the Tower constitutes a "poetic performing": changing one's own situation, modifying one's point of view, empathically grasping the profound sense of "feeling-in" (Origgi, 2013: 68) and reliving past sensations, searching the symbolic meanings of the Tower, which is anything but an artifact of immobile, extinguished, only passive iron.

In those feelings and kinesthetic sensations, all the archetypes of sensation mingle and consecrate the Tower as a poetic object, "reduced to that simple line whose sole mythic function is to join, as the poet says, *base and summit*, or again, *earth and heaven*", writes Roland Barthes (1964; Eng. trans. 1985: 237), that is, the Tower as a virtually empty sign which is pure and ineluctable, "*because it means everything*". Understanding what the artwork "says to us", observes Hans-Georg Gadamer (1976, reprint 2000: 185), is therefore a "self-encounter", in which the artwork "confronts us itself" and all that is "familiar is eclipsed"; but

> as an encounter with the authentic, as a familiarity that includes surprise, the experience of art is *experience* in a real sense and must master ever anew the task that experience involves: the task of integrating it into the whole of one's own orientation to a world and one's own self-understanding. The language of art is constituted precisely by

the fact that it speaks to the self-understanding of *every* person, and [. . .] just this expansion of the hermeneutical perspective to include the language of art makes it obvious how little the subjectivity of the act of meaning suffices to denote the object of understanding. But this fact has a general significance, and to that extent aesthetics is an important element of general hermeneutics.

The profound life of the body and the kinesthetic sensations that Barthes calls into question in his semiotics of the Eiffel Tower, together with Gadamer's hermeneutical observations on the experience of art as *"experience in a real sense"*, lead us back to American philosophical pragmatism and, in particular, to the philosophy of mindfulness and somaesthetics of Richard Shusterman. I have already underlined in Chapter 3 the emphasis of Richard Shusterman on the performative character of our aesthetic experience with respect to his philosophical reflection on photography. Photography, emphasizes Shusterman (2012), must be understood not only through the analysis of the photograph itself, as a definite artefact, but also as a process of creating a photograph. And, in order to take a photograph—we have observed—one has to perform with all his/her senses. Thence, the external senses of sight, touch, smell, hearing and taste act together with internal kinesthetic senses to perform the practice of taking the photograph. Shusterman also emphasizes this point in his critical annotations on the phenomenological philosophy of the perception and of the "flesh" of Maurice Merleau-Ponty, in which he writes that, lacking

> in Merleau-Ponty's superb advocacy of the body's philosophical importance is a robust sense of the real body as a site for practical disciplines of conscious reflection that aim at reconstructing somatic perception and performance to achieve more rewarding experience and action.
>
> (2008: 75)

However, adds Shusterman (2008: 75), it seems possible "to combine this pragmatist reconstructive dimension of somatic theory with Merleau-Ponty's basic philosophical insights about the lived body and the primacy of unreflective perception" because the phenomenological philosophy of Maurice Merleau-Ponty "has its own pragmatic flavor".

The performativity of the aesthetic experience is so significant according to the philosophical pragmatism that, according to John Dewey's thought, the aesthetic experience could do without defining itself aesthetically and instead being recognized for what it is: the experience *tout court*, that is to say, to carry out experiences highly relevant in the fullness of their meaning. Aesthetics, notes Dewey (1934/1987: 52–53) "is no intruder in experience from without, whether by way of idle luxury or transcendent ideality"; it is, instead, "the clarified and intensified development of traits that belong to every normally complete experience", even though

> we have no word in the English language that unambiguously includes what is signified by the two words "artistic" and "esthetic". Since "artistic" refers primarily to the act of production and "esthetic" to that of perception and enjoyment, the absence of a term designating the two processes taken together is unfortunate.

Every time we separate works of art from their creation process, "a wall is built around them that renders almost opaque their general significance, with which esthetic theory deals", writes John Dewey (1934/1987: 9); and therefore, aesthetic philosophy has the task of restoring continuity between their "refined and intensified forms of experience" and the "everyday events, doings, and sufferings that are universally recognized to constitute experience". This is a task that reverberates the philosophical opposition of Luigi Pareyson to the limitation of the aesthetic experience around the arts that we have discussed earlier in various parts of this book, and in particular in Chapter 5. It is precisely "the dynamic and developing experiential activity through which" the work of art is both "created and perceived"—emphasizes Shusterman (2001: 102)—that the pragmatist philosophy of John Dewey privileges "over the material object which ordinary, reified thinking identifies (and then commodifies and fetishizes) as the work of art".

I shall conclude this section by underlining that the performative philosophical sensibility reveals the common ground between Continental philosophy and, in particular, the Merleau-Ponty phenomenology, the post-structuralist semiotics of Barthes, the personal hermeneutics of Pareyson, the aesthetic hermeneutics of Gadamer and the American pragmatism of Dewey and Shusterman.

In the next and final section, I will illustrate how the aesthetic, hermeneutic and performative philosophical sensibilities are connected-in-action with the aesthetic, archeological, artistic and empathic-logical approaches to the study of organization.

6.3 Giving Form: Philosophical Sensibilities and Organizational Theory

The "aesthetic", "hermeneutic" and "performative" philosophical sensibilities illustrated in the two previous sections of this chapter represent three *soft* concepts that are capable of portraying and interpreting the hybridization of organizational theory and aesthetic philosophies (Strati, 2016). However, these three sensibilities are *not* able to distinguish, separate and circumscribe organizational aesthetics research in three clearly different correspondent ambits. In other words, none of the three philosophical sensibilities can establish such a close relationship with an approach to the study of organization that excludes any influence from the other two philosophical sensibilities.

Furthermore, my illustration and the discussion of the three philosophical sensibilities have emphasized that they are very different from one another but not clearly separated from one another. If, for example, we have seen them against each other regarding the importance of "flesh" or "language", on other topics it is rather the diversity in the emphasis given to the argument that distinguishes them. For example, we have seen that

- corporeality is not only linked to phenomenology, but also to pragmatism and also to hermeneutics;
- interpretation is not just linguistic, but embodied for all the three philosophical sensibilities;
- lived and relived experience is a fundamental assumption in each of these three sensibilities;
- the artistic and aesthetic experience is not limited to the "art worlds" in both pragmatism and in personal and aesthetic hermeneutics, as well as in phenomenology;
- the user, the reader or the spectator of the work of art represents an active protagonist of the process of creation and of its enjoyment in all three philosophical sensibilities.

Now, what are the connections-in-action between the aesthetic, hermeneutic and performative philosophical sensibilities and the aesthetic, archeological, artistic and empathic-logical organizational approaches?

First of all, it is important to acknowledge that these connections-in-action do not involve all the organizational aesthetics research, but only various fragments of it in addition to the *Art Firm* book of Pierre Guillet de Monthoux (2004) and my *Organization and Aesthetics* (Strati, 1999). As I pointed out in Chapter 1, a large part of the study on the aesthetics of organization shows no interest in philosophy and, instead, reveals and witnesses that it is sensible to conduct research and study of the aesthetic dimension of organization even without founding it in aesthetic philosophies.

If you look at organizational aesthetic research and avoid considering just the "photograph" of it because you want to see the process of creating it, that is, the ways in which it has been configured through debates, teachings and publications in the last thirty years, you may note the following:

1. Its *humus* is represented by the intellectual activities performed to understand symbolically the organization and the organizational life

in terms of organizational cultures (Alvesson and Berg, 1992; Gagliardi, 1990; Hatch, 2006; Martin, 2002; Strati, 1998; Turner, 1990).

2. Its *inner voices* resound the ongoing debates in art-practice studies, cultural studies, feminist gender studies, post-structuralist Foucauldian studies, organizational emotions studies, and visual studies during the *Cultural Turn* of the 1980s (Strati, 2010b), because, as Jean-François Chanlat (2004: XI) observes, organizational aesthetics research has sought very different sources, ranging from the history of art to sociology and the principal theories of the social; therefore, methods of research are hybrid and experimental (Strati, 2009; Taylor and Ladkin, 2009; Warren, 2009; Zanutto and Piras, 2013), as the artistic performance in organization studies attests (Guillet de Monthoux, 2000; *Organizational Aesthetics*, 2016; Scalfi Eghenter, 2018; Steyaert and Hjorth, 2002).

3. Its *European roots* emphasize the critical analysis of the aestheticization of organization (Ramirez, 2005), and they are in a polemic against the aesthetic exploitation of the participants in the organizational life, as is evident in the essays that have reviewed the literature on the aesthetic dimension of organization with an eye to the future configuration of organizational aesthetics research (Beyes, 2016; Dean, Ramírez and Ottensmeyer, 1997; Gagliardi, 2006; Meisiek and Barry, 2014; Strati, 2013; Taylor and Hansen, 2005).

4. Its *intellectual collective construction* touches a variety of organizational subjects, as documented above by all collective publications, such as:

    (a) the international journals devoted to art and aesthetics in organization, that is, *Aesthesis. International Journal of Art and Aesthetics in Management and Organizational Life*, which was published from 2007 to 2009, and the online journal *Organizational Aesthetics* (https://digitalcommons.wpi.edu/oa/);

    (b) the special issues of journals dedicated to aesthetics and organization (*Organization*, 1996); organizing aesthetics (*Human Relations*, 2002); art and management (*Scandinavian Journal of Management*, 2014); art and aesthetics in work, management and organization (*Consumption, Markets and Culture*, 2002; *Culture and Organization*, 2006; *Dragon*, 1987; *Marketing Theory*, 2006; *Tamara: Journal of Critical Postmodern Organization Science*, 2002); and aesthetics and memories of organizational life (*Aesthesis. International Journal of Art and Aesthetics in Management and Organizational Life*, 2008);

    (c) the anthologies on the study of the aesthetics of organization (Linstead and Höpfl, 2000) and its artifactual landscape (Gagliardi, 1990); on the artistic interventions in organizations

(Johansson Sköldberg, Woodilla and Berthoin Antal, 2016); on art, design and aesthetics as experiencing organizations (King and Vickery, 2013); and on the "aesthetic turn" in management (Minahan and Wolfram Cox, 2007);

(d) the monographs on aesthetics and organization (Strati, 1999); on art, management and organization (Guillet de Monthoux, 2004); and on the beauty of social organization (Ramírez, 1991);

(e) the various essays, published in journals, handbooks and encyclopedias, which participate with an aesthetic lens in the organizational study of topics such as the body, the senses and "Practice-based Studies" (Gherardi and Strati, 2012; *Scandinavian Journal of Management*, 2013); as the visual and the organization (Bell, Warren, and Schroeder, 2014); as passion, desire and learning in organization (*Organization*, 2007); as the aesthetics of leadership (Guillet de Monthoux, Gustafsson, and Sjöstrand, 2007); and as play and its interaction with creativity and entrepreneurship (*Organization Studies*, 2018).

5. Its *dialogue with aesthetic philosophies* takes the form of a dialogue between "fragments of knowing"—which we have seen in Chapter 1— that is, through the process of evocative knowledge for which fragments of organizational knowledge evoke fragments of philosophical knowledge that throw a new light on the aesthetics of organization. Furthermore, the dialogues between organizational theories and aesthetic philosophies take place in the contest of the other ongoing dialogues between organizational theory and philosophy—as, for instance, is the case of corporeality and organizational ethics (Pullen and Rhodes, 2014) or of organizational theories and pragmatist philosophy (Lorino, 2018), process philosophy (Helin et al., 2014), and philosophy *tout court* (Mir, Willmott and Greenwood, 2016).

6. Its *weak philosophical appeal*, which is underlined by the rare essays published by researchers and scholars of philosophical aesthetics on the aesthetic discourse on organization. Among these contributions, David A. White (1996) and Dan Eugen Ratiu (2017) conduct a philosophical reflection on the whole area of research of aesthetics and organization theory: the first when the development of this area of organizational theory was at its debut; the second, when, instead, the organizational aesthetics research became a legitimate and institutionalized strand of organization studies. Ole Thyssen (2003), instead, discusses the theme of "organizational aesthetics" in the light of philosophy of communication. Joseph Chytry (2008), on the other hand, examines some of the principal writings in the area of organizational aesthetics research together with other well-known

publications that deal with the theme of the aestheticization of management in contemporary society.

Along the variegated and hybridized scene described before of the writings concerning the study of the aesthetic side of organization, I found (Strati, 2009) that four different research styles have taken "form" (Table 6.1).

Primarily, I wrote (Strati, 1999: 188–190) that the study of art and aesthetics in organizational contexts was not just a single approach—a sort of approach-umbrella—and that the configuration of this strand of organizational studies was instead articulated in three approaches that

Table 6.1 The four research approaches to the study of organization

Approach to the study of organization	Researcher's style	Emphasis on
Aesthetic Formerly: *Empathic-aesthetic* Strati, 1992, 1999	• empathic understanding • imaginary participant observation • aesthetic judgment • evocative process of knowing • "open text" for communicating the outcomes	• collective everyday negotiation of artistic and mundane organizational aesthetics • aesthetics and organizational citizenship • practices in organizations
Archeological Berg, 1987; Berg and Kreiner, 1990	guise of • an archeologist • an historian of art using qualitative research design and methods	• art and aesthetics to study organization as cultures • symbolism of art and aesthetics in organizational life
Artistic Guillet de Monthoux, 2004	• artistic performance in organization • hybridization of artistic creative energy and ratiocinative capacity	• creativity and playfulness of organizational interactions • insights from the management of art for the art of management
Empathic-logical Gagliardi, 1990, 2006	three phases: 1. observation through empathic immersion 2. empathic and logical interpretation 3. logical-analytical illustration of the outcomes	• pre-cognitive knowledge thanks to the pathos of organizational artefacts • organizational control exercised through aesthetics

were forged during the second half of the 1980s, especially in the ambit of the organizational symbolism approach to the study of organization and, more generally, in the contest of the controversy against the paradigm rationalist and positivist:

1. the *archeological approach* (Berg, 1987; Berg and Kreiner, 1990), in which the researcher "assumes the guise of an archaeologist, a social historian of art, an art critic who investigates organizational artefacts" and studies organizational aesthetics in view of a more sophisticated and subtle understanding of the symbolic construction of the organization and of the organizational artifacts;
2. the *empathic-logical approach* (Gagliardi, 1990, 2006), in which the researcher "acts in the twofold guise of a seeker after both empathic and logico-analytic understanding" starting from the empathic immersion to finish with the rigorous logical analysis of the aesthetic findings along three distinct phases of research: observation, interpretation and writing of acquired results;
3. the *empathic-aesthetic approach*—now simply the *aesthetic approach* (Strati, 1992, 1999)—in which the researcher "sets out to obtain aesthetic-intuitive information about the organization using the empathic-aesthetic understanding", observes reflectively this immersive knowledge-gathering process and writes an "open text" to produce the conditions for a process of aesthetic and evocative knowing.

Thus, it was not a single approach that was being used to study the aesthetics of the organization, but three different approaches—which, however, shared a common ground and also overlapped each other in conducting empirical research and of theoretical and methodological reflections. However, later on, just by reflecting on the research methodologies for the chapter " 'Do you do beautiful things?': aesthetics and art in qualitative methods of organization studies" (Strati, 2009) for *The Sage Handbook of Organizational Research Methods*, edited by David Buchanan and Alan Bryman, I noticed that there was also another style of research that had established itself in organizational aesthetic research, even if only more recently:

4. the *artistic approach* (Guillet de Monthoux, 2004), in which the researcher deals with organizational performance as an experiential flow and focuses on the artistic experience in order to gain insights for the management of organizational dynamics and processes, even out of the art world. The researcher—as organizational scholar, art performer or theoretician of art—explores the creativity, the play and the pleasure of inventiveness in the experiential flux of managing organizational life.

The connections-in-action between the aesthetic, hermeneutic and performative philosophical sensibilities and the aesthetic, archaeologic, artistic and empathic-logical approaches are variegated and subjected to hybridization and metamorphosis. What we cannot avoid noticing is that, while the hermeneutic and the performative sensibilities influence all four approaches, the aesthetic philosophical sensibility is fundamental to the aesthetic approach and instead has a much more modest relevance to the archeological approach, in which the symbolic aesthetics of Ernst A. Cassirer (1923–29) and Susanne K. Langer (1942) are particularly influential. On the other hand, the archeological approach is particularly attentive to the study of the symbolism of the aesthetic dimension of the organization, something which, it's nice to stress, is relevant for all four approaches.

Then, just as a homage to the beginnings of the aesthetic discourse on organization within the *humus* of the symbolic approach to the study of organizations as cultures, I would like to close this section by quoting from Langer's *Philosophy in a New Key* the following philosophical annotations:

> Everybody knows that language is a very poor medium for expressing our emotional nature. [. . .] There is, however, a kind of symbolism peculiarly adapted to the explication of "unspeakable" things, though it lacks the cardinal virtue of language, which is denotation. The most highly developed type of such pure connotational semantic is music. We are not talking nonsense when we say that a certain musical progression is significant, or that a given phrase lacks meaning, or a player's rendering fails to convey the import of a passage.
>
> (1942: 100–101)

Concluding Remarks

Chapter 6 closes Part II of the book dedicated to the three philosophical sensibilities that emerged in my reflections on the ongoing dialogues between "fragments of organizational knowledge" and "fragments" of aesthetic philosophy—fragments that have little in common with *ad hoc* cropping because their boundaries are not delimited, but interrupted, as we saw in Chapter 1. In these conclusive considerations, I shall only emphasize the characteristics of the concept of *philosophical sensibility* that has been used in Part II and, more generally, throughout the book, and which must be understood as an organizational "root metaphor" rather than a "sociological typology".

My intent, in fact, is to portray the creation process of the strand of organizational theories that deals with the aesthetic dimension of organization by considering it in its complex and composite configuration that is due, on the one hand, to the influence of three philosophical sensibilities—aesthetic, hermeneutic, and performative—and, on the other hand, to its articulation in four approaches to the study of organization—aesthetic, archeological, artistic and empathic-logical. With the awareness that these concepts—the philosophical sensibility and the approach—are "incomplete or unfinished concepts designating emergent phenomena", as John Shotter (2011: 256) points out, I want to use them anyway to draw the attention of scholars and students of organizational phenomena to their future oriented characteristics, since—as in the case of Shotter's *"prospective, descriptive concepts"*—the concepts of philosophical sensibility and of approach to the study of the aesthetic dimension of organizational life

> cannot be "summed up" as having an essence, they work by helping us to pick out from an otherwise amorphous background, certain distinctive features or crucial aspects relevant to our current ends-in-view. In other words, their practical use is of a hermeneutical kind, in the sense that, by tacking back and forth between them and a particular event or phenomenon, we can bring to light *general* features within such an otherwise *unique* event, such that the words we use in the descriptions we provide, can arouse in us appropriate anticipations of what we next might expect to happen.

So, in this chapter, I highlighted the principal philosophical foundations of organizational aesthetics research. While acknowledging the wide variety of philosophies taken into due account in the study of art and aesthetics in organization, I illustrated the roots of the aesthetic discourse on organization in the thought of the founders of philosophical aesthetics—Addison, Vico, Baumgarten and Kant—during the Enlightenment, as well as in the work of more recent philosophers, sociologists and semiologists: Roland Barthes, John Dewey, Hans-Georg Gadamer, Luigi Pareyson, Michel Polanyi, Maurice Merleau-Ponty, Michel Serres, Georg Simmel and Richard Shusterman.

Other philosophers and social scientists have also been mentioned—from Rosi Braidotti to Ernst Cassirer, Roberto Esposito, Susanne Langer, Donna Haraway and Jacques Rancière—because they participate in composing the wide range of philosophies and social theories considered along the intellectual collective construction of the field of studying art and aesthetics in organization. Nevertheless, my focus has been on the authors and themes that could characterize distinctively the aesthetic, hermeneutic and performative philosophical sensibilities that I consider to constitute the principal philosophical influences on the four approaches to the study of organization, which characterize and articulate this rather recent area of organizational theory, that is, on the "aesthetic approach", the "archeological approach", the "artistic approach" and the "empathic-logical approach".

With Chapter 6, my reflections on the relevance of aesthetic philosophies for organizational theories have reached their end. Before concluding this book with the Epilogue, however, the rhythm of the words will be interrupted and distracted by the visual language of the photopoem in *Interlude VI: Homage to Niki de Saint Phalle*.

References

Addison, J. (1712). On the pleasures of the imagination, *The Spectator*, in Addison, J. and Steele, R. (eds.), *Selections from The Tatler and Spectator*. Ed. Ross, A. London: Penguin, 1982.

Aesthesis. International Journal of Art and Aesthetics in Management and Organizational Life (2008). Special themed issue on "Aesthetics/The construction and re-construction of memories of organizational life", 2 (1). Edited by Guillet de Monthoux, P. and A. Strati. (A selection of articles is available at the Aesthesis Archive: https://digitalcommons.wpi.edu/aesthesis)

Alvesson, M. and Berg, P. O. (1992). *Corporate Culture and Organizational Symbolism. An Overview*. Berlin: de Gruyter.

Barbaras, R. (2009). *La perception. Essai sur le sensible*. Paris: Librairie Philosophique J. Vrin.

Barthes, R. (1964). *La Tour Eiffel*. Photographs by A. Martin. Paris: Delpire. (Partial English trans.: Barthes, R., *A Barthes Reader*. Ed. Sontag, S. New York: Hill and Wang, 1985, pp. 236–250).

Baudrillard, J. (1978). *La précession des simulacres*. Paris: Éditions de Minuit. (English trans.: *Simulacra and Simulations*. Ann Arbor, MI: University of Michigan Press, 1994).

Baumgarten, A. G. (1735). *Meditationes philosophicae de nonnullis ad poema pertinentibus*. Halle: Grunert.

Baumgarten, A. G. (1750–58). *Aesthetica*, Vol. I–II. Frankfurt am Oder: Kleyb. (Photostat: Olms: Hildesheim, 1986).

Bell, E., Warren, S. and Schroeder, J. (eds.) (2014). *The Routledge Companion to Visual Organization*. London: Routledge.

Berg P. O. (1987). Some notes on corporate artifacts, *Scos Note-Work*, 6 (1): 24–28.

Berg, P. O. and Kreiner, K. (1990). Corporate architecture: turning physical settings into symbolic resources, in Gagliardi, P. (ed.), *Symbols and Artifacts: Views of the Corporate Landscape*. New York: Berlin de Gruyter, pp. 41–67.

Beyes, T. (2016). Art, aesthetics and organization, in Czarniawska, B. (ed.), *A Research Agenda for Management and Organization Studies*. Cheltenham: Elgar, pp. 115–125.

Biernoff, S. (2005). Carnal relations: embodied sight in Merleau-Ponty, Roger Bacon and St Francis, *Journal of Visual Culture*, 4 (1): 39–52.

Binet, L. (2015). *La septième fonction du langage*. Paris: Éditions Grasset et Fasquelle. (English trans.: *The Seventh Function of Language*. New York: Farrar, Straus and Giroux, 2017).

Brady, E. (2013). *The Sublime in Modern Philosophy: Aesthetics, Ethics, and Nature*. Cambridge: Cambridge University Press.

Braidotti, R. (2013). *The Posthuman*. Cambridge: Polity Press.

Bubbio, P. D. (2009). Introduction. Luigi Pareyson: the third way to Hermeneutics, in Pareyson, L. (ed.), *Existence, Interpretation, Freedom: Selected Writings*. Ed. Bubbio, P. D. Aurora, CO: The Davies Group, pp. 1–32.

Calabrese, O. (1985). *Il linguaggio dell'arte*. Milano: Bompiani.

Caroutch, F. Y. (2002). *La licorne: symboles, mythes et réalités*. Paris: Pygmalion/ Gérard Watelet.

Cassirer, A. E. (1923–29). *Philosophie der symbolischen Formen, I–III*. Berlin: Bruno Cassirer. (English trans.: *The Philosophy of Symbolic Forms, I–III*. New Haven, CT: Yale University Press, 1955–57).

Cassirer, A. E. (1932). *Die Philosophie der Aufklärung*. Tübingen: J. C. B. Mohr. (English trans.: *The Philosophy of the Enlightenment*. Princeton, NJ: Princeton University Press, 1951).

Chanlat, J. F. (2004). Préface, in Strati A. (ed.), *Esthétique et organization*. Sainte-Foy, QC: Les Presses de l'Université Laval, pp. vii–xiii.

Chytry, J. (2008). Organizational aesthetics: the artful firm and the aesthetic moment in contemporary business and management theory, *Aesthesis: International Journal of Art and Aesthetics in Management and Organizational Life*, 2 (2): 60–72, http://digitalcommons.wpi.edu/aesthesis/23.

Consumption, Markets and Culture (2002). Special Issue on "Aesthetics and management—Business bridges to art", 5 (1). Edited by Guillet de Monthoux P. and A. Strati.

Crossley, N. (1995). Merleau-Ponty, the elusive body and carnal sociology, *Body & Society*, 1 (1): 43–63.

Culture and Organization (2006). Special issue on "Art of management and organization conference series", 12 (1). Edited by Watkins, C., King, I. and S. Linstead.

Dean, J. W., Ramírez, R. and E. Ottensmeyer (1997). An aesthetic perspective on organizations, in Cooper, C. and Jackson, S. (eds.), *Creating Tomorrow's Organizations: A Handbook for Future Research in Organizational Behavior*. Chichester: Wiley, pp. 419–437.

Deleuze, G. and Guattari, F. (1980). *Mille plateaux: capitalism et schizophénie*. Paris: Éditions de Minuit. (English trans.: *A Thousand Plateaus: Capitalism and Schizophrenia*. Ed. Massumi, B. Minneapolis: University of Minnesota Press, 1987).

De Gendt, A. M. (2016). Du masculin au féminin: le changement de sexe des cinq sens au seuil de la Renaissance, in Duhl, O. A. and Fritz, J. M. (eds.), *Les cinq sens entre Moyen Âge et Renaissance*. Dijon: Éditions Universitaires de Dijon, pp. 71–93.

Dewey, J. (1934/1987). *Art as Experience—The Later Works, 1925–1953*. Vol. 10: 1934. Ed. Boydston, J. A. Carbondale: Southern Illinois University Press.

Dragon, the Journal of SCOS (1987). Special issue on "Art and organization", 2 (4). Edited by P. J. Benghozi.

Duhl, O. A. (2016). Vers une esthétique du sensible, in Duhl, O. A. and Fritz, J. M. (eds.), *Les cinq sens entre Moyen Âge et Renaissance*. Dijon: Éditions Universitaires de Dijon, pp. 19–27.

Erlande-Brandenburg, A. (1989). *The Lady and the Unicorn*. Paris: Éditions de la Réunion des musées nationaux.

Esposito, R. (2010). *Pensiero vivente: Origine e attualità della filosofia italiana*. Torino: Einaudi. (English trans.: *Living Thought. The Origins and Actuality of Italian Philosophy*. Stanford, CA: Stanford University Press, 2012).

Fritz, J. M. (2016). Les cinq sens au prisme de la littérature: allégorie et sérialité, in Duhl, O. A. and Fritz, J. M. (eds.), *Les cinq sens entre Moyen Âge et Renaissance*. Dijon: Éditions Universitaires de Dijon, pp. 7–18.

Gadamer, H. G. (1976). Aesthetics and hermeneutics, in Gadamer, H. G. (ed.), *Philosophical Hermeneutics*. Ed. Linge, D. E. Berkeley: University of California Press, pp. 95–104. Reprinted in Cazeaux, C. (ed.) (2000). *The Continental Aesthetics Reader*. London: Routledge, pp. 181–186.

Gadamer, H. G. (2006). Classical and philosophical hermeneutics, *Theory, Culture & Society*, 23 (1): 29–56.

Gagliardi, P. (ed.) (1990). *Symbols and Artifacts: Views of the Corporate Landscape*. Berlin: de Gruyter.

Gagliardi, P. (2006). Exploring the aesthetic side of organizational life, in Clegg, S. R., Hardy, C., Lawrence, T. B. and Nord, W. R. (eds.), *The Sage Handbook of Organization Studies*. London: Sage, pp. 701–724.

Gherardi, S. and Strati, A. (2012). *Learning and Knowing in Practice-based Studies*. Cheltenham: Edward Elgar.

Gherardi, S. and Strati, A. (2017). Luigi Pareyson's *Estetica: Teoria della formatività* and its implication for organization studies, *Academy of Management Review*, 42 (4): 745–755.

Ghiazza, S. (2005). *La metafora tra scienza e letteratura*. Firenze: Le Monnier Università.

Guattari, F. (1992). *Chaosmose*. Paris: Éditions Galilée. (English trans.: *Chaosmosis. An Ethico-aesthetic Paradigm*. Sidney: Power Publications, 1995).

Guillet de Monthoux, P. (2000). Performing the absolute: Marina Abramović organizing the unfinished business of Arthur Schopenhauer, *Organization Studies*, 21 (0): 29–51.

Guillet de Monthoux, P. (2004). *The Art Firm: Aesthetic Management and Metaphysical Marketing from Wagner to Wilson*. Stanford, CA: Stanford Business Books.

Guillet de Monthoux, P., Gustafsson, C. and Sjöstrand, S. E. (eds.) (2007). *Aesthetic Leadership: Managing Fields of Flow in Art and Business*. Basingstoke: Palgrave Macmillan.

Haraway, D. J. (1991). *Simians, Cyborgs, & Women: The Reinvention of Nature*. New York: Routledge.

Hatch, M. J. (2006). *Organization Theory: Modern, Symbolic, and Postmodern Perspectives*. With Ann L. Cunliffe. Oxford: Oxford University Press. 1st edn. 1997.

Helin, J., Hernes, T., Hjorth, D. and Holt, R. (eds.) (2014). *The Oxford Handbook of Process Philosophy and Organization Studies*. Oxford: Oxford University Press.

Human Relations (2002). Special Issue on "Organising aesthetics", 55 (7). Edited by Strati, A. and P. Guillet de Monthoux.

Johansson Sköldberg, U., Woodilla, J. and Berthoin Antal, A. (eds.) (2016). *Artistic Interventions in Organizations: Research, Theory and Practice*. London: Routledge.

Kant, I. (1790). Kritik der Urteilskraft, in Kant, I. (ed.), *Werke in zwölf Bänden*, Vol. X. Ed. Weischedel, W. Frankfurt am Main: Suhrkamp, 1968. (English trans.: *The Critique of Judgement*. Ed. Meredith, J. C. Oxford: Oxford University Press, 1952).

King, I. W. and Vickery, J. (eds.) (2013). *Experiencing Organisations: New Aesthetic Perspectives*. Faringdon: Libri Publishing.

Küpers, W. M. and the Senses (2013). The sense-making of the senses—perspectives on embodied aesthesis & aesthetics in organising & organisations, in King, I. W. and Vickery, J. (eds.), *Experiencing Organisations: New Aesthetic Perspectives*. Faringdon: Libri Publishing, pp. 33–55.

Langer, S. K. (1942). *Philosophy in a New Key: A Study in the Symbolism of Reason, Rite, and Art*. 4th edn. 1963. Cambridge, MA: Harvard University Press.

Legros R. (2005). La naissance de l'individu moderne, in Foccroulle, B., Legros, R., and Todorov, T. (eds.), *La naissance de l'individu dans l'art*. Paris: Grasset, pp. 121–200.

Linstead, S. and Höpfl, H. (eds.) (2000). *The Aesthetic of Organization*. London: Sage.

Lorino, P. (2018). *Pragmatism and Organization Studies*. Oxford: Oxford University Press.

Marketing Theory (2006). Special issue on "Aesthetics, images and vision", 6 (1). Edited by J. E. Schroeder.

Martin, J. (2002). *Organizational Culture: Mapping the Terrain*. Beverly Hills, CA: Sage.

May, T. (2005). To change the world, to celebrate life: Merleau-Ponty and Foucault on the body. *Philosophy & Social Criticism*, 31 (5–6): 517–531.

Meisiek, S. and Barry, D. (2014). The science of making management an art, *Scandinavian Journal of Management*, 30 (1): 134–141.

Merleau-Ponty, M. (1945). *Phénoménologie de la perception*. Paris: Éditions Gallimard. (English trans.: *Phenomenology of Perception*. Ed. Williams, F. and D. Guerrière. London: Routledge, 2012).

Merleau-Ponty, M. (1948). *Sens et non-sens*. Paris: Éditions Nagel. (English trans.: *Sense and Non-Sense*. Ed. Dreyfus, H. L. and P. Allen Dreyfus. Evanston, IL: Northwestern University Press, 1964).

Merleau-Ponty, M. (1960). *Signes*. Paris: Éditions Gallimard. (English trans.: *Signs*. Ed. McCleary, R. C. Evanston, IL: Northwestern University Press, 1964).

Merleau-Ponty, M. (1964). *Le visible et l'invisible*. Paris: Éditions Gallimard. (English trans.: *The Visible and the Invisible*. Evanston, IL: Northwestern University Press, 1964).

Merleau-Ponty, M. (2002). *Causeries 1948*. Paris: Éditions du Seuil. (English trans.: *The World of Perception*. New York: Routledge, 2004).

Minahan, S. and Wolfram Cox, J. (eds.) (2007). *The Aesthetic Turn in Management*. Gower: Ashgate.

Mir, R., Willmott, H. and Greenwood, M. (eds.) (2016). *The Routledge Companion to Philosophy in Organization Studies*. London: Routledge.

Organization (1996). Special Issue on "Essays on aesthetics and organization", 3 (2). Edited by E. Ottensmeyer.

Organization (2007). Special Issue on "The passion for knowing and learning", 14 (3). Edited by Gherardi, S., Nicolini, D. and A. Strati.

Organization Studies (2018). Special issue on "Organizational creativity, play and entrepreneurship", 39 (2–3). Edited by Hjorth, D., Strati, A., Drakopoulou Dodd, S., and E. Weik.

Organizational Aesthetics (2016). Special issue on "Dance", 5 (1). Edited by Biehl-Missal, B. and C. Springborg.

Origgi, G. (2013). L'empathie est-elle une compétence sociale?, in Gefen, A. and Vouilloux, B. (eds.), *Empathie et esthétique*. Paris: Hermann Éditeurs, pp. 57–70.

Pareyson, L. (1943). *Studi sull'esistenzialismo*. Firenze: Sansoni. (Partial English trans.: Pareyson, L., *Existence, Interpretation, Freedom: Selected Writings*. Ed. Bubbio, P. D. Aurora, CO: The Davies Group, 2009).

Pareyson, L. (1954). *Estetica. Teoria della formatività*. Torino: Edizioni di "Filosofia". Reprinted 1988, Milano: Bompiani. (Partial English trans.: Pareyson, L., *Existence, Interpretation, Freedom: Selected Writings*. Ed. Bubbio, P. D. Aurora, CO: The Davies Group, 2009).

Polanyi, M. (1958). *Personal Knowledge: Towards a Post-critical Philosophy*. 2nd edn. 1962. London: Routledge and Kegan Paul.

Prezzo, R. (2004). Il primato di un paradosso, in Merleau-Ponty, M. (ed.), *Il primato della percezione e le sue conseguenze filosofiche*. Milano: Medusa, pp. 5–14.

Pullen, A. and Rhodes, C. (2014). Corporeal ethics and the politics of resistance in organizations, *Organization*, 21 (6): 782–796.

Ramírez, R. (1991). *The Beauty of Social Organization*. Munich: Accedo.

Ramírez, R. (2005). The aesthetics of cooperation. *European Management Review* 2, pp. 28–35.

Rancière, J. (2004). *Malaise dans l'esthétique*. Paris: Éditions Galilée. (English trans.: *Aesthetics and its Discontents*. Cambridge: Polity, 2009).

Rancière, J. (2011). *Aisthesis. Scènes du régime esthétique de l'art*. Paris: Éditions Galilée. (English trans.: *Aisthesis: Scenes from the Aesthetic Regime of Art*. London: Verso, 2013).

Ratiu, D. E. (2017). The aesthetic account of everyday life in organizations: a report on recent developments in organizational research, *The Journal of Arts Management, Law, and Society*, 47 (3): 178–191.

Sartre, J. P. (1943). *L'être et le néant. Essai d'ontologie phénoménologique*. Paris: Éditions Gallimard. (English trans.: *Being and Nothingness. An Essay on Phenomenological Ontology*. Ed. Barnes, H. New York: Philosophical Library, 1956).

Scalfi Eghenter, A. (2018). Organizational creativity, play and entrepreneurship, *Organization Studies*, 39 (2–3): 169–190.

Scandinavian Journal of Management (2013). Special issue on "Body, senses and knowing in organization", 29 (4). Edited by Gherardi, S., Meriläinen, S., Strati, A., and A. Valtonen.

Scandinavian Journal of Management (2014). Special issue on "Art and management", 30 (1). Edited by Meisiek, S. and D. Barry.

Serres, M. (2003). *Les cinq sens*. Paris: Hachette Littératures (or. edn 1985). (English trans.: *The Five Senses: A Philosophy of Mingled Bodies*. Trans. Sankey, M. and P. Cowley. London: Bloomsbury, 2009).

Shotter, J. (2011). Knowledge in transition: the role of prospective, descriptive concepts in a practice-situated, hermeneutical-phronetic social science, *Management Learning*, 43 (3): 245–260.

Shusterman, R. (2001). Pragmatism: Dewey, in Gaut, B. and Lopes, D. McIver (eds.), *The Routledge Companion to Aesthetics*. London: Routledge, pp. 97–106.

Shusterman, R. (2008). *Body Consciousness. A Philosophy of Mindfulness and Somaesthetics*. Cambridge: Cambridge University Press.

Shusterman, R. (2012). Photography as performative process, *The Journal of Aesthetics and Art Criticism*, 70 (1): 67–77.

Simmel, G. (1908). *Soziologie. Untersuchungen über die Formen der Vergesellschaftung*. Leipzig: Dunker & Humblot. (English trans.: *Sociology. Inquiries into the Construction of Social Forms*, Vol. I–II. Ed. Blasi, A. J., Jacobs, A. K. and M. Kanjireathinkal. Leiden: Brill, 2009).

Steyaert, C. and Hjorth, D. (2002). "Thou art a Scholar, Speak to It . . ."—on spaces of speech: a script, *Human Relations*, 55 (7): 767–797.

Strati, A. (1992). Aesthetic understanding of organizational life, *Academy of Management Review*, 17 (3): 568–581.

Strati, A. (1998). Organizational symbolism as a social construction: a perspective from the sociology of knowledge, *Human Relations*, 51 (11): 1379–1402.

Strati, A. (1999). *Organization and Aesthetics*. London: Sage.

Strati, A. (2003). Knowing in practice: aesthetic understanding and tacit knowledge, in Nicolini, D., Gherardi, S. and Yanow, D. (eds.), *Knowing in Organizations: a practice-based approach*. Armonck: M.E. Sharpe, pp. 53–75. Reprinted in Gherardi, S. and Strati, A. (2012). *Learning and Knowing in Practice-based Studies*. Cheltenham: Edward Elgar, pp. 16–38.

Strati, A. (2007). Sensible knowledge and practice-based learning, *Management Learning*, 38 (1): 61–77. Reprinted in Gherardi, S. and Strati, A. (2012). *Learning and Knowing in Practice-based Studies*. Cheltenham: Edward Elgar, pp. 77–93.

Strati, A. (2009). "Do you do beautiful things?": aesthetics and art in qualitative methods of organization studies, in Buchanan, D. and Bryman A. (eds.), *The Sage Handbook of Organizational Research Methods*. London: Sage, pp. 230–245. Reprinted in Gherardi, S. and Strati, A. (2012). *Learning and Knowing in Practice-based Studies*. Cheltenham: Edward Elgar, pp. 194–209.

Strati, A. (2010a). *Che cos'è l'estetica organizzativa*. Roma: Carocci.

Strati, A. (2010b). Aesthetic understanding of work and organizational life: approaches and research developments, *Sociology Compass*, 4 (10): 880–893, https://onlinelibrary.wiley.com/toc/17519020/2010/4/10.

Strati, A. (2013). Becoming or process: what future for the aesthetic discourse in organizations, in King, I. W. and Vickery, J. (eds.), *Experiencing Organisations: New Aesthetic Perspectives*. Faringdon: Libri Publishing, pp. 223–248.

Strati, A. (2016). Aesthetics and design: an epistemology of the unseen, in Mir, R., Willmott, H. and Greenwood, M. (eds.), *The Routledge Companion to Philosophy in Organization Studies*. London: Routledge, pp. 251–259.

Tamara: Journal of Critical Postmodern Organization Science (2002). Special Issue on "Art and aesthetics at work", 2 (1). Edited by Carr, A. and P. Hancock.

Taylor, S. S. and Hansen, H. (2005). Finding form: looking at the field of organizational aesthetics, *Journal of Management Studies*, n. 42 (6): 1211–1231.

Taylor, S. S. and Ladkin, D. (2009). Understanding arts-based methods in managerial development, *Academy of Management Learning & Education* 8 (1): 55–69.

Thyssen, O. (2003). *Aesthetisk ledelse. Om organisationer og brugskunst*. Copenhagen: Gyldendal. (English trans.: *Aesthetic Communication*. Basingstoke: Palgrave Macmillan, 2011).

Turner, B. A. (ed.) (1990). *Organizational Symbolism*. Berlin: de Gruyter.

Vico, G. (1725). *Principi di una scienza nuova*. Napoli: Mosca. 3rd edn. 1744. (English trans.: *The New Science of Giambattista Vico*. Ed. Bergin, T. G. and M. H. Fisch. Ithaca, NY: Cornell University Press, 1968).

Warren, S. (2009). Visual methods in organizational research, in Buchanan, D. and Bryman, A. (eds.), *The Sage Handbook of Organizational Research Methods*. London: Sage, pp. 566–582.

White, D. A. (1996). "It's working beautifully!": philosophical reflections on aesthetics and organization theory, *Organization*, 3 (2): 195–208.

Zanutto, A. and Piras, E. (2013). Researching the aesthetics of organization, in King, I. W. and Vickery, J. (eds.), *Experiencing Organisations: New Aesthetic Perspectives*. Faringdon: Libri Publishing, pp. 177–192.

nterlude VI: *Homage to Niki de Saint Phalle*, 2018

le Leica M, software Adobe Photoshop

Epilogue
Playing with Philosophical Aesthetics to Understand Organization

In the Epilogue, I shall return to the relevance of philosophy in organizational theory to conclude *Organizational Theory and Aesthetic Philosophies* underlining an important feature of the dialogue that organizational scholars and students can establish with philosophy more generally, but, *in specie*, with the aesthetic philosophy: this dialogue is grounded in playfulness, creativity, irony and self-irony, and reflective feeling. And, in fact, although I am not a philosopher, but a sociologist of organizations and an art photographer, in this book I have been "playing" with aesthetic philosophies, researching and creating connections-in-action between "fragments" of organizational knowledge and "fragments" of philosophical aesthetics.

These fragments, as I have pointed out in various parts of the book, are not made up of *ad-hoc* cut-outs; on the contrary, they are fragments that have interrupted edges—in the manner of Gaudí, as we saw in Chapter 1—which often emerged only in a *casual* way during my empirical research and, also, in the methodological and theoretical study.

There is indeed a philosophical basis for my playing with the aesthetic philosophies: "everyone has a right to this excitement, to this taste, to this play", observes the Italian writer and philosopher Ermanno Bencivenga (1988; Eng. trans. 1994: IX), to the aesthetic experience of excitement and the "intense, sensual taste that feeds" the research of philosophers.

Bencivenga argues on several occasions that philosophy *is defined* as a "play". First of all, he underlines that (Bencivenga, 2013: 130) "with all due respect to Descartes", it is not really true that "the mind gives us clearer and more distinct ideas than the body does"; in the mind "there usually reigns great obscurity and confusion" that the corporeal performance of physical movements can dissipate, as happens, for example, in practices in organizations—practices such as that of "writing". Secondly, "philosophy as a play" is not just a metaphor for philosophical research. It is, instead, the definition of philosophy, because of the "creativity and passion—and transgression, learning, and risk" which characterize the philosophical work, and because "a philosophy is worthy of our attention and participation if it displaces us and fascinates us, it irritates us and flatters us, makes us live repeated *Ah-ha experiences* and raises us objections and disagree to no end" (Bencivenga, 2013: 140–141).

I illustrated in Chapter 1 my surprise when "discovering" the organizational aesthetics—as I like to call it ironically—occurred during my sociological research concerning the introduction of the departmental level in the structure of the Italian university at the beginning of the 1980s. In the same chapter, I also described how important my "discovery" of philosophical aesthetics was to achieving a more subtle and refined understanding of the university department as a symbolic construction of organizational cultures.

Always in Chapter 1, I pointed to some of the principal characteristics of my "aesthetic approach" to the study of organizational life, such as attention to practices in organizations and the emphasis on personal knowledge, sensible performing, the tacit dimension of knowing, metaphorical and poetic understanding, and aesthetic judgment. In Chapters 4 and 5, I then discussed more extensively the aesthetic philosophies with which my "aesthetic approach" is in dialogue, as well as the phenomenological and post-humanist awareness that characterize the approach.

Photography and art photography have been used in the book, especially in Part I, both as a metaphor for the area of organizational aesthetics research and as an empirical field in which to explore, illustrate and discuss the relevance of philosophical aesthetics in organizational theory. I have emphasized in this way the blurred, equivocal and hybridized relations between art, design and worldly aesthetics, and at the same time I have underlined the crucial importance to aesthetically appreciate an organizational artefact, or even an ephemeral and impalpable organizational event, to comprehend aspects of the creation process, elements of aesthetic negotiation and the citizenship of aesthetics in the performance of the practices in organizations. The English director of the Design Museum in London, Deyan Sudjic, underlines these characteristics of organizational aesthetics, observing that the "design", in our society,

> makes uses of all the senses. The smell of leader or wood or ink transforms our responses to a car or an interior or a book fresh from the printer. Fragrances are prepared with the skill of generations of experts to convey a wide range of messages, relying on associations based on memory. The soft touch of a fabric, the coldness of metal, the quality of travertine that has been warmed in the sun, the sound of a keyboard in use or a switch operating, or a camera shutter, have also to take on symbolic qualities which are considered and manipulated as much as any visual signal. Preparing food and making wine are not generally described as design, but they are very closely related to it. And our sense of taste determines our responses to so many objects—not least the china or the glass that we use for our eating utensils.

The most successful designs are those that make simultaneous use of all of these qualities, and do it with conscious understanding of what they can do.

(2008: 89)

Equally important is my emphasis throughout this book on the freedom that aesthetic understanding gives to human beings in their interactions with other living beings and the pre-cognitive agency of the *pathos* of the artefacts. The aesthetic study of organizations is of particular importance, I have emphasized elsewhere, to "give form" to

> how organisational citizenship and democracy can be shaped in the everyday routine work, since it investigates how individuals and groups operate by listening to their feelings, desires, tastes, talents and passions, and by negotiating them—achieving success or failure—in interactions where they deploy their organisational expertise, which is not merely mental, but on the contrary rooted in the corporeality of sensible knowledge.
>
> The aesthetic approach studies, in fact, how, through the negotiative processes that distinguish interaction in organisations, the tastes of people at work are educated, because one way of working is defined as elegant, another as clumsy, yet another as disgusting or revolting. That is to say, it studies how negotiated aesthetic judgements are formulated on the basis of feelings which give salience to the *pathos* of the materiality of everyday life in organisations constituted by corporeality and artifacts to which aesthetic, though impalpable, form is given and which makes them beautiful or horrendous, or just kitsch, to the taste of those concerned.
>
> (Strati, 2014: 126)

The philosopher Dan Eugen Ratiu (2017: 181–182) sees in this—that is, in the fact that "organizations should be understood in terms of relationships between aesthetics and materiality"—a fundamental principle of the distinction he proposes between this "strong" version of organizational aesthetics research and the "weak" version of it, which

> is concerned more with "organization *plus* aesthetics", and accepts and compounds a dualism between the rational and the non-rational in which the latter is demoted to a secondary interest. The "strong" version instead obviates this dualism; moreover, it involves opening up new questions about the experiences of organizational life and making fundamentally new claims about the ontology of organization or ways of organizing by appreciating that "organization *is* aesthetic". [. . .]

Such a strand is apparent in the work of Strati, Pasquale Gagliardi, Guillet de Monthoux, Taylor and Hansen, to name some of the OA's

[Organizational Aesthetics] proponents. Against the approaches that privilege the mental, cognitive, and rational dimensions of social action, the approaches within the "strong" version of OA focus on the *material*, *sensible*, and *emotional* dimensions of everyday life and work relations in organizations (Strati, 2010: 885), and especially on that fundamental part of the human experience which was neglected by the rationalist-utilitarian paradigms, "the way we perceive and feel reality and the sensory experience" (Gagliardi, 2007: 332).

In this sense, in the Special Issue dedicated to the philosophy of design by the journal *Figures de l'art* (2013), edited by Bernard Lafargue and Stéphanie Cardoso, an important distinction—both from a sociological and a philosophical point of view—between "strong" and "weak" design is underlined by Claire Azéma (2013), drawing on the philosophy of "Weak thought" of Gianni Vattimo, of which we discussed in Chapter 1, and the philosophy of pragmatism of John Dewey that we saw in Chapter 6. The "weak design", writes Azéma (2013: 71), introduces "a discontinuity between producer and user, produces experiences of resistance that promote awareness of the present" and the conscious use that "makes us aware of the resistance that exists between our organism and our environment daily" and which allows us to reclaim our lived experience and "to become aware of our singularity through that of experience".

These considerations evoke the debates on "aesthetic capitalism" (Murphy and de La Fuente, 2014) that we saw in Chapter 3, as well as on the subject of the art, aesthetics and design that "anesthetize" our aesthetic understanding (Strati and Guillet de Monthoux, 2002), our sensible knowing and judging, as emphasized by the German philosopher Odo Marquard (1989) in his reflections based on hermeneutic and skeptical philosophy.

Furthermore, Luc Boltanski and Ève Chiapello (1999; Eng. trans. 2005: 326) observe that even the art critique against the new spirit of capitalism "was, rather, the result of its seeming success and the ease with which it found itself recuperated and exploited by capitalism". The demand for autonomy, creativity, authenticity and liberation that were at the basis of art critique were recuperated in various forms by capitalism, and this did not even "bring about a transfer to the social critique" (Boltanski and Chiapello, 1999; Eng. trans. 2005: 327). However, Wolfgang Welsh, another German philosopher who pays particular attention to postmodernist themes, specifies that aestheticization in contemporary society should neither "be affirmed nor rejected without qualification" (1996: 19).

This is the philosophical debate on art, aesthetics and design in our contemporary societies that emphasizes the photopoem *Homage to Niki de Saint Phalle* shown in *Interlude VI*. It does so with a tribute to the

"Nanas" created by the French artist Niki de Saint Phalle, who was inspired by the sculptures in the Park Güell realized by the Catalan architect Antoni Gaudí in the Gràcia district of the city of Barcelona, Spain.

As for the "Nanas" of the photopoem *Homage to Niki de Saint Phalle*, the reader can also imagine the parts of the scene where the two "Nanas" are situated that are not visible in *Interlude VI*. In fact, on the red cloth that serves as background for the two "Nanas", few words appear, both in French and in English: "ELLES MANGENT, MANGENT, MAN-GENT . . ."/"THEY EAT, AND EAT, AND EAT . . .". Voilà, once again, the language—as we saw with the sixth tapestry, *À mon seul désir*, which we discussed in Chapter 6—to constitute the carnal "I" of the two "Nanas".

"ELLES MANGENT, MANGENT, MANGENT . . ."/"THEY EAT, AND EAT, AND EAT . . .", however, is not the title of this artwork by Niki de Saint Phalle. The title is *Le Thé chez Angeline*, that is, the tea at Angeline's home, and it is a painted sculpture realized in polyester in 1971 that belongs to the series "The Devouring Mothers" and is now at the Museum of Moderne Kunst in Wien.

The last thing I shall say about *Homage to Niki de Saint Phalle* is that it provides only a detail of *Le Thé chez Angeline*, in black and white, and that this photopoem is composed of several digital photographs that I took with my Leica M during the exhibition held in 2014 at the Grand Palais in Paris, France. I then manipulated the digital photographs with the Adobe Photoshop software, creating an image that reveals how it was made, showing the overlap of the different files made to give a sense of the texture of the table, the flowers and the cups, as well as the hands, the faces and bodies of the "Nanas".

I also invented a third "Nana", the shadow, that is, which, being a silhouette, brings into evidence the corporeity of the other subjects—the two "Nanas", the table, the cups, the flowers, the floor and the walls—and also the kitsch that pervades the ceremonial *pathos* of the rite of having tea at Angeline's place. We already encountered this rite of tea in Chapter 3, when I illustrated and discussed the principal aspects of the new philosophical strand of the "Everyday Aesthetics".

In Part II of the book, especially, we saw the connections-in-action between the organizational and the philosophical "fragments". They depict a panorama of the organizational theory in which three philosophical sensibilities—aesthetic, hermeneutic and performative—emerge that characterize the principal aspects of organizational aesthetics research.

These connections-in-action, I pointed out, concern only a part of the organizational aesthetics research, because the study of the aesthetics of organization can be conducted even without taking into due consideration the aesthetic philosophies.

However, as regards the organizational aesthetics research in which philosophy is considered important, the panorama of connections-in-action between aesthetic, hermeneutic and performative philosophical sensibilities and the aesthetic, archeological, artistic and empathic-logical approaches does not depict interactions that are well defined and delimited. On the contrary, this panorama is made up of a thousand colors, which continuously change color, as in a "metamorphosis".

The Italian artist and designer Bruno Munari (1966; Eng. trans. 1971: 80–82) gives a nice and poetic image of the process of the metamorphosis act of thousands of colors which, moreover, resonates with the millions of colors expected for the screens that pervade our working life in the organization, from the mobile phone to the smartphone, to the computer, to the monitor, to the television:

> Red, green, yellow, blue, white, brown, violet, orange, turquoise, grey . . . a list of colours such as this ends almost as soon as it has begun, but there are in fact twelve thousand colours in existence, like cockleshells all in a row. Twelve thousand colours. Think of it. Maybe it is not possible to tell them all apart, but they are all the same. [. . .] You will now realize that twelve thousand colours exist, even if you cannot distinguish one from its neighbour. But the story of colours does not end there. Every colour changes according to the material in which is fixed, just as in music the same note sounds one way played on a trumpet and quite another when played on the mandolin.

The interactions between philosophical sensibilities and organizational approaches have been described in these terms in the book, as a continuous metamorphosis resulting from the hybridization of fragments of organizational knowledge with fragments of aesthetic philosophy. That is a flow, rather than a sequence, as it can be appreciated by looking at one of the three *Metamorphosis* prints created by the Dutch graphic artist Maurits Cornelis Escher, which are woodcut prints of different lengths, realized from 1937 to 1968 and based on tessellated patterns that turn into a new pattern, thus giving shape to a new image.

If we look, for instance, at *Metamorphosis II*, made in 1939–40 and measuring 19 cm × 390 cm, we can notice that it commences with the language, the Dutch word *metamorphose*; thus, it becomes a checkered pattern that becomes reptile, nesting bee, insect, fish, bird, three-dimensional block, the small town of Atrani on the coast of Amalfi, in Italy, a chessboard—and finally ends up again with the language as it began, that is, the Dutch word *metamorphose*. One must avoid selecting a tessellated pattern, such as a fish or honeycomb, and create a single frame separated from the others, because to be aesthetically appreciated is the flux that *Metamorphosis II* depicts.

This is what this book tells us about organizational theories and aesthetic philosophies. It does not provide the reader with fixed tessellated patterns, but with the flux of the continuous metamorphosis of them into new tessellated patterns, since it avoids choosing a number of colors. Because it is their continuous color change, paradoxically, which is what metaphorically pictures the connections-in-action between philosophical sensibilities and aesthetic discourse on organization.

Philosophy, writes Maurice Merleau-Ponty (1960; Eng. trans. 1964: 112), "is indeed, and always, a break with objectivism and a return from *constructa* to lived experience, from the world to ourselves", to "an intersubjectivity that gradually connects us ever closer to the whole of history". Consideration that evokes the personal "connoisseurship", namely connoisseurship as the art of knowing, as we saw with Michael Polanyi in Chapter 6, the "I do not know what" that organizational scholars, students and researchers cannot avoid owning and to master, given that, as I pointed out in my essay a long time ago (Strati, 1992: 576–577), they "have their own direct experience of the aesthetic dimension of the organization being studied", collect organizational phenomena of an aesthetic nature, and "have their own aesthetic experiences of the relationship with the interlocutor", organizational artefacts, other living beings, organizational theory and other social theories, such as aesthetic philosophies.

The connoisseur, writes Hans-Georg Gadamer (1977; Eng. trans. 1986: 52–53), "represents the opposite extreme to kitsch", and goes "to the opera because Callas is singing, rather than because a particular opera is being performed", because, when

> the complete experience of a work of art is genuine, however, what amazes us is precisely the unobtrusiveness of the performers. They do not display themselves, but succeed in evoking the work and its inner coherence with a kind of unforced self-evidence. Thus we have two extremes here: on the one hand, an artistic intent that manipulates us for a particular purpose and finds expression in kitsch; and on the other, total obliviousness to the real appeal that the work of art addresses to us in favor of a quite secondary level in which we delight in aesthetic taste for its own sake. [. . .] The work of art, transforms our fleeting experience into the stable and lasting form of an independent and internally coherent creation. It does so in such a way that we go beyond ourselves by penetrating deeper into the work.

I now want to conclude *Organizational Theory and Aesthetic Philosophies*. But before doing that, as textual Interlude this time rather than the visual Interludes that compose, together with the written text, the architecture of this book, I want to recount the fact that, while I was writing it, on random occasions, I had around me, on my desk, in my library, in my case, the *Six Memos for the Next Millennium* written by the Italian writer Italo Calvino (1988). There, Calvino proposes to take into due consideration in the new millennium—where we are now—five qualities or values of literature: "lightness", "quickness", "exactitude", "visibility" and "multiplicity". I have always loved lightness as a peculiarity of writing. It is based on the substraction, on the removal of the weight from the subjects treated and from the argumentation—something that I did, subtracting the topics and removing their treatment to make the architecture of this text more agile.

Now, remaining on the architectural image, in the following considerations the Canadian-American architect Frank O. Gehry focuses on something that resonates with my treatment of the relationships between organizational theory and aesthetic philosophies and the relationship between Polanyi's personal knowledge, Pareyson's personal hermeneutics and the philosophical aesthetics:

> When I make a building, I tell clients at the start that we are going to be in a liquid state for a lot of the time. In the liquid state, there is information gathering and agonizing about program issues like adjacencies, land use, materials, and bureaucracies that we have to deal with. During that liquid period, we make a lot of study models, and some models are pretty scary looking. When we show them to a client, they get pretty nervous. We call them *schreck* models. [. . .]
> Staying liquid allows the freedom to make choices for quite a long time in the process so that there are a lot of opportunities for the design of the building.
>
> (Gehry, 2004: 20–21)

These words by Frank Gehry evoke the thematic continuity between my book *Organization and Aesthetics* published by Sage in 1999 and this book by Routledge, *Organizational Theory and Aesthetic Philosophies*, which appears twenty years after. That's why I would like to conclude the Epilogue—and the book—with the considerations of Frank O. Gehry about his recent architectural work for the Business School Building of the University of Technology in Sidney, Australia. I will do this because I feel that in the expressions of Gehry, there is the aesthetic pleasure "that seeks certain words in view of sharing and communication" of the sensible—*Le partage du sensible* (Rancière, 2000)—in the performance of "play" that would otherwise evoke the sense of the incommensurability of tastes, and, therefore, of solitude and impossible interaction (Lontrade, 2004: 8).

The concept of play, observes Hans-Georg Gadamer (1977; Eng. trans. 1986: 22–23), "is of particular significance", above all because "play is so elementary a function of human life that culture is quite inconceivable without this element", but also because "play appears as a self-movement that does not pursue any particular end or purpose so much as movement *as* movement, exhibiting so to speak a phenomenon of excess, of living self-representation", in the "form of nonpurposive activity". Furthermore, in my emphasis on playing with philosophy in order to understand organization and organizational life, I guard a touch of *ironie serieuse*, that is, of self-irony that resounds in the following conversation between Lisa Naar and Frank Gehry (Naar and Clegg, 2015: 67):

Lisa Naar: Can I ask you a couple of questions that are kind of a breakdown between philosophy, design and your view of education?
Frank Gehry: I haven't got any philosophy.
Lisa Naar: Is it curiosity that characterizes your approach?
Frank Gehry: Yeah, I think so.

References

Azéma, B. (2013). Un design comme la vie, pour une pragmatique de la pensée faible, *Figures de l'art*, 25: 61–74.

Bencivenga, E. (1988). *Tre dialoghi: un invito alla pratica filosofica*. Torino: Bollati Boringhieri. (English trans.: *Philosophy in Play: Three Dialogues*. Indianapolis, IN: Hackett Publishing, 1994).

Bencivenga, E. (2013). *Filosofia in gioco*. Roma-Bari: Laterza.

Boltanski, L. and Chiapello, È. (1999). *Le nouvel esprit du capitalisme*. Paris: Gallimard. (English trans.: *The New Spirit of Capitalism*. London: Verso, 2005).

Calvino, I. (1988). *Lezioni americane. Sei proposte per il prossimo millennio*. Milano: Garzanti. (English trans.: *Six Memos for the Next Millennium*. Cambridge, MA: Harvard University Press, 1993).

Figures de l'art (2013). Special Issue on 'Philosophie du design', 25. Edited by Lafargue, B. and S. Cardoso.

Gadamer, H-G (1977). *Die Aktualität des Schönen. Kunst als Spiel, Symbol und Fest*. Stuttgart: Phillip Reclam Jr. (English trans.: The relevance of the beautiful. Art as play, symbol, and festival, in Gadamer, H. G. (eds.), *The Relevance of the Beautiful and Other Essays*. Cambridge: Cambridge University Press, 1986, pp. 3–53).

Gagliardi, P. (2007). The collective repression of "pathos" in organization studies, *Organization*, 14 (3): 331–338.

Gehry, F. O. (2004). Reflections on designing and architectural practice, in Boland, R. J. and Collopy, F. (eds.), *Managing as Designing*. Stanford: Stanford Business Books, pp. 19–35.

Lontrade, A. (2004). *Le Plaisir esthétique: naissance d'une notion*. Paris: l'Harmattan.

Marquard, O. (1989). *Aesthetica und Anaesthetica: Philosophische Überlegungen*. Paderborn: Schoningh.

Murphy, P. and de La Fuente, E. (eds.) (2014). *Aesthetic Capitalism*. Leiden: Brill.

Merleau-Ponty, M. (1960). *Signes*. Paris: Éditions Gallimard. (English trans.: *Signs*. Edited by McCleary, R. C. Evanston, IL: Northwestern University Press, 1964).

Munari, B. (1966). *Arte come mestiere*. Bari: Laterza. (English trans.: *Design as Art*. London: Penguin, 1971).

Naar, L. and Clegg, S. (eds.) (2015). *Gehry in Sidney: The Dr Chau Chak Wing Building, UTS.* Melbourne: Image Publishing.

Rancière, J. (2000). *Le partage du sensible. Esthétique et politique.* Paris: La fabrique éditions. (English trans.: *The Politics of Aesthetics.* London: Continuum, 2004).

Ratiu, D. E. (2017). The aesthetic account of everyday life in organizations: a report on recent developments in organizational research, *The Journal of Arts Management, Law, and Society,* 47 (3): 178–191.

Strati, A. (1992). Aesthetic understanding of organizational life, *Academy of Management Review,* 17 (3): 568–581.

Strati, A. (2010). Aesthetic understanding of work and organizational life: approaches and research developments, *Sociology Compass,* 4 (10): 880–893, https://onlinelibrary.wiley.com/toc/17519020/2010/4/10.

Strati, A. (2014). The social negotiation of aesthetics and organisational democracy, in Murphy, P. and de La Fuente, E. (eds.), *Aesthetic Capitalism.* Leiden: Brill, pp. 105–127.

Strati, A. and Guillet de Monthoux, P. (2002). Introduction: organizing aesthetics, *Human Relations,* 55 (7): 755–766.

Sudjic, D. (2008). *The Language of Things.* London: Penguin.

Welsh, W. (1996). Aestheticization processes. Phenomena, distinctions and processes, *Theory, Culture & Society,* 13 (1): 1–24.

Index

Note: **bold** page numbers indicate a table on the corresponding page.

Printed in the United States
by Baker & Taylor Publisher Services

Printed in the United States
by Baker & Taylor Publisher Services